Vowels and Consonants

This book should be for Jenny, but a major part of it already belongs to her. Many of the sentences are hers, and she compiled everything on the CD.

Vowels and Consonants

An Introduction to the Sounds of Languages

Peter Ladefoged
University of California, Los Angeles

BLACKWELL
Publishers

First published 2001

2 4 6 8 10 9 7 5 3 1

Blackwell Publishers Inc.
350 Main Street
Malden, Massachusetts 02148
USA

Blackwell Publishers Ltd
108 Cowley Road
Oxford OX4 1JF
UK

Library of Congress Cataloging-in-Publication Data
Ladefoged, Peter.
    Vowels and consonants : an introduction to the sounds of languages /
Peter Ladefoged.
        p.   cm.
    Includes bibliographical references and index.
    ISBN 0-631-21411-9 (alk. paper) — ISBN 0-631-21412-7 (pbk. : alk. paper)
    1. Phonetics.   I. Title.
P221.L244   2000
414—dc21   00-023130

British Library Cataloguing in Publication Data
A CIP catalogue record for this book is available from the British Library.

Typeset in 10/12.5pt Palatino
by Graphicraft Limited, Hong Kong
Printed in Great Britain by T.J. International, Padstow, Cornwall

This book is printed on acid-free paper.

Contents

15 Putting Vowels and Consonants Together 169

Figures

Tables

The Compact Disk

The following recordings, color figures, and videos are on the CD that accompanies this book. The CD can be used on any computer that can use a net browser, such as Netscape Navigator or Microsoft Explorer. It has been optimized for use on the particular version of Netscape Navigator which is included (with permission from Netscape) on the disk. You should use this program to browse the CD (and the web) as it has a special application included, theWebPlayer, which not only plays each recording when you open it, but also brings up a menu that allows you to make an acoustic analysis of the sound that has been played.

The material on the CD is also available and updated on:
   http://hctv.humnet.ucla.edu/departments/linguistics/VowelsAndConsonants

Recording 1.1   Sounds illustrating the IPA symbols

Recording 2.1   The tones of Standard Chinese (table 2.1)
Recording 2.2   The tones of Cantonese (table 2.2)
Recording 2.3   *I'm going away* said as a normal unemphatic statement
Recording 2.4   *Where are you going?* said as a normal unemphatic question
Recording 2.5   *Are you going home?* said as a regular question
Recording 2.6   *Where are you going?* said with a rising pitch
Recording 2.7   *Are you going away?* said with some alarm
Recording 2.8   *When danger threatens your children, call the police*
Recording 2.9   *When danger threatens, your children call the police*
Recording 2.10   *Jenny gave Peter _instructions_ to follow*
Recording 2.11   *Jenny gave Peter instructions to _follow_*

Recording 2.12   An utterance in which there are no words, but in which
                        the speaker sounds contented
Recording 2.13   An utterance in which there are no words, but in which
                        the speaker sounds upset or angry
Also in chapter 2:
Video of the vibrating vocal folds
Photographs of the vocal folds producing a sound at three different pitches

Recording 3.1   Spanish vowels
Recording 3.2   Hawaiian vowels
Recording 3.3   Swahili vowels
Recording 3.4   Japanese vowels
Recording 3.5   General American vowels
Recording 3.6   BBC English vowels

Recording 4.1   Whispered *heed, hid, head, had, hod, hawed*
Recording 4.2   The words *had, head, hid, heed* spoken in a creaky voice

[There are no recordings for chapter 5.]

Recording 6.1   English consonants

Recording 7.1   *A bird in the hand is worth two in the bush* (synthesized)
Recording 7.2   *A bird in the hand is worth two in the bush* (F1)
Recording 7.3   *A bird in the hand is worth two in the bush* (F2)
Recording 7.4   *A bird in the hand is worth two in the bush* (F3)
Recording 7.5   *A bird in the hand is worth two in the bush* (F1, F2, F3)
Recording 7.6   *A bird in the hand is worth two in the bush* (F1, F2, F3 plus
                        fixed resonances)
Recording 7.7   *A bird in the hand is worth two in the bush* (fricative noises)
Recording 7.8   *A bird in the hand is worth two in the bush* (F1, F2, F3 plus
                        fixed resonances plus fricative noises)
Recording 7.9   *A bird in the hand is worth two in the bush* (fully synthesized)

Recording 8.1   The words *leaf* and *feel*, recorded forwards and backwards
Recording 8.2   High-quality speech synthesis

[There are no recordings for chapters 9–11.]

In chapter 11:
Video of the articulations of vowels

Recording 12.1   Burmese nasals
Recording 12.2   A comparison of English **b, p** and Spanish **b, p**

Preface

This book is about the sounds of languages. There are thousands of distinct languages in the world, many of them with sounds that are wildly different from any that you will hear in an English sentence. People trill their lips and click their tongues when talking, sometimes in ways that are surprising to those of us who speak English. Of course, some of the things that we do, such as hearing a difference between *fin* and *thin*, or producing the vowel that most Americans have in *bird* are fairly amazing to speakers of other languages, as we will see.

There are about 200 different vowels in the world's languages and more than 600 different consonants. There is no way that I can discuss all these sounds in an introductory book. I've just tried to give you the flavor of what happens when people talk, explaining most of the well-known sounds, and giving you a glimpse of some of the more obscure sounds that I've found interesting. As a result, this is a book of personal favorites. If you want a more systematic account of phonetics, there are many textbooks available, including one of my own.

Many of the sounds discussed are reproduced on the accompanying CD, which will work on any current Macintosh or Windows computer. If possible, you should listen to the sounds while you read. I hope you will be entertained by what you hear and read here, and will look at the suggestions for further reading at the end of the book. I've been thrilled by a lifetime chasing ideas in phonetics. Who knows, perhaps you, too, will go on to become a phonetician. Enjoy.

P.L.

Acknowledgments

Many people have contributed wonderful ideas and comments for this book. Foremost among them is my colleague Pat Keating, who offered nuggets of teaching wisdom that I have incorporated, and suggested corrections for numerous errors (but don't blame her for those I have added since she read the draft version). Other helpful commentators include (in alphabetical order): Vicki Fromkin, Yoshinari Fujino, Tony Harper and his colleagues and students at New Trier High School, Bjorn Jernudd, Sun-Ah Jun, Olle Kjellin, Jody Kreiman, Peggy MacEachern, Yoshiro Masuya, Pam Munro, Peter Roach, Janet Stack, and Jie Zhang. I am indebted to Caroline Henton for comments on speech synthesis and speech recognition, and to Mark Hasegawa Johnson for making me restructure the speech recognition chapter. Victoria Anderson let me use her palatography pictures, Didier Demolin gave me the MRI pictures, and Bruce Gerratt took the photographs of the larynx; many thanks to all of them. I am also very grateful to the many people from all over the world who kindly made recordings for me. Special thanks to Jean Acevedo who encouraged me to write a book of this kind.

Sources for the data on the vowels of different dialects are as follows:

General American English: Peterson, G.E., and Barney, H.L. (1952). Control methods used in a study of the vowels. *Journal of the Acoustical Society of America*, 24: 175–184.

Californian English: Hagiwara, R.E. (1995). Acoustic realizations of American English /r/ as produced by women and men. *UCLA Working Papers in Phonetics*, 90: 1–187.

Northern Cities (US): Hillenbrand, J., Getty, L.A., Clark, M.J., and Wheeler, K. (1995). Acoustic characteristics of American English vowels. *Journal of the Acoustical Society of America*, 97(5): 3099–3111.

BBC English: Deterding, D. (1990). Speaker normalisation for automatic speech recognition. Unpublished PhD dissertation, University of Cambridge.

The mean tongue positions in chapter 11 are based on data and factor analyses reported in Harshman, R.A., Ladefoged, P., and Goldstein, L.M. (1977). Factor analysis of tongue shapes. *Journal of the Acoustical Society of America*, 62: 693–707.

CONSONANTS (PULMONIC)

	Bilabial	Labiodental	Dental	Alveolar	Postalveolar	Retroflex	Palatal	Velar	Uvular	Pharyngeal	Glottal
Plosive	p b			t d		ʈ ɖ	c ɟ	k ɡ	q ɢ		ʔ
Nasal	m	ɱ		n		ɳ	ɲ	ŋ	N		
Trill	ʙ			r					R		
Tap or Flap				ɾ		ɽ					
Fricative	ɸ β	f v	θ ð	s z	ʃ ʒ	ʂ ʐ	ç ʝ	x ɣ	χ ʁ	ħ ʕ	h ɦ
Lateral fricative				ɬ ɮ							
Approximant		ʋ		ɹ		ɻ	j	ɰ			
Lateral approximant				l		ɭ	ʎ	L			

Where symbols appear in pairs, the one to the right represents a voiced consonant. Shaded areas denote articulations judged impossible.

CONSONANTS (NON-PULMONIC)

Clicks	Voiced implosives	Ejectives
ʘ Bilabial	ɓ Bilabial	ʼ Examples:
ǀ Dental	ɗ Dental/alveolar	pʼ Bilabial
ǃ (Post)alveolar	ʄ Palatal	tʼ Dental/alveolar
ǂ Palatoalveolar	ɠ Velar	kʼ Velar
ǁ Alveolar lateral	ʛ Uvular	sʼ Alveolar fricative

OTHER SYMBOLS

ʍ Voiceless labial-velar fricative

w Voiced labial-velar approximant

ɥ Voiced labial-palatal approximant

H Voiceless epiglottal fricative

ʢ Voiced epiglottal fricative

ʡ Epiglottal plosive

ɕ ʑ Alveolo-palatal fricatives

ɺ Alveolar lateral flap

ɧ Simultaneous ʃ and x

Affricates and double articulations can be represented by two symbols joined by a tie bar if necessary.

k͡p t͡s

VOWELS

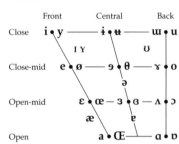

Where symbols appear in pairs, the one to the right represents a rounded vowel.

SUPRASEGMENTALS

ˈ Primary stress

ˌ Secondary stress

ˌfoʊnəˈtɪʃən

ː Long eː

ˑ Half-long eˑ

˘ Extra-short ĕ

| Minor (foot) group

‖ Major (intonation) group

. Syllable break ɹi.ækt

‿ Linking (absence of a break)

DIACRITICS   Diacritics may be placed above a symbol with a descender, e.g. ŋ̊

̥ Voiceless	n̥ d̥	̤ Breathy voiced	b̤ a̤	̪ Dental	t̪ d̪		
̬ Voiced	s̬ t̬	̰ Creaky voiced	b̰ a̰	̺ Apical	t̺ d̺		
ʰ Aspirated	tʰ dʰ	̼ Linguolabial	t̼ d̼	̻ Laminal	t̻ d̻		
̹ More rounded	ɔ̹	ʷ Labialized	tʷ dʷ	̃ Nasalized	ẽ		
̜ Less rounded	ɔ̜	ʲ Palatalized	tʲ dʲ	ⁿ Nasal release	dⁿ		
̟ Advanced	u̟	ˠ Velarized	tˠ dˠ	ˡ Lateral release	dˡ		
̠ Retracted	e̠	ˤ Pharyngealized	tˤ dˤ	̚ No audible release	d̚		
̈ Centralized	ë	̴ Velarized or pharyngealized ɫ					
̽ Mid-centralized	e̽	̝ Raised	e̝	(ɹ̝ = voiced alveolar fricative)			
̩ Syllabic	n̩	̞ Lowered	e̞	(β̞ = voiced bilabial approximant)			
̯ Non-syllabic	e̯	̘ Advanced Tongue Root	e̘				
˞ Rhoticity	ɚ a˞	̙ Retracted Tongue Root	e̙				

TONES AND WORD ACCENTS

LEVEL		CONTOUR	
e̋ or ˥ Extra high	ě ˩ Rising		
é ˦ High	ê ˥ Falling		
ē ˧ Mid	e̍ ˦ High rising		
è ˨ Low	e̖ ˩ Low rising		
ȅ ˩ Extra low	e̗ ˧ Rising-falling		
↓ Downstep	↗ Global rise		
↑ Upstep	↘ Global fall		

THE INTERNATIONAL PHONETIC ALPHABET (revised to 1993, corrected 1996)

1

Sounds and Languages

1.1 The Sounds of Language Evolve

Once upon a time, the most important animal sounds were those made by predators and prey, or by sexual partners. As mammals evolved and signaling systems became more elaborate, new possibilities emerged. Nowadays undoubtedly the most important sounds for us are those of language. Nobody knows how vocal cries about enemies, food, and sex turned into language. But we can say something about the way the sounds of languages evolved, and why some sounds occur more frequently than others in the world's languages.

Although we know almost nothing about the origins of language, we can still consider the evolution of languages from a Darwinian point of view. Remember that Darwin himself did not know anything about the origin of life. He was not concerned with how life began but with the origin of the various species he could observe. In the same spirit, we will not consider the origin of language; but we will note the various sounds of languages, and discuss how they got to be the way they are. We will think of each language as a system of sounds subject to various evolutionary forces.

We should also consider why people speak different languages. There are many legends about this. Some say it was because God was displeased when the people of Babel tried to build a tower up to heaven. He smote them so that they could not understand each other. Others say that the Hindu God Shiva danced, and split the peoples of the world into small groups. Most linguists think that languages just grew apart as small bands of people moved to different places. We know very little about the first humans who used language. We do not even know if there was one origin of language, or whether people started talking in different parts of the world at about the same time. The most likely possibility is that speech developed in one place, and then, like any wonderful cultural development, it spread out as the advantages of talking became obvious.

We do know that languages change, often quite rapidly, so that elderly people cannot readily understand what their grandchildren are saying. My 11-year-old granddaughter does not know what I'm talking about when I mention a *milliner* (hat-maker) or a *davenport* (couch), and old words are constantly being replaced by new ones (when buying *shoes* I now look for a store that sells *footwear*). When people are isolated from their neighbors, living in places where travel is difficult, different ways of speaking soon become established. Even when travel is comparatively simple, as it is along rivers in many tropical areas, prehistoric groups became self-sufficient. They had no need to interact with other people as long as they had sufficient food. When a small group of people live by themselves they develop their own way of speaking after only a generation or so, producing a new dialect that their neighbors will understand only with difficulty. In a few hundred years they will have a new language which is different from that of their ancestors and everybody else around them.

There are about 7,000 languages in the world all together. Nearly 4,000 of them are spoken by small tribes in two tropical areas, one extending across Africa from the Ivory Coast to the Congo and beyond, and the other centered on Papua New Guinea. In these areas there is ample rainfall and the people have been relatively self-sufficient for many generations. Until recently they had no great need to talk to other people. They had the resources to live and talk in their own way. Quite often they developed new sounds, constrained only by the general pressures that affect all human speech.

What are the pressures affecting the sounds that languages can use? In the first place, we are constrained by what we can do with our tongues, lips, and other vocal organs. Secondly, we are limited by our ability to hear small differences in sounds. These and other constraints have resulted in all languages evolving along similar lines. No language has sounds that are too difficult for native speakers to produce within the stream of speech (although, as we will see, some languages have sounds that would twist English-speaking tongues in knots). Every language has sounds that are sufficiently different from one another to be readily distinguishable by native speakers (although, again, some distinctions may seem too subtle for ears that are unfamiliar with them). These two factors, articulatory ease and auditory distinctiveness, are the principal constraints on how the sounds of languages develop.

There are additional factors that shape the development of languages, notably, from our point of view, how our brains organize and remember sounds. If a language had only one or two vowels and a couple of consonants it could still have half a dozen syllables, and make an infinite number of words by combining these syllables in different orders. But many of the words would be very long and difficult to remember. If words are to be kept short and distinct so that they can be easily distinguished and remembered, then the language must have a sufficient number of vowels and consonants to make more than a handful of syllables.

It would be an added burden if we had to make a large number of sounds that were all completely different from one another. It puts less strain on our ability to produce speech if the sounds of our languages can be organized in groups that are articulated in much the same way. We can think of the movements of our tongues and lips as gestures, much like the gestures we make with our hands. When we talk we use specific gestures – controlled movements – to make each sound. We would like to use the same gestures over and over again. This is a principle that we will call gestural economy. Typically, if a language has one sound made by a gesture involving the two lips such as **p** as in *pie*, then it is likely to have others such as **b** and **m**, as in *by* and *my* made with similar lip gestures. If you say *pie, by, my*, you will find that your lips come together at the beginning of each of them. If a language has *pie, by, my*, and also a sound made with a gesture of the tongue tip such as **t** in *tie*, then it is also likely to have other sounds made with the tongue tip, such as **d** and **n** in *die* and *nigh*. You can feel that your tongue makes a similar gesture in each of the words *tie, die, nigh*. The sounds that evolve in a language form a pattern; and there is a strong pressure to fill gaps in the pattern.

Societies weight the importance of the various constraints – articulatory ease, auditory distinctiveness, and gestural economy – in different ways, producing mutually unintelligible languages. But despite the variations that occur, the sounds that all languages use have many features in common. For example, every language uses both vowels and consonants to produce a variety of words. All languages use outgoing lung air in all words (though some may use ingoing air in parts of a word). And all languages use variations in the pitch of the voice in a meaningful way.

1.2 Language and Speech

The main point of a language is to convey information. Nowadays a language can take various forms. It can be spoken or written, or signed for those who cannot hear, represented in Braille for the blind, or sent in morse code or semaphore or many other forms when necessity arises. Speech is the most common way of using language. But speech is not the same as language. Think of what else you learn just by listening to someone talking. There are all sorts of non-linguistic notions conveyed by speech. You need only a few seconds to know something about a person talking to you, without considering the words they use or their meaning. You can tell whether they come from the same part of the country as you. You know the social group they belong to, and you may or may not approve of them. Someone talking with a so-called Harvard accent may sound pretentious. In Britain the differences between accents may be even more noteworthy. As Bernard Shaw puts it in the Preface to *Pygmalion*: "It is impossible for an Englishman to open his mouth without making some other Englishman despise him." The accent someone uses conveys information about what sort of person they are, but this is different from the kind of information conveyed by the words of the language itself.

Another aspect of speech that is not part of language is the way speech conveys information about the speaker's attitude to life, the subject under discussion, and the person being spoken to. We all know people who have a bright, happy way of talking that reflects their personalities – perhaps someone like Aunt Jane who was always cheerful, even when she was dying of cancer. Of course, people who sound happy may be just putting on a brave front. But, true or false, their speech conveys information that is not necessarily conveyed by their words. Whenever someone talks, you get an impression of their mood. You know whether they are happy, or sad, or angry. You can also assess how they feel about whatever you are discussing. They may sound interested or indifferent when they reply to your comments. In addition you can tell from their tone of voice what they think about you. They may be condescending, or adoring, or just plain friendly. All these attitudinal aspects of speech are wrapped up together in information conveyed by speech. You may be wrong in whatever inferences you make, but, true or false, whenever someone talks, their speech is conveying information of this sort.

The final kind of non-linguistic information conveyed by speech is the identity of the speaker. You can often tell the identity of the person who is speaking without looking at them. Again, you may be wrong, but when someone telephones and simply says 'Hi', you may be able to say whether it is a member of your family or a friend you know. You can get this kind of information from the aspects of speech we have just been discussing, the regional accent and the attitude that the speaker has. But there is often something more. You can tell which person it is from that region, and you can say who they are whatever their current emotions. I know my wife's voice on the phone, even when I am expecting a call from one of her relatives, and irrespective of whether she is cross because she has just had her purse stolen, or delighted because she has won the lottery. She still sounds like Jenny. (To be truthful, I have never had the opportunity to test the last part of this observation; I don't really know whether I could identify her voice when she has won the lottery.)

1.3   Describing Speech Sounds

In this book we will refer to the sounds of languages in three different ways. We will describe the sound waves in acoustic terms; we will note the gestures

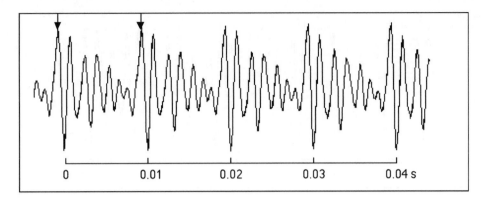

Figure 1.1 Part of the sound wave of the vowel **a** as in *father*. The arrows indicate a section that is repeated every one-hundredth of a second.

of the vocal organs used to produce them (the articulations); and we will label them using the symbols of the International Phonetic Alphabet (the IPA). We will discuss the latter two possibilities, the articulations and symbols, later, although we can note here that sounds illustrating all the IPA symbols are on the attached CD in recording 1.1. If you listen to the sounds illustrating the IPA symbols now, remember that they are the typical sounds represented by these symbols in many different languages. They may not be equivalent to any of the sounds of your accent of English or any other particular language.

Phonetic symbols should not be confused with letters of the alphabet used in spelling words. I always put phonetic symbols in bold, thus: **a, e, i, o, u**. Whenever I am referring to letters I put them in quotes: 'a, e, i, o, u'. Another convention I adopt in this book is to put words in italics when I am referring to the word as spoken. I might, for example, refer to the consonant **p** as in *pie*.

We will begin our description of the sounds of languages by considering the sound waves that are produced when we talk. Whenever you speak you create a disturbance in the air around you, a sound wave, which is a small but rapid variation in air pressure spreading through the air. Figure 1.1 shows part of the sound wave of the vowel **a** as in *father*. During this sound the air pressure at the speaker's lips goes up and down, and a wave with corresponding fluctuations is generated. When this sound wave reaches a listener's ear it causes small movements of the eardrum, which are sensed by the brain and interpreted as the sound **a** as in *father*, spoken with a particular pitch and loudness.

We can start thinking about the sound waves that form the acoustic structure of speech by considering the ways in which sounds can differ. Speech sounds such as vowels can differ in pitch, loudness, and quality. You can say the vowel **a** as in *father* on any pitch within the range of your voice. You can also say it softly or loudly without altering the pitch. And you can say many different vowels, without altering either the pitch or the loudness.

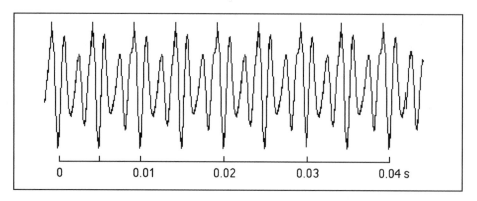

Figure 1.2 Part of the sound wave of the vowel **a** as in *father* said on a pitch corresponding to a frequency of 200 Hz, making it an octave higher than the sound in figure 1.1.

The pitch of a sound depends on the rate of repetition of the changes in air pressure. A short section of the sound wave of the vowel **a** as in *father* in figure 1.1 repeats itself every one-hundredth of a second. The frequency of repetition is 100 times a second, or, in acoustic terms, 100 Hz. (Hz is the abbreviation for hertz, the unit of frequency.) This particular frequency corresponds to a fairly low pitch in a male voice. Figure 1.2 shows the same vowel with the higher frequency of 200 Hz, which means that it had a higher pitch. This vowel was said on a pitch an octave above the sound in figure 1.1. It is in the higher part of the male voice range.

The loudness of a sound depends on the size of the variations in air pressure. Figure 1.3 shows the sound wave of another utterance of the vowel **a** as in *father*. On this occasion the sound wave has an amplitude (the size of the pressure variation) which is about half the amplitude of the vowel in figure 1.1. You can see that the peaks of air pressure in figure 1.3 are about half the size of those in figures 1.1 and 1.2. The only difference between figures 1.1 and 1.3 is in the amplitude (the size) of the wave. In all other respects the waves have exactly the same shape. Differences in amplitude are measured in decibels (abbreviated dB). The difference in amplitude between the sounds in figures 1.1 and 1.3 is 6 dB, but, because of the complex way in which dB differences are calculated, there is no easy way of putting an amplitude scale on these figures. The wave in figure 1.1 sounds a little more than twice as loud as the one in figure 1.3.

The third way in which sounds can differ is in quality, sometimes called timbre. The vowel in *see* differs in quality from the first vowel in *father*, irrespective of whether it also differs in pitch or loudness. The symbol for the quality of the vowel in *see* is **i**, corresponding to the letter 'i' in French, Italian, or Spanish *si*. (In English we rarely use **i** for this sound, but we do in *police*.) As

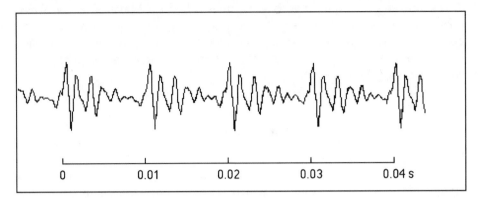

Figure 1.3   Part of the sound wave of the vowel **a** as in *father* produced with approximately half the loudness of the sound in figure 1.1.

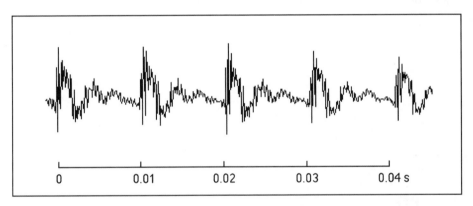

Figure 1.4   Part of the sound wave of the vowel **i** as in *see* said on the same pitch and with approximately the same loudness as the sound in figure 1.1.

we have seen, the symbol for the quality of the first vowel in *father* is **a**, a script letter 'a'.

Differences in vowel quality have more complex acoustic correlates, loosely summed up as differences in the shape of the sound wave (as opposed to its repetition rate and size). Figure 1.4 shows the sound wave of the vowel **i** in *see*. This wave, like the waves in figures 1.1 and 1.3, has a frequency of 100 Hz, in that the wave repeats every hundredth of a second. It also has a slightly smaller amplitude than these other waves. The vowel **i** (remember, this is the internationally agreed-upon symbol for the vowel in *see*, not the sound of the word *I*) is usually less loud – has less amplitude – than the vowel **a** because the mouth is less open for **i** than for **a**. In general, the wider you open your mouth, the louder the sound.

The shape of a sound wave is sometimes called the waveform. The wave-forms in figures 1.1 and 1.4 repeat every one-hundredth of a second, so that both sounds have the same pitch. The waveform in figure 1.4 has a greater number of small variations than that in figure 1.1. It is the waveform of a sound with a different quality.

1.4 Summary

This chapter has discussed the principal constraints on the evolution of the sounds of the world's languages, which are ease of articulation, auditory dis-tinctiveness, and gestural economy. It has also discussed the differences be-tween speech and language, and outlined some of the main acoustic distinctions among sounds. In the next chapter we will consider how one of the acoustic distinctions, that corresponding to pitch, is used in the world's languages.

2

Pitch and Loudness

2.1 Tones

In English, and most European languages, the meaning of a word remains the same irrespective of whether it is said on a rising pitch or a falling pitch. You can say *Chocolate?* with a questioning intonation, or *Chocolate!* with a demanding one. The differences in pitch will make the phrase mean different things, but you will still be talking about chocolate. However, pitch changes of this kind may cause a word to have a different meaning in languages spoken in other parts of the world. In Standard Chinese (Mandarin) the meaning of a syllable is very much affected by changes in pitch. The syllable **ma**, for example, has four different meanings, depending on the pitch on which it is spoken, as shown in table 2.1. Cantonese is another language spoken in China. (From a linguistic point of view Cantonese is a separate language, not just a dialect.) In Cantonese, a syllable such as **si** can have up to six different meanings, as shown in table 2.2. Differences in pitch that can change the meaning of a word are called differences in tone. The tables show the Chinese characters for each of these words in the first column. The second column shows the IPA tone symbol indicating the pitch during the word. The vertical bar at the right of the tone symbol marks the range of the speaker's voice, and the position and shape of the line attached on its left shows the pitch during the word. The next column provides a verbal description of how the pitch varies. You can hear the words in recordings 2.1 and 2.2.

We can use the tone marks in tables 2.1 and 2.2 to make a point that will apply to our use of symbols throughout this book. Symbols can represent only the major linguistic aspects of an utterance. When we make a pitch track – a

Table 2.1   Examples of the pronunciation of the syllable **ma** with different pitches, forming words differentiated by tone in Standard Chinese. These words are illustrated in recording 2.1

	Standard Chinese **ma**		
Chinese character	Tone symbol	Tone description	English gloss
媽	˥	high level	'mother'
麻	˦	high rising	'hemp'
馬	˩	low falling rising	'horse'
罵	˥	high falling	'scold'

Table 2.2   Examples of the pronunciation of the syllable **si** to form words differentiated by tone in Cantonese. These words are illustrated in recording 2.2

	Cantonese **si**		
Chinese character	Tone symbol	Tone description	English gloss
詩	˥	high falling	'poem'
試	˧	mid level	'to try'
事	˨	low level	'matter'
時	˩	extra low	'time'
使	˦	high rising	'to cause'
市	˧	mid rising	'city'

record of the frequency of the voice – we find that the curves of each of the words in recordings 2.1 and 2.2 are not the same as the schematized versions in tables 2.1 and 2.2. Figures 2.1 and 2.2 show pitch tracks produced by computer analyses of recordings 2.1 and 2.2. As you can see, the tone symbols in the tables (and the short descriptions of the tones) are only rough descriptions of what actually happened when these words were said. In figure 2.1 one of the most notable differences is in the third word, 'horse', which is described as low falling rising. This word is typically pronounced with a kind of hoarse raspy voice, that we will later call creaky voice, at the beginning, so that there is no real pitch and the computer analysis produces only a few isolated points in the low frequency range. I've joined these points up so that they produce a curve illustrating the pitches that you hear. The final word, 'scold', also differs from the conventional tone mark in table 2.1 in that the pitch does not, on this occasion, fall to the bottom of the speaker's range.

The pitch tracks for the Cantonese words in figure 2.2 differ even more from the conventional descriptions in table 2.2. The fall in the first word is very short, right at the end of the word. The next two tones are described as being level, but in the particular utterances recorded here they both fall considerably. The

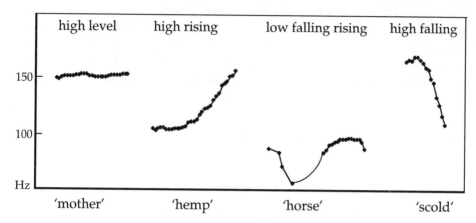

Figure 2.1   Pitch tracks of the words in table 2.1.

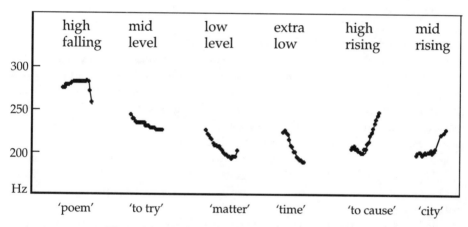

Figure 2.2   Pitch tracks of the words in table 2.2.

extra low tone also falls (to a lower point than the other low tone). The high rising and mid rising tones are somewhat as these terms suggest.

The symbols (and short descriptions) used for all these tones are abstractions intended to describe the general appearance of the tones in the two languages, Standard Chinese and Cantonese. They cannot be taken literally when considering any particular utterance. Nor, rather obviously, are the exact frequency values important. The Standard Chinese examples were spoken by a man and were on a lower pitch than the Cantonese examples, which were spoken by a woman. If a woman had spoken the Standard Chinese examples, they would all have been on a higher pitch. The absolute values are never important from a linguistic point of view. The changes in meaning are conveyed by the relative pitch changes. The pitch range used is a property of the speaker, not the language.

Standard Chinese has four tones as shown in table 2.1, and Cantonese has six tones on the syllable **si** as shown in table 2.2. (Cantonese has three more tones that can be used on other syllables, so that it has nine tones in all.) Although tonal differences are rare or non-existent in most languages spoken in Europe and India, well over half the languages spoken in the world use tones to differentiate the meanings of words.

2.2   English Intonation

In English we use pitch changes in a different way. In our case it is the meaning of a group of words – a sentence or a phrase – that is changed, rather than the meanings of individual words. A difference in pitch that changes the meaning of a group of words is called a difference in intonation.

Everyone can hear and produce the tunes required for differences in intonation. Some people think that they cannot be producing tunes because they consider themselves to be tone-deaf. But nobody is completely tone-deaf, unless they are literally deaf in every respect. One might be tone-deaf in the sense that one cannot hear and produce the different pitches required in a song. People for whom this is true probably did not have music in their background when they were young. Learning to sing is like learning a language, easier to pick up and do with perfection if you are a child, but more difficult when older. Singing differs from speaking in that it holds the pitch of the voice constant, usually for a syllable or two, and then jumps to the next note. In speech the pitch is always changing, never remaining the same, even within a single syllable. But whether one can sing or not, everyone can make the tunes required in speech.

The most obvious tunes in English are those used to mark the end of a sentence. In a statement such as *I'm going away* (recording 2.3) the pitch goes down at the end. Figure 2.3 shows a pitch track of my pronunciation of this phrase. There are small variations at the beginning, a rise for the word *going* (after the virtual silence and lack of any pitch for the initial **g**), and then a small fall until the final major fall at the end.

Questions such as *Where are you going?* (recording and figure 2.4) have a similar pitch pattern. The beginning of the sentence has some small variations, but the pitch is generally high, and there is the lack of any pitch in the **g** at the beginning of *going*. It is not until the final syllable that there is a major fall in pitch. Speakers of American English may have a lower pitch on the first part of the sentence, and a greater rise on the first syllable of *going*, so that the pattern of the tune as a whole can be characterized as a rise–fall, rather than just a fall as it is in my British English.

Questions that can be answered by yes or no, such as *Are you going home?* (recording and figure 2.5), usually rise at the end. The beginning of the sentence

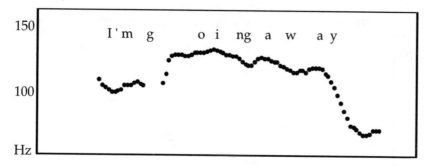

Figure 2.3 Pitch track for the phrase *I'm going away* said as a normal unemphatic statement (recording 2.3).

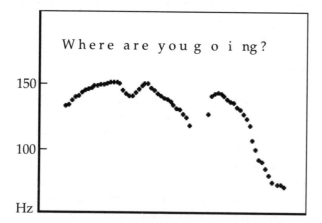

Figure 2.4 Pitch track for the phrase *Where are you going?* said as a normal unemphatic question (recording 2.4).

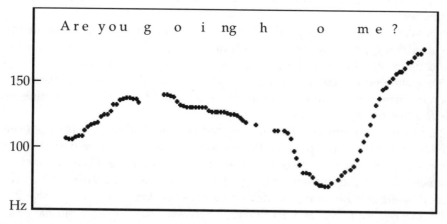

Figure 2.5 Pitch track for the phrase *Are you going home?* said as a regular question (recording 2.5).

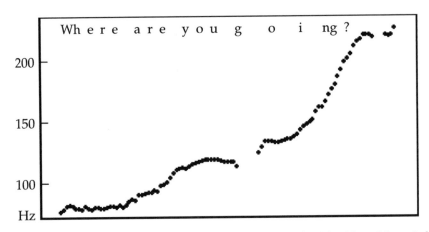

Figure 2.6 Pitch track for the phrase *Where are you going?* said with a rising pitch.

is similar to the other sentences we have been considering. After a small initial rise, there is a small fall until the beginning of the word *home*, in which there is a considerable fall followed by an even more considerable rise. In this particular utterance the last word was said with some emphasis, so that this tune can be characterized as a fall–rise. Unemphatic yes–no questions typically have just a rise at the end.

It is difficult to generalize about the pitch changes that can occur in a language. One can say *Where are you going?* with a rising pitch (recording and figure 2.6), which makes it a question indicating surprise. In the case of the utterance illustrated, the pitch went from a low of about 80 Hz to a high of around 220 Hz. A pitch change of this magnitude might indicate utter amazement, as if I were asking a question in reply to my wife calmly saying, "I'm off to the South Pole." (Thankfully, she has never said this. I don't like cold climates.)

Similarly, a question expecting the answer yes or no, which is normally said with a rising pitch, can be said with this tune partially reversed. Recording and figure 2.7 illustrate the phrase *Are you going away?* said with a falling–rising pitch on the last word. This makes it sound like a question expressing some alarm, the sort of question intonation I would use when lamenting my wife's departure.

Intonation is important for marking the clauses that go to make up a sentence. We can use the pitch of the voice to make subtle grammatical differences in the breaks between clauses that would have been marked by punctuation in the written language. Recordings 2.8 and 2.9 and the corresponding figures illustrate the difference between *When danger threatens your children, call the police,* and *When danger threatens, your children call the police.* In each utterance the sentence as a whole has a downward movement of the pitch. Both sentences have three major peaks, one on the first syllable of

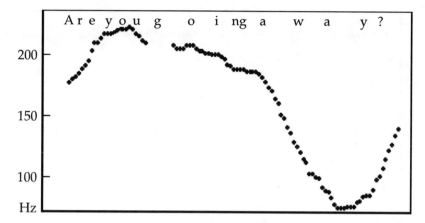

Figure 2.7 Pitch track for the phrase *Are you going away?* (recording 2.7).

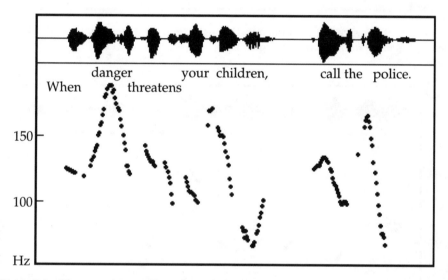

Figure 2.8 The waveform and pitch track for the sentence *When danger threatens your children, call the police* (recording 2.8).

danger, one on the first syllable of *children*, and the third on the second syllable of *police*. This last syllable also has a fall to the lowest pitch in each utterance. In the first sentence (figure 2.8), there is a fall to the same low pitch at the end of *children*, but the listener is made aware that this is not the end of the sentence by the rise in pitch at the very end of this word. This sort of fall followed by a small rise is the usual way of marking the fact that this is just the end of a clause and there is something more to come.

As can be seen in figure 2.9, the second sentence has a pause after *threatens*, and it is the end of this word that has a small rise indicating that this is only

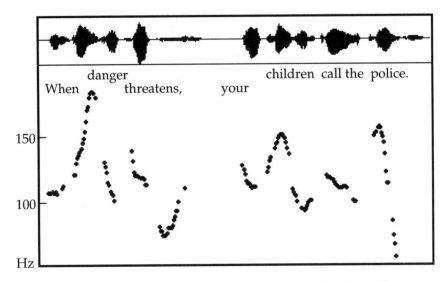

Figure 2.9 The waveform and pitch track for the sentence *When danger threatens, your children call the police* (recording 2.9).

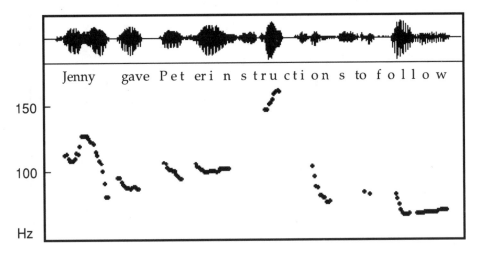

Figure 2.10 The waveform and pitch track for the sentence *Jenny gave Peter instructions to follow* (recording 2.10).

the end of a clause and there is more to come within the sentence. The peaks are still on the first syllables of *danger, children,* and *police,* and the major fall indicating the end of the sentence is still on the last syllable of *police.*

Some different tunes on sentences are not even marked by the punctuation; the reader (or listener) has to get them from the context. Recordings and figures 2.10 and 2.11 show that we can tell the difference between sentences

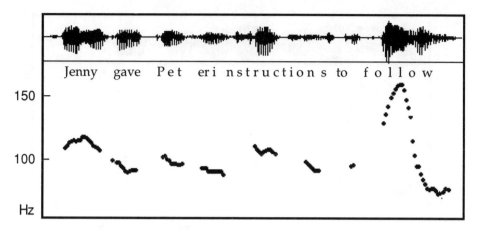

Figure 2.11 The waveform and pitch track for the sentence *Jenny gave Peter instructions to <u>follow</u>* (recording 2.11).

such as *Jenny gave Peter <u>instructions</u> to follow* and *Jenny gave Peter instructions to <u>follow</u>*. The first means that Peter was given some instructions and he has to follow them, and the second that Jenny told Peter to follow after her. The words are the same in the two sentences, but the meaning is different because of the differences in pitch and rhythm. In figure 2.10 the high point in the sentence is on the second syllable of *instructions*. In figure 2.11 the whole first part of the sentence is said on a low pitch, and the major rise and fall in pitch comes on the first syllable of *follow*.

Other pitch changes in speech can be used to convey different kinds of information. We can usually tell whether a speaker is angry or loving by listening to the tune without even hearing the words. The pitch of the voice carries much of the emotional content of speech. Listen to recordings 2.12 and 2.13 and look at the corresponding figures. There are no distinguishable words, but it is obvious which was spoken in anger and which when happy. In the first of these two utterances (figure 2.12) there are large changes in pitch, with the 'sentence' as a whole having a generally falling pitch. The second utterance (figure 2.13) has slightly smaller peaks, but they are sharper, without the rounded tops, and the 'sentence' as a whole has an increasing pitch.

Finally, we should reiterate the point made above about the tone language examples. It is the relative pitch change that matters. All the English examples were produced by a male speaker with a fairly deep voice (mine). The low point in these phrases is usually around 80 Hz. Except when expressing surprise or a high degree of emotion, the high point does not go above 180 Hz. If the whole pattern were shifted up 20 or 30 Hz, it would simply sound as if a man with a higher-pitched voice were saying the same thing with the same meaning. A woman or a child could produce the same pitch patterns in a higher range without changing the meaning.

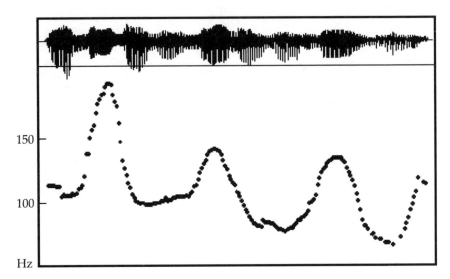

Figure 2.12   The waveform and pitch track for an utterance in which there are no words, but in which the speaker sounds contented (recording 2.12).

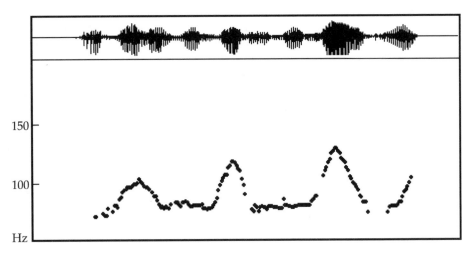

Figure 2.13   The waveform and pitch track for an utterance in which there are no words, but in which the speaker sounds upset or angry (recording 2.13).

2.3   The Vocal Folds

So far we have been talking just about sounds. Now let's see how people make pitch changes such as those we have been considering. The pitch of the voice depends mainly on the tension of the vocal folds, two small muscular flaps in the larynx. With the aid of a mirror in the back of the throat, it is possible to

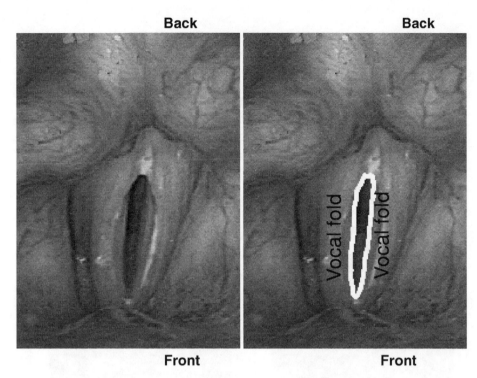

Figure 2.14 A view of the vocal folds. In the copy of this picture on the right the vibrating inner edges of the vocal folds have been outlined.

see the vocal folds. This is how the picture of my vocal folds in figure 2.14 was produced (color versions of this and other figures in this chapter are on the CD). Between the vocal folds you can see down into the trachea (the windpipe).

Figure 2.15 shows a sequence of vocal fold positions. In the first figure, at the top on the left, they are closed. In the second photograph, a few thousandths of a second later, they are less tightly closed, and in the third photograph they are beginning to come apart. They are fully open by the time of the first picture in the second row, and from then on they start closing again. You can see them vibrating (in color) in the material for this chapter on the CD.

The vibrations of the vocal folds are the result of the air from the lungs blowing them apart, and then sucking them together so that they can be blown apart again. They behave in some ways like the lid of a boiling kettle. When the pressure of the steam below the lid becomes too great it is blown upward, releasing the pressure. When there is no pressure beneath it, it falls down; and then the pressure builds up again. In the case of the vocal folds there is a slight complication. The pressure of the air in the lungs will blow them apart, but, when the pressure is less and air is escaping between them, they do not simply collapse together. There is an additional mechanism drawing them

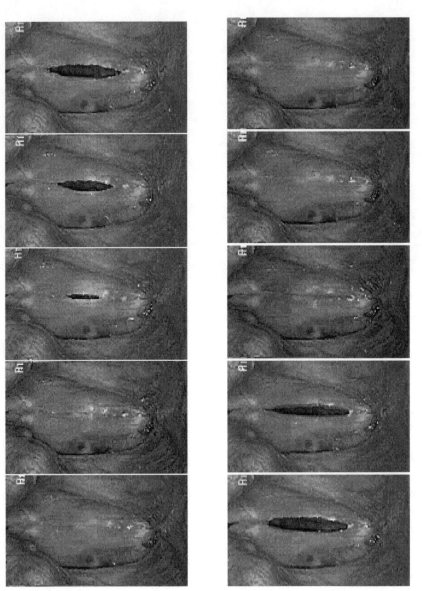

Figure 2.15   The vibrating vocal folds.

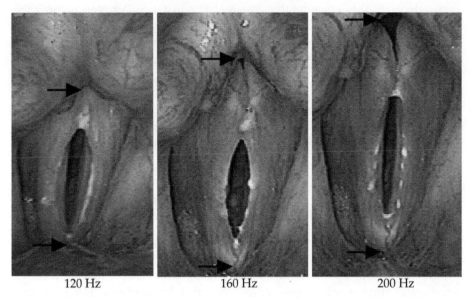

| 120 Hz | 160 Hz | 200 Hz |

Figure 2.16 Views of the vocal folds vibrating at different pitches. The arrows indicate comparable points on the vocal folds.

towards one another. The vocal folds are actively sucked together by the air passing between them. Air traveling at speed through a narrow gap causes a drop in pressure. (You have probably noticed this when traveling in a car. When another car traveling in the opposite direction passes close by, you can feel the pull as the two cars are sucked towards one another.) This suction causes the vocal folds to be pulled together faster than they were blown apart. The rapid, repetitive closing of the vocal folds is what produces the sound of the voice. Each time the vocal folds close, the air in the throat and mouth is set into vibration so that a sound wave is produced.

The vocal folds can be stretched so that they become longer and thinner. As a result, like a guitar string that has been stretched, they vibrate more quickly, producing a higher pitch. Figure 2.16 shows three pictures of my vocal folds as I said a vowel at three different pitches. (Color versions of these pictures are on the CD.) In the first picture my vocal folds were vibrating about 120 times a second. As we saw in chapter 1, the rate of vibration is measured in hertz (Hz), so we can say that I was producing a note with a frequency of 120 Hz. For the second picture I had increased the frequency to 160 Hz. The parts of the vocal folds that are vibrating do not seem to be longer than those in the first picture, but this may be just an accident dependent on the moment in the vibration that was captured by the camera. With the equivalent of a camera speed of 1,200 frames per second, each complete vibration is represented by less than 10 frames. What is apparent, however, is that the distance between the front of the vocal folds (which are at the bottom of the picture) and the back (at the top) is considerably greater. The distance between comparable points on the vocal folds (marked by arrows) has increased by about 28 percent in the second picture. In the third picture, when my vocal folds were vibrating at approximately 200 Hz, the distance between comparable points had increased by about 48 percent. In this picture the chink between my vocal folds at the back (by the upper arrow), which was just beginning to show at the top of the second picture, is much larger. When the vocal folds are fully stretched there tends to be an opening in this region, which remains throughout the vibration – at least in the case of untrained singing voices such as mine.

2.4   Loudness Differences

We all know that we can speak loudly or softly. We can shout at unruly children or murmur confidential secrets. Kids can yell at actors on a movie screen, and then murmur how stupid they feel for doing so. Even within a normal conversation differences in loudness are important. They can be used to distinguish meanings, particularly when they are also accompanied by differences in pitch. We produce differences in loudness by using greater activity of our respiratory muscles so that more air is pushed out of the lungs. Very often when we do this we also tense the vocal folds so that the pitch goes up. Syllables with a greater amount of respiratory energy (and, usually, increased tension of the vocal folds) are called stressed syllables. In English we use differences in stress to distinguish between many nouns and verbs: *an insult* versus *to insult, an export* versus *to export,* and *an overflow* versus *to overflow.*

The act of pushing more air out of the lungs has several consequences: it makes the amplitude of the vibrations of the vocal folds larger and hence louder; it increases the pitch; and it usually makes the syllable longer. As we saw, the vocal folds vibrate because the air from the lungs pushes them apart and then sucks them together again. A larger push will result in their being pushed apart more rapidly; and a greater flow of air between them will cause them to be sucked together more rapidly. The result is that they will vibrate at a higher frequency, and the pitch will go up. The increase in pitch is the major cue to the position of the stressed syllable in an English word. Some of the pitch increase is due to increased respiratory activity, the extra push of air from the lungs, and some is due to the accompanying increase in vocal fold tension.

You can see the effect of just pushing more air out of the lungs for yourself by performing a very simple experiment. Stand against a wall, take a deep breath, and say a long vowel such as a. Try to keep the vowel on a steady pitch. Now, ask a friend to press the lower part of the rib cage while you are saying the vowel, so that more air is pushed out of your lungs. The result will be that the vowel will become louder; but there will also be a very noticeable increase in pitch. All that you and your friend have done is to increase the pressure of the air in the lungs, and the result is an increase in pitch as well as loudness.

In English, the stress occurs on different syllables in ways that are somewhat predictable. As we have seen, there are noun–verb pairs in which the stress is on the first syllable for the noun and the last for the verb, such as *a record* versus *to record*, *a convict* versus *to convict*. There are also sets of words in which the stress moves from the first syllable to the second and then to the one before the last, depending on whether an added suffix forms another noun or an adjective: **pho**tograph, pho**tog**rapher, photo**graph**ic, and **dip**lomat, dip**lo**macy, diplo**mat**ic.

Some languages have fixed stress, which always comes on a certain syllable in the word. Polish words nearly always have stress on the next-to-last syllable, for example: *komin* 'chimney', *kominek* 'fireplace', *komisariat* 'police station'. The only exceptions are a few verb forms and foreign words such as: *opera, ceramika, minimum.* Swahili, a very different language from Polish in most other respects, nevertheless also generally stresses words on the next-to-last syllable: *dawa* 'medicine', *daraja* 'bridge', *chandalua* 'mosquito net'. In Swahili, a sound such as **m** before a consonant such as **p** may count as a syllable, as in *nilimpa* 'I gave it to him', in which the **m** is the next-to-last syllable and therefore stressed.

In nearly every language – certainly in all those that we have been discussing – what we hear as stress is more a matter of increasing the pitch and length of the syllables concerned than of increasing their loudness. From the speaker's point of view it involves extra effort, an extra push of air out of the lungs, and increased tension of the vocal folds. What is most important to the listener is the increase in pitch that occurs, not the increase in loudness.

2.5 Summary

The pitch of the voice can be used to produce different tones, which change the meanings of words. Most of the world's languages are like Standard Chinese in that they use pitch in this way. All languages also use pitch to produce different intonations which show the clause structure and other grammatical aspects of sentences. English typically uses a fall for ending statements and questions that do not expect the answer yes or no, a rise for ending questions expecting the answer yes or no, as well as for clauses within a sentence, and rise–fall and fall–rise intonations in more special circumstances. Variations in pitch also reflect the speaker's emotions.

Pitch differences are caused by varying the rate of vibration of the vocal folds, two small bands of muscles in the larynx. Tensing the vocal folds makes them vibrate faster, so that the pitch increases. Increased loudness is caused by pushing more air out of the lungs. Stressed syllables are produced by the speaker pushing more air out of the lungs, and usually, at the same time, increasing the tension of the vocal folds. Both these actions increase the pitch, which is the important cue for stress.

3

Vowel Contrasts

3.1 Sets of Vowels in a Language

How many vowels are there in English? If you went to school in a country where English is the national language, you probably learned that there are five or six, "A E I O U, and sometimes Y". But if we are considering sounds, and not letters, there are actually many more vowels. As you may also have learned at school, each of the vowel letters represents two sounds, one when it is by itself, and another when it is accompanied by a silent 'e'. This is how we write the ten different vowels in the English words 'mat-mate, pet-Pete, kit-kite, cod-code, cut-cute'. But if we think of a vowel as the core of nearly every spoken syllable, then more than ten sounds qualify as vowels of English. The vowel in *good*, for example, is not one of the ten we have just noted. In this book we will consider a vowel to be any sound occurring in the middle of a syllable, provided that it is produced without any kind of obstruction of the outgoing breath. Sounds that have some obstruction to the breath stream, such as the bringing of the lips together, are consonants.

Every language has a number of vowels that contrast with one another so that they make different words. Many languages use just the five vowels that can be represented by the letters 'a, e, i, o, u'. Languages as diverse as Spanish, Hawaiian, Swahili, and Japanese manage with these five vowel sounds, forming words such as those in table 3.1. As is evident from recordings 3.1, 3.2, 3.3, and 3.4, the qualities of the vowels are not exactly the same in each of these languages, but they are all appropriately written with the letters 'a, e, i, o, u'.

Table 3.1   Words illustrating the vowels **a, e, i, o, u** in Spanish, Hawaiian, Swahili, and Japanese (the qualities of the vowels are not exactly the same in each of these languages)

Spanish		Hawaiian		Swahili		Japanese	
masa	'dough'	**kaka**	'to rinse'	**pata**	'hinge'	**ma**	'interval'
mesa	'table'	**keke**	'turnstone'	**peta**	'bend'	**me**	'eye'
misa	'mass'	**kiki**	'to sting' (bee)	**pita**	'pass'	**mi**	'fruit, nut'
mosca	'fly'	**koko**	'blood'	**pota**	'twist'	**mo**	'algae'
musa	'muse'	**kuku**	'to beat' (tapa)	**puta**	'thrash'	**mu**	'nothing'

3.2   English Vowels

The number of vowels in English varies considerably, with some forms of Scottish English having only 10 distinct vowels and some old-fashioned British English speakers having 21. (We are, of course, concerned with the number of sounds that can occur as vowels in English syllables, and not the various ways vowels can be spelled in the written language; English spelling is notoriously odd.) One difficulty in describing, or even listing, these vowels is that there are so many different forms of English. We will begin by considering just two, the form of English used by national newscasters in Britain, and the corresponding form used in the USA and Canada. The former is often called 'BBC English'. We will refer to its US and Canadian counterpart as 'General American English', noting that there are more differences among American national newscasters than occur in BBC English (which is, nevertheless, fairly diverse).

In General American English there are 14 or 15 different vowels. We cannot find a single set of English words differing only in the vowels as we did for most of the languages in table 3.1, but we can demonstrate the possibilities that can occur by considering the sets of words shown in table 3.2. The final column in the table shows a way of transcribing these vowels in the symbols of the International Phonetic Alphabet. We will discuss these symbols later in this book. Recording 3.5 illustrates a typical American pronunciation of these words.

The vowels in the first five sets of words in table 3.2 are distinguished in all major dialects of English, British as well as American. It is only when we come to rows 6 and 7 that we run into differences that can be observed even among the General American English of national newscasters. Probably most Americans do not distinguish between the vowels in the words in these two rows. They make no difference between the words *cot* and *caught*, and similar pairs like *hock* and *hawk*, and *knotty* and *naughty*. People living in the Midwest or Far West are often surprised when they realize that many speakers on the East coast (and all speakers of BBC English) distinguish these words.

Table 3.2 English vowel sounds that can occur between **b** and **d**, **b** and **t**, **h** and **d**, and **k** ('c') and **t** in General American English, the form of English used by many national newscasters in the USA and Canada, together with a set of IPA symbols that can be used to transcribe them

	b__d	b__t	h__d	k__t	IPA symbols
1	bead	beat	heed		iː
2	bid	bit	hid	kit	ɪ
3	bayed	bait	hayed	Kate	eɪ
4	bed	bet	head		e
5	bad	bat	had	cat	æ
6	bod(y)	bot(tom)	hod	cot	ɑː
7	bawd	bought	hawed	caught	ɔː
8	bud(dhist)		hood		ʊ
9	bode	boat	hoed	coat	oʊ
10	booed	boot	who'd	coot	uː
11	bud	but	Hudd	cut	ʌ
12	bird	Bert	heard	curt	ɝ
13	bide	bite	hide	kite	aɪ
14	bowed	bout	howd(y)		aʊ
15	Boyd		(a)hoy	quoit	ɔɪ

There are no other differences in the number of vowels used in General American English. There are always either 14 or 15 distinct vowels, although they may be pronounced in various ways in different parts of the country.

The vowel in the words in row 8 is comparatively rare. Many speakers of American English do not use it between **b** and **d**, pronouncing the word *buddhist* with the same vowel as in *booed*. But everyone uses it in some very common words, such as *could*, *good*, and *look*.

The vowel in the words in row 12 is among the most common in American English, although it is among the rarest vowels in the world. This combination of vowel plus 'r' has become a single sound in American English. People often think that a word such as *bird* contains a sequence of a vowel followed by **r**, but it doesn't. Listen carefully to a word such as *err* as pronounced by a speaker of General American English, and you'll hear that the **r** quality is present from the beginning. The only other well-known language in which this sound occurs is Standard Chinese, and even there it is fairly infrequent.

The vowels in the last three rows are diphthongs – sounds that have a change in vowel quality during the course of the syllable. They each count as a single vowel because each of these words is a single syllable. The vowels in rows 3 and 10 are also usually diphthongs, but the change in vowel quality during the syllable is somewhat smaller. Remember that we are discussing sounds, not letters. The word *beat* is spelled with two vowel letters although most speakers say it with an unvarying quality. The word *bite* (or *fight*) has a single vowel letter in the middle, but nearly everybody makes the quality of the vowel at the beginning of this word different from the quality at the end.

Table 3.2 leaves out the most common vowel in American (and British) English, the small, indistinct sound that occurs in the usual pronunciation of many little words, such as *a, the, to, at*. We sometimes pronounce the word *a* as if it rhymed with *hay* or *bay*, but we usually say it with a vowel similar to (but, for many people, not quite the same as) that in *bud* or *but*. It gets left out of table 3.2 as it is not, strictly speaking, a vowel that contrasts with any of the other vowels in the table. It occurs only in syllables that are not receiving any particular stress. It does contrast with other vowels when it occurs in an unstressed syllable of a word with more than one syllable. It makes a difference between the ends of words such as *Texas* and *taxes* for many people, and even distinguishes (for some people) words such as *Rosa's* and *roses*. The phonetic symbol for this vowel is ə, an upside-down letter 'e'.

In the form of British English used by national newscasters ('BBC English') there are 20 different vowels. Table 3.3 shows some sets of contrasts. For the

Table 3.3 English vowel sounds that can occur between **b** and **d**, **b** and **t**, **h** and **d**, and **k** ('c') and **t** in BBC English, together with a set of IPA symbols that can be used to transcribe them. The last four rows have different consonantal contexts

	b__d	b__t	h__d	k__t	IPA symbols
1	bead	beat	heed		iː
2	bid	bit	hid	kit	ɪ
3	bayed	bait	hayed	Kate	eɪ
4	bed	bet	head		e
5	bad	bat	had	cat	æ
6	bard	Bart	hard	cart	ɑː
7	bod(y)	bot(tom)	hod	cot	ɒ
8	bawd	bought	hawed	caught	ɔː
9	bud(dhist)		hood		ʊ
10	bode	boat	hoed	coat	əʊ
11	booed	boot	who'd	coot	uː
12	bud	but	Hudd	cut	ʌ
13	bird	Bert	heard	curt	ɜː
14	bide	bite	hide	kite	aɪ
15	bowed	bout	howd(y)		aʊ
16	Boyd		(a)hoy	quoit	ɔɪ
17	beer	peer	here		ɪə
18	bare	pear	hair	care	eə
19	byre	pyre	hire		aə
20	boor	poor			ʊə

words in the last four rows the consonants differ from those at the head of the column. Recording 3.6 illustrates my pronunciation of these words.

The first five rows in table 3.2 are identical with the corresponding rows in table 3.3. The sixth row illustrates a vowel that occurs in BBC English because the **r** that still occurs in a syllable after a vowel in American English has been lost. Nobody quite knows why, but many years ago it became fashionable in British English to change the consonant **r** into a vowel, when it occurred at the end of a word or before another consonant. As a result BBC English has some new vowels where General American English still has a vowel followed by **r** or an r-colored vowel. In row 6, instead of vowel plus **r** there is a new vowel quality. This vowel quality distinguishes pairs of words such as *cart* and *cot*, and *card* and *cod*. American English speakers often report that they hear some r-coloring in these words in BBC English but this is not the case. BBC English also distinguishes the words in rows 7 and 8, so there is a three-way distinction between the words *cart*, *cot*, and *caught*, all without any r-coloring.

The loss of **r** has produced some other notable differences between BBC English and General American English. The words in rows 12 and 13 are distinguished by just the vowels, without any r-coloring. More strikingly, BBC English has four more diphthongs, illustrated in rows 17 to 20. All of these are single-syllable words, each with a vowel that starts with one quality and then moves so that the quality at the end is more like that in BBC English *bird*. Some old-fashioned speakers of this form of English even have one more vowel. They have a diphthong in words such as *more* and *lore*. For these speakers *more* and *lore* are distinct from *maw* and *law*.

Parts of the northeastern seaboard of the United States follow British English in the loss of **r** after a vowel. It seems that people in the seaports such as Boston were influenced by the British speakers from around London and adopted their speech habits. As a result they, too, have r-less dialects. They have a vowel somewhat between BBC English **æ** as in *had* and **ɑː** as in *hard*, which they use in words such as *park* and *car*.

As in General American English, we must note that the most common vowel in speech is not in table 3.3. This is the vowel that occurs in dozens of words such as *the*, *a*, and *that*. If you say any of these words in isolation, you will probably do so with one of the vowels in table 3.3. But in connected speech each of them will usually have the reduced vowel we are symbolizing as **ə**. Sometimes, as in the case of *that*, a word will be pronounced with a full vowel in one meaning, and with **ə** in another. *That* always has the vowel in *bad* when in phrases such as *This and that*, or *I know that man*, and **ə** when it is in a phrase such as *I know that I'm wrong*.

English is a language in which the differences between dialects are largely in the vowels. (This is not the case in Spanish. The Spanish of Mexico and other Latin American countries differs from the Castilian Spanish of Spain mainly in the consonants.) There are more differences among the vowels of different dialects of English than we can discuss here. Many Scottish speakers

do not distinguish the vowels in *hood* and *who'd* (or *look* and *Luke*). Some
Northern English speakers do not distinguish between *look* and *luck*. Speakers
of Canadian English are often distinguishable by the quality of the diphthong
in words such as *out* and *about*.

There are also differences in the qualities of the vowels that occur in different consonantal contexts. Everybody distinguishes the vowels in *seen* and *sin*,
but only one of these two vowels can occur before 'ng'. For speakers of BBC
English the vowel in *sing* is very like that in *sin*; but for many speakers of
American English, notably those from California, it is almost identical with the
vowel in *seen*. British speakers have three different vowels in the words *merry*,
Mary, and *marry*, but most Americans do not distinguish all these vowels
before 'r'. Californian English speakers typically pronounce all three of these
words in exactly the same way.

3.3   Summary

Many languages, like Spanish and Japanese, have only five vowels. General
American English as spoken by national newscasters has 14 or 15 distinct
vowels that can contrast in monosyllabic words. The corresponding form of
British English, BBC English, has 20 distinct vowels.

4

The Sounds of Vowels

4.1   Acoustic Structure of Vowels

We all know what a vowel sounds like, but there are no popular terms for describing how the quality of one vowel differs from that of another. We need to consider more than the acoustic properties we have been considering so far, the frequency (pitch) and intensity (loudness) of different sounds. Vowels can be produced on any pitch within the range of a speaker's voice. I can say the vowels in *heed, hid, head, had* on a low pitch, when the vocal folds are vibrating about 80 times a second (a low E), and then I can say them again with vocal folds vibrating 160 times a second (the E an octave above). The pitch of my voice will have changed, but the vowels will still have the same quality. I can also say any vowel loudly or softly. The quality, the factor that distinguishes one vowel from another, remains the same when I shout or talk quietly.

Different vowels are like different instruments. One can play concert pitch A on a piano, a clarinet, or a violin. In each case it will be the same note because the rate of repetition of the sound wave as a whole – the fundamental frequency – is the same. The quality will be different because the smaller variations within each repetition of the sound wave – the overtones – will be different. Similarly, vowels will retain their individual qualities irrespective of the pitch produced by the vocal folds.

When we listen to a vowel or a musical note, we can tell which vowel it is, or which instrument produced it, by the overtones that occur. The reed of the clarinet or the vocal folds may be vibrating 100 times a second, but the sound that is produced at the mouth of the clarinet or at the lips will contain characteristic groups of overtones at higher frequencies. We can see an indication of

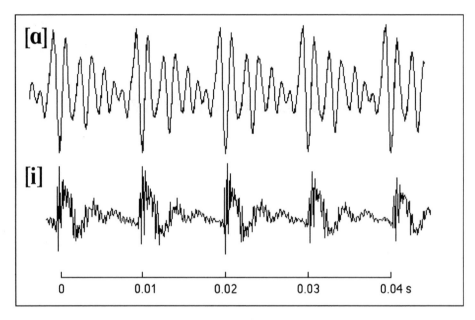

Figure 4.1   The vowel **a** as in *father* (from figure 1.1) and the vowel **i** as in *see* (from figure 1.4), showing the different overtones that occur when these vowels are said on the same pitch.

these higher frequencies in the waveforms of the vowels **a** as in *father* and **i** as in *see*, which were reproduced in figures 1.1 and 1.4 and are shown here together in figure 4.1. In both cases the wave as a whole repeats itself one hundred times a second. Within one-hundredth of a second in the upper wave there are seven peaks in air pressure. Seven peaks in one-hundredth of a second corresponds to 700 peaks in a second. It is as if there is a 700 Hz wave that starts up and then diminishes every one-hundredth of a second. But within one-hundredth of a second in the lower wave, there is a wave that starts up and repeats itself a little over twice in one-hundredth of a second, and a number of other, smaller, waves that repeat themselves over 20 times in this interval. For my voice (all these figures show sound waves that I produced), the vowel **a** is characterized by a group of overtones around 700 Hz; and the vowel **i** is characterized by two groups of overtones, one around 250 Hz, and the other around 2,100 Hz. As we will see later, the situation is actually a little more complicated than this, as the vowel **a** has two groups of overtones in the 700 range, and the vowel **i** also has additional overtones that we must take into account.

If we looked at some other vowels, we would see that for the vowel in *head* the most prominent overtones will be at about 550 and 1,600 Hz. For the vowel in *had* they will be around 750 and 1,200 Hz. These overtones will occur although the vocal folds may be vibrating at any rate from about 80 to around 250 Hz for a male speaker.

To see how these higher frequencies arise, we can liken the air in the mouth and throat to the air in a bottle. When you blow across the top of a bottle the air inside it will be set in vibration. The resonance of the bottle – the note that it produces when the air vibrates – will depend on the size and shape of the body of air inside it. If the bottle is full of air, with nothing else in it, it will have a low-pitched resonance. Pouring water into it so that the body of air becomes smaller makes the pitch go up. Smaller bodies of air vibrate more quickly. They have a higher resonant frequency.

Producing different vowels is like altering the size and shape of the bottle. For a vowel the relevant shape is the tube formed by the mouth and throat, which is known as the vocal tract. The air in this tube is set in vibration by the pulses of air from the vocal folds. Every time they open and close, the air in the vocal tract above them will be set in vibration. Because the vocal tract has a complex shape, the air within it will vibrate in more than one way. Often we can consider the body of air behind the raised tongue (i.e. in the throat) to be vibrating in one way, and the body of air in front of it (i.e. in the mouth) to be vibrating in another. In the vowel in *heed* the air behind the tongue will vibrate at about 250 Hz, and the air in front of it at about 2,100 Hz.

The resonances of the vocal tract are called formants. Trying to hear the separate formants in a vowel is difficult. We are so used to a vowel being a single meaningful entity that it is difficult to consider it as a sound with separable bits. But it is possible to say vowels so that some of their component parts are more obvious. One possibility is to whisper a series of vowels, as I have done in recording 4.1. When whispering, the vocal folds do not vibrate; they are simply drawn together so that they produce a random noise like that of the wind blowing around a corner. Because this noise is in the pitch range of one of the resonances of the vocal tract, we can hear that resonance more plainly. If you whisper you will not hear a note with a specific pitch; but you will be able to hear the changes in the vowel resonances. Try whispering *heed*, *hid*, *head*, *had*, *hod*, *hawed*, as in recording 4.1; there will be a general impression of a descending pitch.

Another way of making one of the resonances more obvious is to say a series of words on a very low pitch. Say the vowel in *had* on as low a pitch as you can, and then try to go even lower so that you produce a kind of creaky voice. Now say the words *had*, *head*, *hid*, *heed* in this kind of voice, as I have done in recording 4.2. You may be able to hear not only the constant low buzzing sort of pitch associated with the vocal folds, but also a changing pitch in one of the overtones. When saying the words *had*, *head*, *hid*, *heed*, this pitch goes down.

The sound that you hear when whispering is mainly that of the vibrations of the air in the front of the mouth. Conversely, the pitch changes associated with saying *had*, *head*, *hid*, *heed* in a creaky voice are due to the vibrations of the air in the back of the vocal tract. This resonance is the lower in pitch of the two, and is called the first formant. The height of the bars in figure 4.2 shows the

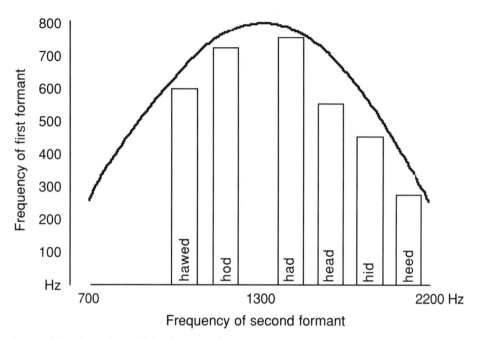

Figure 4.2   The values of the first two formants in some English vowels. The solid curve marks the limits of the possible vowel space.

mean pitch of this formant in the vowels in *hawed*, *hod*, *had*, *head*, *hid*, *heed*. The words are listed from left to right mainly in order of increasing frequency of the overtone that is heard when whispering (the second formant). The highest first formants will be when the second formant is in the middle of its range. The lowest first formants will be when the second formant is very high (as you can hear it is when you whisper *heed*). The solid curve in the figure shows the limits on the first and second formant frequencies that can occur, given an average-size male vocal tract.

There is a gap on the left of the curve in figure 4.2 where English could have had an additional vowel or two. As we will see, this is because in most dialects of English the vowels in *hood* and *who'd* at one time occupied this space. They are now pronounced with formants that would place them more in the middle of the diagram. If you say *moo*, the sound a cow is conventionally supposed to make, you may produce something more like the vowel that would be in the lower left of the figure.

You can hear a descending pitch when you say the words *hod*, *hawed*, *hood*, *who'd* in a creaky voice, just as you did when you said *had*, *head*, *hid*, *heed* in that way. This is because the first formant goes down in pitch in both these sets of words. It is the second formant that has shifted upwards in the last two words so that the vowels in these words are more in the center of the space.

4.2 The Acoustic Vowel Space

We will now return to the question of why so many languages have the five vowels **a**, **e**, **i**, **o**, **u**, pronounced as in the Spanish words *masa*, *mesa*, *misa*, *mosca*, *musa*. Figure 4.3 shows the five Spanish vowels in relation to the boundaries of the formant space that can be produced by an average male speaker. The scale used for the second formant frequency has the frequency values unequal distances apart. They have been arranged this way because the ear hears the higher frequencies as if they were closer together on the scale.

In the case of Spanish (and many other languages with five vowels) the vowel **u** has a low second formant. It thus occupies the space on the left of the diagram, where the English vowel in *who* might have been, and indeed was until comparatively recent times. In most English dialects the vowel in *who* now has a higher second formant than the corresponding Spanish vowel.

The Spanish vowels are fairly evenly distributed near the perimeter of the vowel space. The three vowels **i**, **a**, **u** are near the corners of this space, and thus as far apart from each other as possible. The other two vowels, **e** and **o**, are spaced at intermediate distances. Because the three vowels **i**, **a**, **u** are as auditorily distinct as possible, they are very effective ways of distinguishing words, and many languages make use of them. If we think of languages from an evolutionary point of view, it is hardly surprising that by far the majority have evolved so that they have vowels similar to the three Spanish vowels **i**, **a**, **u**, which provide such efficient means of communication. If there are two further vowels, as in Spanish, they are likely to be placed so that the resulting set of five vowels is distributed in the possible vowel space in the most efficient way. This will involve arranging the vowels as shown in figure 4.3 for Spanish. These vowels are as auditorily distinct as any five vowels can be.

When we consider the development of vowel systems we must note that the vowel systems of the world's languages also show evidence of another constraint discussed in chapter 1, the pressure to form patterns. Given that the auditory space for possible vowels is somewhat triangular, the selection of the three most distant vowels **i**, **a**, **u** is obviously beneficial. It would be possible for languages to add just one vowel to these basic three, and, indeed, some languages do have only four vowels. But it turns out that far more languages have five or seven vowels than have four or six. With five or seven vowels it is possible to have a nicely symmetrical triangular vowel space.

If a language uses a still larger number of vowels, then they may be distinguished not only by differences in their formant frequencies but also by other differences such as length. English has several vowels that are kept distinct in this way. For example, the vowel in *heed* is different from that in *hid* not only by having a lower first formant, but also by being longer. In the next chapter

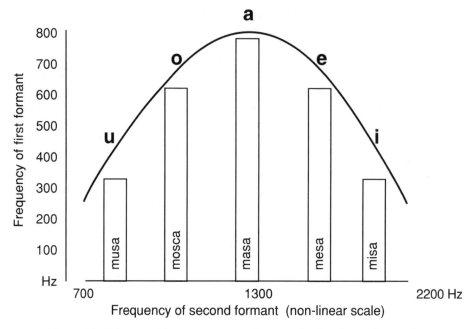

Figure 4.3   The possible vowel space, showing the five Spanish vowels.

we will see how we can represent the English vowels on a graph showing the formant frequencies.

4.3   Sound Spectrograms

We have been describing vowels as if they were distinguished by only two formants, but actually the situation is more complicated. There is a third formant that is important for distinguishing some sounds, notably the r-colored vowel that occurs in American English pronunciations of words such as *bird*, and the French vowel that occurs in *tu* (you). There are also formants with even higher pitches that add to the overall vowel quality. We can see the more complete set of formants that occur by making a computer analysis of the sound waves in a set of words. The top part of figure 4.4 shows the sound wave of the words *bead, bid, bed, bad*. The lower part of the figure is a computer analysis showing the component frequencies (in the form of a sound spectrogram). Time runs from left to right, as for the sound wave. The frequency scale (shown on the left) goes up to 4,000 Hz. The dark bands with white lines running through their centers are the formants, with the degree of loudness (the amplitude) of each formant being shown by the darkness of the band. The

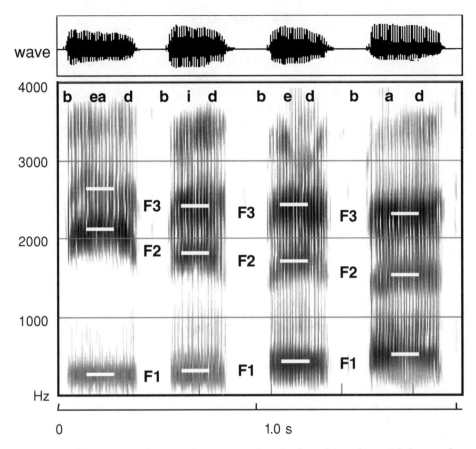

Figure 4.4 Upper part: the sound waves produced when the author said the words *bead, bid, bed, bad*. Lower part: a spectrogram of these sound waves in which the complex sound waves are split into their component frequencies (overtone pitches), the amplitude (loudness) of each frequency being shown by the darkness. The three principal groups of overtones (the first three formants) are marked by white lines, labeled F1, F2, and F3.

white lines are not part of the computer analysis but were added so as to make the locations of the formants more obvious. Sound spectrograms of this kind (with or without the white lines) are powerful tools for describing speech sounds, and we will be using them extensively in this book.

In this spectrogram, the formants are far from straight lines. But in general you can see that the first formant frequency in the first word is lower than it is in the second word, and gets steadily higher in each succeeding word. You can hear this change in pitch when you say these words with a creaky voice. The second formant frequency goes steadily down, as it does when you whisper them. The third formant also moves down slightly.

4.4 Summary

The principal characteristics of the sounds of vowels are the groups of over-tone pitches, known as formants, which are produced by the vibrations of the body of air in the vocal tract. The acoustic vowel space can be considered to be an area bounded by the possible ranges for the frequencies of the first two formants. Computer analysis of speech can be used to produce spectrograms, graphical displays in which the formants appear as dark bars.

5

Charting Vowels

5.1 Formants One and Two

Earlier in this book, when we were considering the information conveyed by the pitch of the voice, we noted that men's and women's voices differed substantially in pitch, but they conveyed the same information. What mattered was the relative pitch within a sentence, whether it went up or down at the end, or which word stood out from the others because of a difference in pitch. It is the pattern of pitch changes that counts, not the exact frequencies involved. We must keep the same considerations in mind when discussing vowels.

The vowels of a particular speaker can be described precisely by stating their formant frequencies. But some speakers with big heads will have large resonating cavities, producing formants with comparatively low frequencies; and others will have higher formant frequencies because they have smaller vocal tracts. In order to represent the vowels of a language we need to show the average values of the formants.

The most useful representation of the vowels of a language is a plot showing the average values of formant one and formant two for each vowel as spoken by a group of speakers. We can also get this plot to reflect the approximate tongue positions in vowels by arranging the scales appropriately. When you say the vowel i as in *heed*, you pull the tongue up so that it is high and in the front of the mouth. Breathe in while holding the position for i, and you will be able to feel the cold air rushing through the narrow gap between the tongue and the roof of the mouth. Now say the vowel u as in *who'd*. If you hold this position while breathing in you will find that the tongue is still high in the mouth, but you can feel the rush of cold air further back in the mouth.

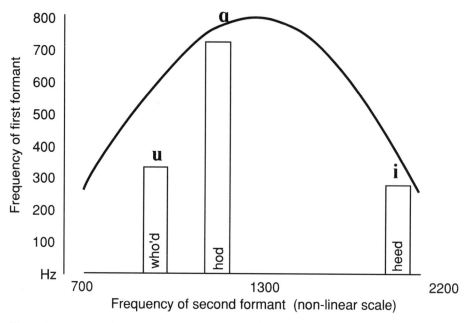

Figure 5.1   A modified version of figure 4.2, showing the first two formants of the vowels in the words *hod* and *heed*, as in that figure, and adding the vowel in *who'd*.

The vowel **ɑ** as in *hod* has a very low tongue position. Look in a mirror and you will see that the mouth is wide open and the body of the tongue is very far back in the mouth. We should also note that when you say **i** as in *heed*, the corners of your lips are spread apart, but for the vowel **u** as in *who'd* the corners of the lips are more together. We can characterize these two lip positions as being unrounded in **i** as in *heed*, as opposed to rounded in **u** as in *who'd*.

Now let us think about these facts in relation to the formant frequencies. Figure 5.1 is a modified version of part of figure 4.2, showing the first two formants of the vowels in the words *hod*, *heed*, and *who'd*. The principal modification of the earlier figure is that the bar for *who'd* has been added to the vowels in *hod* and *heed*. Its first formant is similar to that of the corresponding Spanish vowel, so the bar is about the same height. But it has a higher second formant than the corresponding Spanish vowel, so the bar is placed more to the right on the horizontal scale.

As we saw when we first discussed formants, the first formant has a low pitch for **i** (*heed*), a high pitch for **ɑ** (*hod*), and a low pitch again for **u** (*who'd*). This is the opposite of what the tongue does (high in *heed*, low in *hod*, and high again in *who'd*). So if we want to make a chart that shows both the vowel formants and an approximation of the tongue positions, we have to make the scale for the first formant go downwards, with low values at the top and high values at the bottom. By turning figure 5.1 upside down, as in figure 5.2, we

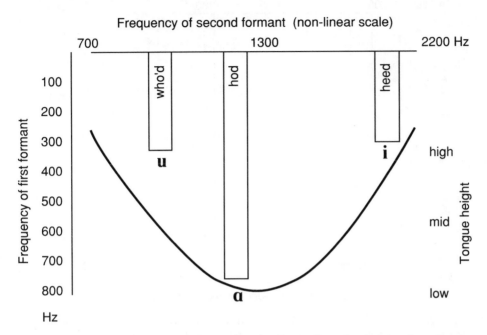

Figure 5.2 Figure 5.1 inverted, with an added scale on the right showing how the first formant relates to tongue height.

can plot the formants in a way that will match the articulations in this respect. An indication of the tongue height has been added on the right of the figure.

We also saw that the second formant is high for **i** (*heed*) and lower for **u** (*who'd*). The tongue is in the front of the mouth for **i** (*heed*) and in the back in **u** (*who'd*). Traditional phonetic diagrams have the front of the mouth on the left and the back on the right. We can achieve this pattern by reversing figure 5.2, making the scale go from right to left, so that a low value suitable for **u** (*who'd*) will be on the right and high values like those in **i** (*heed*) will be on the left, as in figure 5.3. The only problem with this figure is that it is not a simple representation of the front–back position of the tongue. The tongue is certainly in the front of the mouth for **i** (*heed*) and towards the back for **u** (*who'd*), but the vowel in which the tongue is furthest back in the mouth is **a** (*hod*). So it is apparent that the frequency of the second formant is related to something else as well as tongue position. The answer is that a major part of the lowering of the second formant is due to the increase in lip rounding. The lips are much closer together for **u** (*who'd*) than they are for **a** (*hod*). Accordingly, the scale should be taken as reflecting lip rounding as much as the backness of the tongue, as indicated at the bottom of the picture.

The five vowels of Spanish, which we first illustrated in figure 5.3, can be represented in this way, as shown in figure 5.4, a reversed and inverted version of figure 5.3. In this case the bars for each vowel have been replaced by points. This kind of representation of vowels is known as a formant chart.

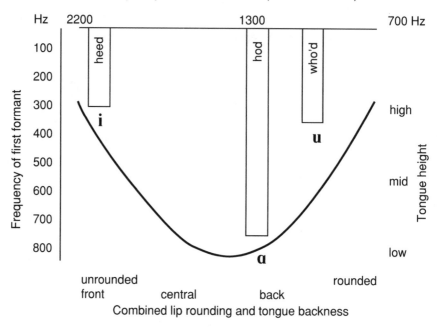

Figure 5.3 Figure 5.1 inverted and reversed, with added scales showing how the first formant relates to tongue height and the second formant to the front–back position of the tongue and the degree of lip rounding.

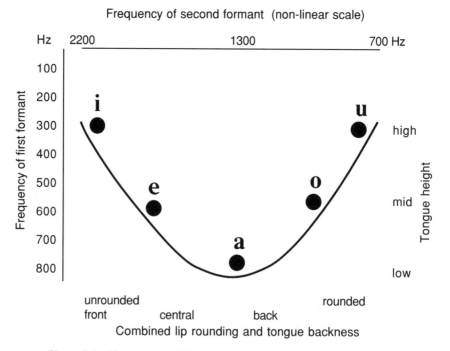

Figure 5.4 The vowels of Spanish represented on a formant chart.

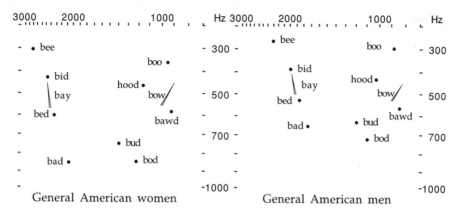

Figure 5.5 Formant charts of a conservative style of General American English. The vowels in *bay* and *bow* (rhyming with *hoe*, not *how*) are represented by lines rather than points, as these vowels are diphthongs.

5.2 Comparing English Vowels

Figure 5.5 is a formant chart of the vowels of one form of General American English. Most of the vowels are represented by points, but the vowels in *bay* and *bow* (as in *bow tie*) are indicated by lines, to show that these vowels are diphthongs, starting with one vowel quality and ending with another. The scales in this figure (and in all the formant charts in this book) have been arranged to reflect how people hear the distances between vowels. The points representing the vowels in *bee* and *bid* are about as far apart as those for *bid* and *bed*, which is how listeners judge the distances between these pairs of vowels. The vowels in *bid* and *bod* are much further apart, in accordance with the fact that listeners hear these two vowels as being very different. Remember that these charts are for one form of General American English, so the vowels may not be the same as those with which you are familiar. They are based on data from speakers in the eastern part of the United States, who were recorded in the 1950s. Accordingly they represent a more old-fashioned dialect than that of most readers of this book.

The first thing to note about these charts is the difference between the women on the left of the figure, and the men on the right. The men's vowels have lower formant frequencies, resulting in their chart being more compressed, with all the points being moved upward and to the right. This is because men have larger vocal tracts, containing bigger bodies of air. These larger bodies of air vibrate more slowly, so that the formants have lower frequencies. But the pattern of vowels is much the same for both men and women.

Vowel charts provide an excellent way of comparing different dialects of a language. Figure 5.6 shows the average vowels of Southern Californian women and men. There are several differences from the more conservative General

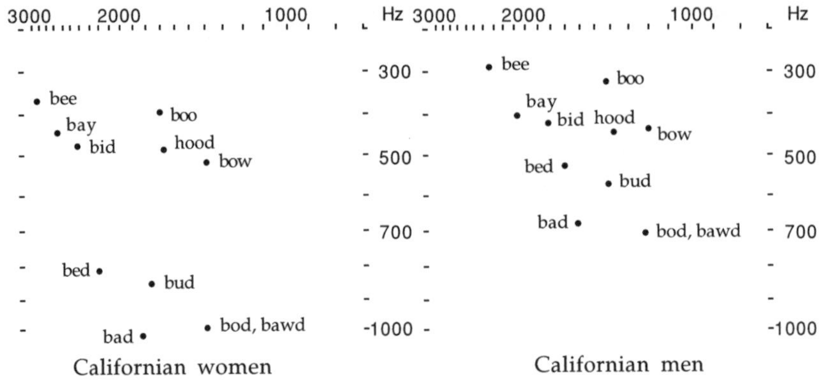

Figure 5.6   Formant charts of Californian English.

American dialect represented in figure 5.5. First, in contemporary Californian English the vowels in *bay* and *bow* have only a small change in quality from beginning to end, so it is possible to represent them by points rather than lines. The quality of the vowel in *bay* is in between that of the vowels in *bee* and *bid*. What is not shown on the chart is that the vowels in *bay* and *bid* (or *bait* and *bit*, to give a minimally contrasting pair) also differ in length. The vowel in *bait* is longer than that in *bit*. Another difference between the two dialects is that the contemporary Californian vowels in *boo* and *hood* have a much higher second formant frequency – they are further to the left in the diagram – than their conservative General American counterparts. Finally, as we noted in chapter 4, Californians do not distinguish between the vowels in *bod* and *bawd* (or *cot* and *caught*), making all these words with a vowel sound having a comparatively high first formant frequency.

There are several other distinct dialects of American English, but we will consider only one of them which is notable because of an interesting sound change that has occurred in comparatively recent years. In many of the northern metropolitan areas of the United States, such as Detroit and Rochester, a form of speech has developed that has come to be known as Northern Cites dialect. Formant charts of this form of speech are shown in figure 5.7. The most striking feature of this dialect is the relative position of the vowels in *bad* and *bed*, which is the reverse of their positions in General American English. The vowel in *bad* has come to have a lower first formant, so it has moved to a higher position on the chart. Although they are close together on the chart, the vowels in *bad* and *bed* are still quite distinct because *bad* is longer and has a slightly diphthongal quality.

The vowels of BBC English are shown in figure 5.8. Many of them are in fairly similar positions to the corresponding vowels shown in figures 5.5 and 5.6 for American English. This is hardly surprising as most of us can readily understand both accents. The major differences are due to the additional vowels

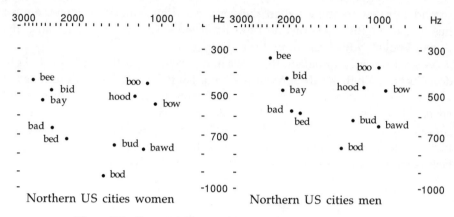

Figure 5.7   Formant charts of US Northern Cities English.

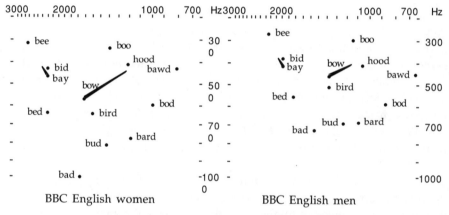

Figure 5.8   Formant charts of BBC (British) English.

of BBC English that we discussed in chapter 4, and the large change in quality that occurs in the diphthong in words such as *no, dough*, and *bow*.

In the middle of the chart in figure 5.8 is the vowel in *bird*, which has the same quality as the first vowel in *about* or the last vowel in *sofa*, and like them has no r-coloring. As a result of this vowel in *bird* occupying the space in the center, the BBC English vowel in *bud* is pushed down so that it is somewhat lower on the chart, with a higher first formant frequency than its General American counterpart. Another additional vowel is that in *bard*, which also has no r-coloring, but is nevertheless distinct from the vowels in *bod* and *bawd*. In BBC English *cart, cot, caught* are all pronounced differently, all of them without any suspicion of an **r** sound. The presence of this new vowel in *bard* and *cart* pushes the vowel in *bod* and *cot* higher on the chart. It has a lower first formant frequency than its General American counterpart. The vowel in *bawd* and *caught* is also pushed higher, and in addition has a considerably lower second formant frequency than the corresponding American vowel, almost pushing it off the chart on the right-hand side. This is largely because the British English vowel has more lip rounding.

As with American English, there are many varieties of British English. London Cockney English differs from BBC English in having large diphthongs in words such as *bay* and *mate*, which sound superficially like those in *buy* and *might*. They are actually somewhat different, and Cockney speakers do not confuse these words. *Bay* has changed so that it begins with a vowel more like that in BBC English *bud*, but *buy* is also different from BBC English in that it begins with a vowel more similar to that in BBC English *father*.

5.3   Formant Three

Formant charts such as those we have been discussing do not take the frequency of the third formant into account. This formant has very little function in distinguishing the vowels shown. For all English vowels, with one notable exception, the third formant frequency can be predicted fairly accurately from the frequencies of the first two formants. The exception is the vowel in most forms of American English *bird*. As with many other sounds associated with *r*, this vowel has a very low third formant frequency. Its first and second formants are often very similar to those in *hood*, but it has a very different quality. It would be misleading to plot it on a chart that shows only the first and second formant frequencies.

The frequency of the third formant is very much affected by the position of the lips. This makes it more important in some languages. It so happens that neither General American English nor BBC English have vowels with the same tongue positions but different lip positions. In English, when the tongue is high in the front of the mouth (as for **i** as in *heed*), the lips are fairly far apart. But in French, German, and many other languages, the position of the lips (and hence the frequency of the third formant) is not so predictable. We will discuss these languages in chapter 14.

5.4   Summary

Vowels can always be accurately described in terms of the frequencies of the first three formants. It is often sufficient to plot the frequencies of the first two formants on a formant chart. Given proper scales that reflect how the differences between vowels are perceived we can give good descriptions of the dialects of English. The only English vowel in which the third formant plays a significant role is the vowel in *bird* as pronounced in General American English.

6

The Sounds of Consonants

6.1 Consonant Contrasts

There are only minor differences in the consonants of the principal dialects of English, so we need not discuss British and American English separately. Table 6.1 shows all the consonants before **e** as in *bet* and **ai** as in *buy*. Recording 6.1 illustrates my pronunciation of these words. The first column in the table lists the appropriate symbols of the International Phonetic Alphabet. Nearly all of them are familiar letters of the alphabet. We will note the special symbols when we refer to them. The final column of this table groups the consonants in accordance with certain features that they have in common. We will discuss the sounds of consonants with reference to these features.

6.2 Stop Consonants

Many consonants are just ways of beginning or ending vowels. This is particularly true of consonants such as **b, d, g,** each of which has a rapid movement of the lips or tongue before or after another sound such as a vowel. They are called stop consonants because the air in the vocal tract is completely stopped at some point. When forming a **b** in a word such as *bib,* the lips are firmly closed at the beginning and end of the word. In the case of **d** as in *did* it is the tip of the tongue that blocks the vocal tract by forming a closure just behind the upper front teeth. For **g** as in *gag,* the back of the tongue is raised to make a closure against the roof of the mouth.

Table 6.1 English consonant sounds, illustrated as far as possible before the vowel **e** as in *bet*, and the vowel **ai** ('i') as in *buy*. The first column shows a set of IPA symbols that can be used to transcribe them, and the final column names a feature that groups sets of consonants together

IPA	Vowel e	Vowel ai		Feature
b	bet	buy		stop
d	debt	die		stop
g	get	guy		stop
p	pet	pie		stop
t	ten	tie		stop
k	ken	kite		stop
w	wet	why		approximant
j ('y')	yet			approximant
l	let	lie		approximant
r	retch	rye		approximant
m	met	my	ram	nasal
n	net	nigh	ran	nasal
ŋ			rang	nasal
f	fed	fie		fricative
θ		thigh		fricative
s	set	sigh		fricative
ʃ	shed	shy	mission	fricative
h	hen	high		fricative
v	vet	vie		fricative
ð	then	thy		fricative
z	Zen	Zion	mizzen	fricative
ʒ			vision	fricative
ʧ	Chet	chime		affricate
ʤ	jet	jive		affricate

Each of these stop consonants forms a quickly changing sound. The resonances of the vocal tract, the formants, are being produced while the stop closure is being formed or is opening. The shape of the vocal tract is changing, and as a result the formant frequencies are moving. Figure 6.1 shows the formant frequency movements associated with the stop consonants **b, d, g** in the words *bab, dad, gag*. The location of each of the first three formants at the start of the syllable is marked by an arrow.

At the beginning of the first word, *bab*, all three formants move rapidly upward. The resonances of the vocal tract when the lips are almost closed are

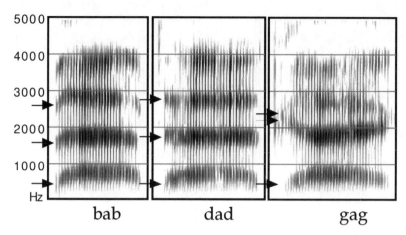

Figure 6.1 Spectrograms of stops in *bab, dad, gag*. The arrows mark the origins of the first three formants.

in the low range. The formant frequencies move up from this low starting point to the higher resonant frequencies that occur in the vowel. At the beginning of the word *dad* the first formant goes up, the second moves very little and the third moves slightly down. The **d** closure, with the tip of the tongue behind the teeth, makes a vocal tract shape that has resonances as shown by the positions of the three arrows. As the stop is released and the vocal tract moves away from this shape, the formants move away from the position indicated by the arrows. For the final word, *gag*, the most notable movements are those of the second and third formants. The shape of the vocal tract when the back of the tongue is almost touching the roof of the mouth, as it does in **g**, makes the second and third formants have very similar frequencies. The resonances of the vocal tract when the stop is being released are as shown by the arrows.

The movements of the second and third formants are the distinguishing characteristics of the stop consonants. The movements of the first formant simply mark them as having a stop closure. For all three of the sounds we have been considering, the frequency of the first formant increases when they are at the beginning of a syllable, and falls when they are at the end. The movements of the other two formants distinguish these sounds from one another. In general, if a word or syllable starts with both the second and third formants increasing in frequency, then the sound is a **b**. If the third formant falls and the second formant has only a small movement it is a **d**. If the second and third formants are close together just after a stop has been formed, then the back of the tongue has contacted the roof of the mouth, as in a **g**.

The stops **b**, **d**, and **g** also affect the formants at the ends of the words in figure 6.1. In each of these words the movements of the formants at the end are the reverse of those at the beginning. The first formant moves down as the stop is formed in all three words. The second and third formants move down

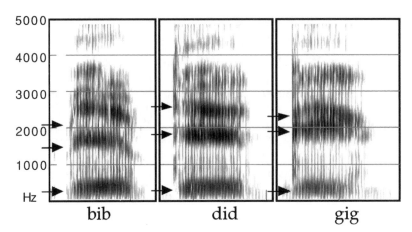

Figure 6.2 Spectrograms of stops in *bib, did, gig*. The arrows mark the origins of the first three formants.

at the end of *bab*, reversing the movement at the beginning of the word. There is very little movement of the formants at the end of *dad*, just as there was little movement at the beginning. With a little imagination one can see that at the very end of *dad* there is a small downward movement of the second formant and an indication of an upward movement of the third formant. At the end of *gag* the second and third formants clearly come together, forming a kind of mirror image of the way they came apart at the beginning of the word.

There are similar movements of the formants when these consonants occur with other vowels. Figure 6.2 shows spectrograms of the words *bib, did, gig*. In these words, too, you can see that the sound **b** is associated with a lowering of all three formants, for **d** the second and third formants are level or pointing upwards, and for **g** the second and third formants are closer together. These formant movements characterize these stop consonants.

English has another set of stop consonants, the sounds **p, t, k**, as in the words *pip, tit, kick*. (We use the symbol **k** for this sound, irrespective of whether it is spelled with 'c', as in *cat*, or 'k' or 'ck' as in *kick*, or 'q' as in *quick*, which can be considered as beginning with **kw**, or even 'x' as in *tax*, which ends in **-ks**.) The sounds **p, t, k** are made with the same gestures of the lips or tongue as **b, d, g**. For **p** and **b** the lips close, for **t** and **d** the tip of the tongue makes contact just behind the teeth, and for **k** and **g** the back of the tongue contacts the roof of the mouth. Consequently the movements of the formants are similar for these two sets of sounds. The difference between the two sets is in the action of the vocal folds. When you say a word beginning with **b, d,** or **g** the vocal folds are vibrating while the lips or tongue are moving apart. But for **p, t,** and **k** the vocal folds are apart at the beginning of the movement. Consequently at the beginning of each of the words *pip, tit, kick* there is a burst of air that produces a different kind of sound. Instead of the sound produced by the

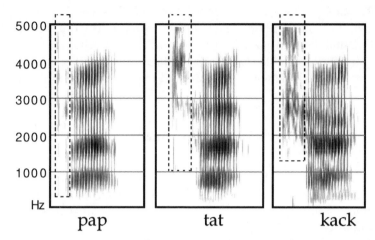

Figure 6.3 Spectrograms of voiceless stops in *pap*, *tat*, *kack* (as in *cackle*).

action of the vocal folds, which has a definite pitch and overtones corresponding to a particular vocal tract shape, there is a more noisy sound with a less
well-defined pitch. You can hear a difference between the noisy bursts that
occur at the beginning and end of each of the words *pip*, *tit*, *kick*, if you say just
the **p**, **t**, **k** sounds by themselves. The bursts of noise for **p** at the beginning and
end of *pip* are very small and with no definite pitch. There is a comparatively
high pitch associated with the burst of noise for **t** in *tit*, and a somewhat lower
pitch for the **k** noise in *kick*.

So that you can compare the sounds **p**, **t**, **k** with **b**, **d**, **g** in *bab*, *dad*, *gag*,
figure 6.3 shows a spectrogram of *pap*, *tat*, *kack*. The first two are real words in
my vocabulary, but the third is a nonsense word beginning in the same way as
cat, but ending so that it rhymes with *back*. The bursts of noise at the beginning
of each of these words are enclosed within dashed lines. (The bursts that
sometimes occur at the ends of these words were not produced when these
words were said. They are more commonly heard when the next word begins
with a vowel.) The burst associated with **p** is fairly faint, and scattered over a
wide range. That associated with **t** is in the higher frequency range, and in fact
extends far above the range of frequencies shown in this analysis. The **k** burst
has its greatest intensity between 2,000 and 3,000 Hz. The burst for **k** is also
slightly longer than that for **t**, and both of them are longer than that for **p**.

You cannot see the movements of the formants at the beginnings of *pat*, *tat*,
cat, as the corresponding movements of the lips and tongue take place during
the noise bursts. But you can see some of the changes that occur for the stops
at the ends of these words. There are small downward movements at the end
of *pap*, just as there were at the end of *bab*. There is very little movement at the
end of *tat*, which is what we found at the end of *dad*. At the end of *kack* there
is a tendency for the second and third formants to come together, as happened
at the end of *gag*. The movements of the formants are not so clear at the ends

of *pat*, *tat*, *kack* because in my speech (as for many speakers of both BBC English and General American English) the vocal folds close tightly together just as the final consonants in words of this type are being made, cutting off the last part of the syllable. This is also the reason why there are no bursts at the ends of these words when they are said in a normal unemphatic way.

6.3 Approximants

The next set of consonants listed in table 6.1 are those in words such as *wet*, *yet*, *let*, and *retch*. The IPA symbols for them are **w**, **j**, **l**, **r**, all of them having the same values as in English words except for **j**, which corresponds to English 'y'. The International Phonetic Association chose **j** to represent the sound at the beginning of *yet*, as 'j' has this value in several Northern European languages such as German and Danish. In these languages words such as *ja* (yes) and *jung* (young) begin with a sound we would write with 'y'. The sounds **w**, **j** ('y'), **l**, **r** are called 'approximants'. They are the opposite of stop consonants in that they do not involve any kind of closure of the vocal tract. Instead there is simply a narrowing at some point. For **w** the lips are close together and the back of the tongue is raised, but air still flows freely out of the mouth. For **j** ('y') it is the front of the tongue that is raised, but not far enough to hinder the airflow. The sound **l** is peculiar in that the tip of the tongue comes up and touches the upper teeth or roof of the mouth much as it did for **d** and **t**, but air flows out freely over the sides of the tongue. The sound **r** is more difficult to describe, partly because different speakers make it in different ways. It usually involves some raising of the tip of the tongue toward a point on the roof of the mouth well behind the upper front teeth.

Each of these gestures is associated with particular formant frequencies. As you can see in figure 6.4, the most conspicuous aspect of the **w** in *wet* is the rising second formant. The first formant also goes up, but less noticeably (partly because it is very faint at the start of the word), and the third formant has much the same frequency at the beginning and end of the word. The **j** ('y') in *yet* has a falling second formant, a more visible rise in the first formant, and a drop in the third formant.

The **l** in *let* differs from the first two sounds (and from the last) in that there is a distinct break in the pattern at the moment indicated by the arrow. Before that time there is a faint formant bar at a very low frequency, and another faint bar at about 1,500 Hz. Immediately after the arrow the formants have a much higher intensity (the bars are darker) and are at a distinctly different frequency. The same kind of change in the pattern also occurs in the higher frequencies above 3,000 Hz. These changes occur because there is an abrupt change in the articulation – the tip of the tongue is in contact with the roof of the mouth for the **l**, and then breaks away from it for the vowel.

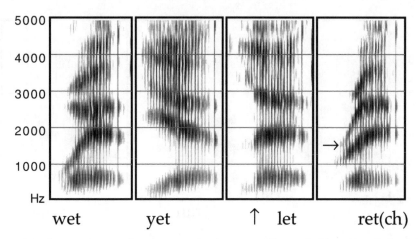

Figure 6.4 Spectrograms of approximants in *wet, yet, let, retch*. The arrow below the third spectrogram marks the moment when the tip of the tongue, which is raised for l, comes away from the roof of the mouth. The arrow in the fourth spectrogram shows the low beginning of the third formant.

The **r** at the beginning of *retch* is characterized by the very low frequency of the third formant. All the formants rise at the beginning of this word, but it is the movement of the third formant that is most significant. Whenever there is an **r** in a word the third formant will be below 2,000 Hz, sometimes, as shown by the arrow in this example, falling to as low as 1,500 Hz.

6.4 Nasals

The next set of sounds listed in table 6.1 are called nasals because they involve sound radiated while air comes out through the nose. The nasal sounds **m, n,** and **ŋ** (the phonetic symbol for 'ng') occur at the ends of the words *ram, ran,* and *rang*. They are like vowels and approximants in that they can be character-ized largely in terms of their formant frequencies, but they differ in that the formants are not as loud as they are in vowels. The nasals are made by block-ing the sound from coming out of the mouth while allowing it to come out through the nose, and this affects the relative amplitude (the loudness) of the formants.

Spectrograms illustrating the three nasals in the words *ram, ran, rang* are shown in figure 6.5. (These spectrograms also provide further illustrations of the **r** with its low third formant at the beginning of each of these words.) Just before the nasals at the end of each of the words in figure 6.5 there is a sharp discontinuity (marked by an arrow) when the lips come together or the tongue comes up to contact the roof of the mouth. After this point there is less

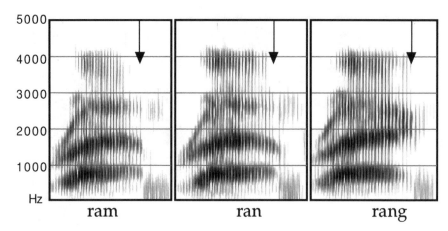

Figure 6.5 Spectrograms of nasals at the ends of the words *ram, ran, rang*.
The arrows mark the onsets of the nasals.

amplitude in the nasal consonant itself. All three nasals have a first formant
which has distinctly less energy (is fainter) than in the preceding vowel, and
which has a very low frequency, around 200 Hz. For each of them there is also
another formant visible in the neighborhood of 2,500 Hz, but there is comparatively little energy in the region normally occupied by the second formant.
This pattern typifies the nasal consonants.

The main differences between the three nasals are not in the wholly nasal
portions, but in the onsets to these portions. The ways the formants move as
the nasal is being formed are very reminiscent of the formant movements in
bab, dad, gag, which we saw in figure 6.1. As the lips close for **m** the formants
(particularly the second) lower in frequency, just as they did before the lip
closure for **b**. The formant frequencies just before the tongue tip closure for **n**
are very similar to those for **m**, but the third formant is very slightly higher.
The ŋ ('ng') at the end of *rang* is far more distinct. The second and third
formants come together just as they did in *gag*.

6.5 Fricatives

There are several consonants that are produced without vibrations of the vocal
folds. Prominent among them are the consonants in the words *fie, thigh, sigh,
shy*, each of which begins with a sound in which the vocal folds are held apart
so that they do not vibrate. In these consonants the noise is made by air being
forced through a narrow gap. Instead of formants – resonances of the vocal
tract – their most prominent acoustic features are higher-pitched, more random,
noises, akin to the screech of the wind as it blows around a corner. The sound
at the beginning of each of the words *fie, thigh, sigh, shy* is called a voiceless

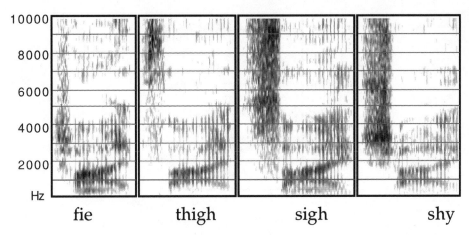

Figure 6.6   Spectrograms of voiceless fricatives in *fie, thigh, sigh, shy*. Note that the frequency scale extends higher in this figure than in the previous figures.

fricative – voiceless because the vocal folds are not vibrating, and fricative to indicate that the noise is produced by the friction, the resistance to the air as it rushes through a narrow gap.

Figure 6.6 shows a spectrogram of the four voiceless fricatives that occur in English. The pattern of the noise that occurs at the beginning of each of the words *fie, thigh, sigh, shy* is similar to the bursts that we saw at the beginning of each of the words *pap, tat, kack* in figure 6.3. In all these voiceless sounds there are no pulses produced by the vocal folds. Whenever the vocal folds are vibrating there is a series of pulses that produce amplitude peaks in the sound wave. These peaks are visible on spectrograms as vertical striations. Figure 6.7 shows an expanded spectrogram of the first part of the word *fie*, with the wave-form showing the vocal fold pulses immediately above. As may be seen, there are about 10 pulses in 100 milliseconds (ms), or one pulse in one-hundredth of a second (10 ms). There are no such regular pulses in the fricative portion before the vowel. The energy is scattered over the higher frequencies. It is not, however, randomly distributed, and each of the four English fricatives has a distinct pattern.

The spectrogram of **f** as in *fie* on the left of figure 6.6 has noise spread over a wide range of frequencies. Insofar as there is a region in which there is greater intensity it is between 3,000 and 4,000 Hz. The spectrogram of **θ** (the phonetic symbol for 'th' as in *thigh*) also shows energy over a range of frequencies, but in this case it is centered in the higher frequency range, above 8,000 Hz. There is often very little difference in the fricative noises of these two sounds – neither of them is very loud. There are, however, differences in the formants of the adjacent vowels. The fourth formant is below 4,000 Hz in *fie* and above it in *thigh*. The second formant in *fie* also starts at a slightly lower frequency, around 1,200 Hz, and then moves noticeably upwards. At the start

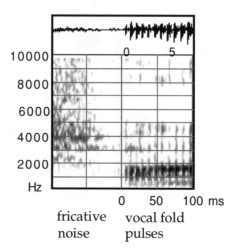

Figure 6.7   A spectrogram of part of the word *fie* in figure 6.6 on an expanded time scale. The waveform of the sound is shown above, with numbers below the fifth and tenth vocal fold pulses.

of *thigh* the second formant is fairly level at around 1,250 Hz. In many circumstances, such as over a telephone or in a room full of people, the fricative noise is inaudible, and the formant movements are the only cues distinguishing these two sounds. But in any case the differences in the fricative noise and in the formant movements are both very small, and it is not surprising that English is one of the few languages in the world that uses both these sounds. Greek and Spanish are the only other well-known European languages that contrast them.

The next fricative is **s** as in *sigh*. It has a large amount of energy in the upper part of the figure, extending even above the 10,000 Hz shown in the figure. There is comparatively little energy below 3,500 Hz, and a noticeable intense band above 5,000 Hz. The sound ʃ (the phonetic symbol for 'sh' as in *shy*) has more energy at a slightly lower frequency, centered at a little above 3,000 Hz. Say a long ʃ ('sh'), as if you were saying *shush* to a child, and then a long **s**, as if you were hissing a villain. The ʃ ('sh') sounds lower in pitch than the **s**. Neither of these sounds said in isolation has a real pitch in the way that a vowel does. For that you have to have a repeating waveform of the kind that is produced by regular repetitive movements of the vocal folds. But you get some impression of pitch from the fact that the energy is in specific parts of the frequency range.

The fricatives **s** as in *sigh* and ʃ as in *shy* are sometimes called sibilants. They have a greater intensity – they are louder – than the other two voiceless fricatives **f** and θ ('th'). As a result there are darker marks in the upper frequency range on the spectrogram. If you make each of the sounds **f**, θ ('th'), **s**, ʃ ('sh') one after the other without any vowel in between, you can hear that the first two fricatives are far less loud than the other two.

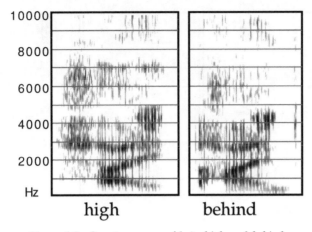

Figure 6.8 Spectrograms of **h** in *high* and *behind*.

The next consonant listed in table 6.1 is **h** as in *high*. It is convenient to discuss it at this point, although it is not really a voiceless fricative as the source of the noise is not air being forced through a narrow gap. Instead the origin of the sound is the turbulence – the random variations in air pressure – caused by the movement of the air across the edges of the open vocal folds and other surfaces of the vocal tract. Because the principal origin of the sound is deep within the vocal tract, rather than near the lips or the front of the mouth, the resonances of the whole vocal tract will be more prominent, and the sound is more like that of a noisy vowel.

Figure 6.8 shows spectrograms of **h** in *high* and *behind*. In *high* there is a noisy third formant at a little below 3,000 Hz, and there are even faint traces of the first two formants. In *behind*, in which **h** is between two vowels, the vocal folds draw apart without completely ceasing the vibrations that occur in the vowels, so that they are still flapping in the airstream. There are noisy forms of the first two formants, as well as energy in the higher frequencies.

Each of the four voiceless fricatives **f**, **θ** ('th'), **s**, **ʃ** ('sh') has a counterpart in which the vocal folds are vibrating while the fricative noise is being formed by forcing air through a gap. The **f** in *fie* contrasts with the **v** in *vie* in this way. A similar contrast occurs in *thigh* and *thy*. In this case English spelling does not distinguish the two forms of 'th'. As we have seen, the phonetic symbol for 'th' as in *thigh* is **θ**. The symbol for 'th' as in *thy* is **ð**, a modified version of the old Anglo-Saxon letter for this sound. The voiceless fricative **s** has a voiced counterpart **z**. The nearest word showing the contrast with **s** in *sigh* is *Zion*. A pair of words that differ only in that one has **s** and the other has **z** is *seal* and *zeal*. The counterpart to **ʃ** as in *shy* occurs in relatively few words, usually between vowels as in the middle of *measure*. This sound, for which the phonetic symbol is **ʒ**, cannot appear at the beginning of a word other than in a foreign name such as *Zsa Zsa*, **ʒa ʒa**. The distinction between **ʃ** and **ʒ** is best

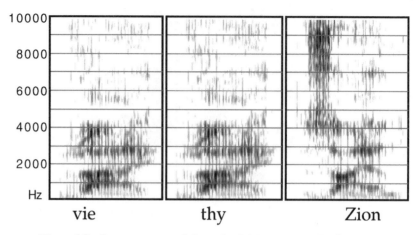

Figure 6.9 Spectrograms of the voiced fricatives in *vie*, *thy*, *Zion*.

exemplified by words such as *mission*, which has ʃ, versus *vision* which has ʒ in the middle.

Voiced fricatives have formants produced by pulses from the vocal folds as well as more random energy produced by forcing air through a narrow gap. Figure 6.9 shows spectrograms of the voiced fricatives in *vie*, *thy*, *Zion*. In all three of these words very faint formants can be seen during the initial fricatives. In the first two words, *vie* and *thy*, there is only a little random energy in the higher frequencies, but in the third word, *Zion*, the effects of the turbulent airstream produced by the friction are clearly visible. We saw in the discussion of figure 6.6 that the corresponding voiceless fricatives, f and θ, had a relatively low-intensity noise in the higher frequencies when compared with s.

The difference between the voiced and voiceless fricatives ʒ and ʃ is illustrated in figure 6.10 (which also shows a further example of the voiced fricative v). The fricatives are in the middle of each word, as indicated by the placement of the phonetic symbols. Under the ʒ in the first word, in the area between the dashed lines, there are vertical striations associated with vibrations of the vocal folds. These indications of vocal fold vibrations are rather difficult to see, so I have added lines at the top of the picture that make them a little clearer. Under ʃ there is only the noise due to the turbulent airstream.

The last sounds to be considered in this chapter, the initial consonants in *chime* and *jive*, are not really single sounds. The 'ch' in words such as *chime* and *chip* consists of the t in *time* or *two*, followed by the ʃ in *shine* or *ship*. You can see this if you compare phrases such as *gray chip* and *great ship*. In the first of these phrases the two consonants are at the beginning of the second word, but in the second phrase the t is at the end of the first word and the ʃ is at the beginning of the second. Similarly 'j' as in *jive* begins with the two consonants d and ʒ, although this cannot be illustrated in the same way, as English words

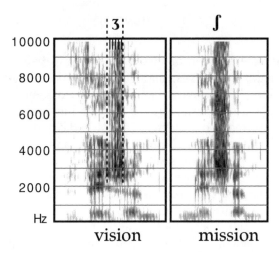

Figure 6.10   Spectrograms showing the contrast between the voiced fricative in *vision* and the voiceless fricative in *mission*.

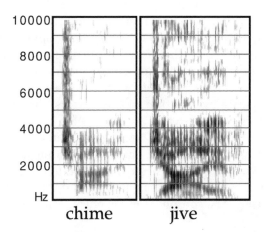

Figure 6.11   Spectrograms showing the contrast between the voiceless affricate in *chime* and the voiced affricate in *jive*.

do not begin with ʒ. The nearest I can get to showing this combination is the pair of phrases *hide Zsa (Zsa)* and *high jar*. The combination of a stop followed by a fricative as in tʃ and dʒ is called an affricate.

Figure 6.11 illustrates these two sounds. There is, of course, little to see for the initial t in *chime*, except for the abrupt beginning of the following ʃ. The vertical striations due to the vibrations of the vocal folds are just visible in ʒ in *jive*. Both the voiceless ʃ and the voiced ʒ are considerably shorter than when they occur on their own.

6.6   Summary

The voiced and voiceless consonants of English can be divided into stops, approximants, nasals, fricatives, and affricates. Spectrograms of stops are marked by the abrupt beginning or ending of the adjacent vowel. The voiced stops **b, d, g** can be distinguished by the formant movements, **b** having a low second and third formant, **d** a second formant in the mid-range, around 1,700 Hz and a high third formant, and **g** having second and third formants that are very close together. The voiceless stops **p, t, k** may have formant movements similar to those of **b, d, g** after a vowel, but at the beginning of a word they are largely distinguished by the frequencies of the bursts of noise that are produced as the stop closure is released. The approximants **w, j** ('y'), **l, r** have their own formant patterns, **w** being similar to a movement away from the vowel **u** as in *boo*, and **j** ('y') being similar to a movement away from the vowel **i** as in *bee*. The approximant **l** has a low-intensity formant at a very low frequency, another low-intensity formant at about 1,500 Hz, and a distinct break in the pattern before a vowel. Whenever there is an **r** in a word the third formant will be very low, usually below 2,000 Hz. The nasals **m, n, ŋ** ('ng') have first formants with a very low frequency, around 200 Hz, another formant visible in the neighborhood of 2,500 Hz, and comparatively little energy in the region normally occupied by the second formant. They have similar formant movements to the corresponding stops. The voiceless fricatives **f** and **θ** ('th') have energy over a wide range of higher frequencies. They are distinguished from each other partly by the formant movements. The other voiceless fricatives, **s** and **ʃ** ('sh'), have greater energy, with **s** being mostly in the high frequency range from about 3,500 Hz upwards, and **ʃ** having most energy somewhat lower, around 3,000 Hz. The corresponding voiced fricatives **v, ð** ('th'), **z, ʒ** (in *vision*) have similar energy distributions, but with the addition of formant resonances. The affricates **ʧ** ('ch') and **ʤ** ('j') are like the sequences **t + ʃ** ('ch') and **d + ʒ**. The consonant **h** has noisy forms of the formants in the adjacent vowels.

7

Acoustic Components of Speech

7.1   The Principal Acoustic Components

When I was a graduate student in the early 1950s I had the good fortune to hear a talk by one of the first people to realize how conversational speech could be fully described in a limited set of acoustic terms. He was an engineer named Walter Lawrence, who broke speech down into parts that he could represent by lines painted on a glass slide. Each line represented one of the ingredients – parameters as he called them – of running speech. He used a beam of light to read the lines that he had painted, and was able to turn them back into speech-like sounds. Lawrence's great insight was that it was possible to break speech into a set of components. We will follow (and slightly enlarge) his original system so that we can summarize the acoustic characteristics of speech that we described in chapter 6.

Let's begin with vowels. They can be distinguished by the frequencies of the first three formants. On a spectrogram you can see higher formants, but they do not vary much from one vowel to another. They differ from person to person and make people sound slightly different from one another, but they have little linguistic function. They distinguish people, not words.

Table 7.1 is the start of a list summarizing the acoustic characteristics of speech, showing the things we need to know other than those required for distinguishing one speaker from another. The table gives both the technical acoustic terms and the terms that we can use to describe what we hear. We'll refer to these as the auditory correlates. The vowels of English and most other languages can be described by stating the values of just the three things shown in the table.

Table 7.1   The major acoustic variables of vowels and their auditory correlates

Acoustic variable	Auditory correlate
Frequency of first formant	Pitch of first group of overtones
Frequency of second formant	Pitch of second group of overtones
Frequency of third formant	Pitch of third group of overtones

Table 7.2   Some additional acoustic variables of speech and their auditory correlates

Acoustic variable	Auditory correlate
Amplitude of first formant	Loudness of first group of overtones
Amplitude of second formant	Loudness of second group of overtones
Amplitude of third formant	Loudness of third group of overtones

Now we must add what we need for consonants. The nasal consonants re-
presented by **m**, **n**, and **ŋ** ('ng'), as at the ends of the words *ram*, *ran*, and *rang*,
can also be characterized largely in terms of their formant frequencies. However, as we have seen, they differ from vowels in that the formants, the groups
of overtones, are not as loud as they are in vowels. The same is true of the
approximants **w**, **r**, l, **j**, as in *what*, *rot*, *lot*, *yacht*. We must add to the list of
the components of speech sounds given in table 7.1 by noting the possibility of
varying the amplitude (loudness) as well as the frequency (pitch) of the three
formants. This adds three more variables to our list, as shown in table 7.2.

Voiceless consonants can be characterized in acoustic terms by adding two
more variables to the list that we have been building up. As we noted, the
major difference between **s** and **ʃ** ('sh') is that **s** has a higher pitch. This corresponds to a difference in the frequency of semi-random noise that occurs.
Roughly speaking, we can say that there is a band of noise, and it has a higher
mid frequency for **s** than for **ʃ** ('sh'). The major difference between **s**, **ʃ** and **f**,
θ ('th') is that **s** and **ʃ** are louder than **f** and **θ**. They have greater amplitude.
With this in mind we can see that we need to specify the noise as shown in
table 7.3. A precise specification of all the aspects of voiceless consonants – the
noise bursts of **p**, **t**, **k** as well as the fricatives **f**, **θ**, **s**, **ʃ** – would be very
complex, and well beyond the scope of this book. The variables in table 7.3
provide only a rough characterization of these sounds, sufficient to distinguish
them from one another.

In order to describe the sounds of speech we have to add one more variable,
which we discussed at the beginning of this book, the pitch of the voice as
controlled by the rate of vibration of the vocal folds. This variable is not
relevant in voiceless sounds such as **f**, **θ**, **s**, **ʃ**. But in all the sounds in which the

Table 7.3 The major acoustic variables required for specifying voiceless sounds, together with their auditory correlates

Acoustic variable	Auditory correlate
Center frequency of the semi-random noise	Pitch of the voiceless components
Amplitude of the semi-random noise	Loudness of the voiceless components

Table 7.4 The major acoustic components of speech and their auditory correlates

Acoustic variable	Auditory correlate
Frequency of first formant	Pitch of first group of overtones
Frequency of second formant	Pitch of second group of overtones
Frequency of third formant	Pitch of third group of overtones
Amplitude of first formant	Loudness of first group of overtones
Amplitude of second formant	Loudness of second group of overtones
Amplitude of third formant	Loudness of third group of overtones
Center frequency of the semi-random noise	Pitch of the voiceless components
Intensity of the semi-random noise	Loudness of the voiceless components
Fundamental frequency of voiced sounds	Pitch of the voice

vocal folds are vibrating, the rate of vibration has to be noted. A more complete set of acoustic variables is therefore as shown in table 7.4. This table summarizes the nine most important acoustic variables of speech. We can characterize nearly all English speech sounds (and by far the majority of those in other languages) in terms of the values of these variables.

7.2 Synthesizing Speech

Walter Lawrence, the engineer who first described running speech in terms of a small set of variables, began by considering only six possibilities. He used a single amplitude variable for all three formants (which meant that his specifications of nasals and approximants were not very good), and he did not distinguish the noise frequencies – the pitch distinction between **s** and ʃ ('sh'). But he was able to show that a limited set of variables could characterize many aspects of speech by building a speech synthesizer, a machine that made noises in accordance with these specifications. He called it PAT, a Parametric Artificial Talker. He painted the required values for each variable on a glass slide, which was scanned to provide the controlling voltages for a vast rack of vacuum tubes that produced and summed up different sound waves.

Lawrence's work was followed up by many people, and he himself went on to build a synthesizer using the nine variables in table 7.4. Many years ago, in the 1960s, Lawrence's colleague John Holmes demonstrated that these variables could be used to synthesize very natural speech. The recordings for this chapter show how they can be used in the synthesis of the sentence 'A bird in the hand is worth two in the bush'. In synthesizing this sentence I used values of the nine variables very similar to those originally used by John Holmes, modifying them slightly to make the utterance sound more like my own voice, and playing them through a computer in the UCLA Phonetics Lab.

Recording 7.1 is the complete synthesized sentence. The following recordings show how this sound was built up. Recording 7.2 is the result of varying just the first formant. It is a computer-synthesized sound wave in which only the pitch and loudness of the first formant are varied. If you listen to this, you can hear something vaguely similar to some of the sounds in the sentence, but if you hadn't heard recording 7.1 first you would have had difficulty in distinguishing any of the sounds in recording 7.2. Recording 7.3 is a sound wave in which only the pitch and loudness of the second formant are varied. It is easier to hear more of the characteristics of the full sentence in this recording. The second formant by itself conveys more information than the first. But, again, if you hadn't heard the full sentence first, you would have had a great deal of difficulty in interpreting just this formant. Recording 7.4 is a sound wave corresponding to the third formant by itself. This rather tinny sound conveys very little information on its own.

When the three sound waves corresponding to the first three formants are added together, as in recording 7.5, the sounds are instantly clearer. They still don't have the full quality of the human voice. We can make a slight improvement by adding some fixed overtones, as in recording 7.6. This recording has the three varying formants, together with fixed higher formants and other resonances you can see on spectrograms. These added fixed components should not be considered as acoustic variables of speech as they do not vary and hence have not been listed in table 7.4. They do not distinguish any of the sounds of speech; they simply add richness to the voice.

If you listen again to recording 7.6 you can hear most of the voiced sounds, both the vowels and the consonants. What's missing is the noise components that do not rely on the vibrations of the vocal folds. The final ʃ 'sh' in *bush* is completely absent, as well as the noises at the ends of *is* and *worth*. Recording 7.7 reproduces the sound waves that correspond to variations in the next two variables, the pitch and loudness of the voiceless components. By themselves, these noises sound very odd. But, as recording 7.8 shows, when they are added in the right places they provide a good approximation to the noisy components of speech.

Recording 7.8 has all the variations in eight of the nine variables listed in table 7.4. When you listen again, note that it is still on a monotone. Recording 7.9 adds the last variable, the variations due to the vibrations of the vocal

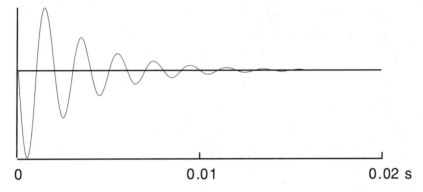

Figure 7.1 A single cycle of a formant with a frequency of 500 Hz.

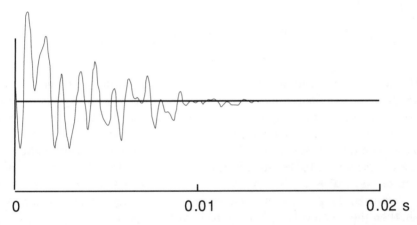

Figure 7.2 A single cycle of a wave corresponding to all the formants in the middle of *bird*.

folds. Adding the pitch for an appropriate intonation makes a big difference. The whole sentence sounds much more natural.

It is worth emphasizing that the 'speech' on the recording was produced entirely on a computer. It is in no sense a recording of a human voice. The values for the variables were obtained by studying a real voice saying this sentence, making spectrograms and other acoustic analyses to find the formants, fundamental frequency, and so on. For example, the first formant was found to be around 500 Hz in the word *bird*. The computer was instructed to calculate a sound wave that corresponded to a first formant frequency of 500 Hz as shown in figure 7.1. Formants with appropriate frequencies and amplitudes were also calculated for the other resonances. When they were all added together the result was a complex wave, as shown in figure 7.2.

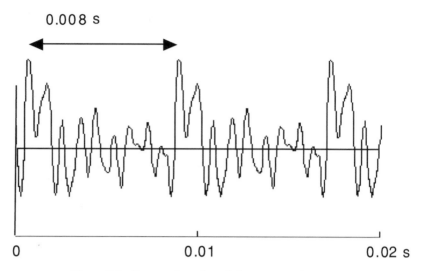

Figure 7.3   Repeated cycles of the wave in figure 7.2.

The next step in forming the vowel in *bird* was to produce a waveform with the right pitch. The computer had to turn the waveform in figure 7.2 into a series of waveforms that were repeated at the correct rate. It did this by adjusting the interval between each repetition of the waveform and smoothing the join between them as shown in figure 7.3. In this particular example the peaks of the waveform are 0.008 seconds apart. This means that there are 125 peaks in one second ($0.008 \times 125 = 1.0$), so the pitch is 125 Hz. If a higher pitch had been required, the peaks would have been pushed closer together; if a lower pitch, then they would have been spread further apart.

The superimposition of the noise components is the only other step required for the synthesis of this phrase. There are, of course, no noise components in the vowel in *bird*. The noises that occur elsewhere in this phrase, such as those in *bush* and *is*, were made by starting with the kind of hissing sound that you hear on a radio when it is not tuned to any station. This was filtered so that it formed a band of noise with the appropriate center frequency. Then the amplitude (loudness) was modified so that the noises made good consonantal sounds.

The recording does not sound exactly like me for two reasons. First, I have simply modified a set of acoustic values originally produced by John Holmes, who was modeling another voice. Many of the characteristics of the original speaker remain, and certainly the credit for producing such a natural-sounding voice must go to him. Second, I synthesized this sentence over 25 years ago, in the early 1970s, on what would now be called a rather primitive computer. Nevertheless, this recording demonstrates very well that we can describe a voice in acoustic terms just by combining a few constants (the fixed resonances) and nine varying features.

7.3 Summary

There are nine principal components of speech sounds: (1–3) the frequencies of the first three formants, (4–6) the amplitudes of the first three formants, (7–8) the frequency and amplitude of the voiceless components, and (9) the fundamental frequency of voiced sounds. Speech can be synthesized by combining sound waves specified in these terms. In order to add naturalness and to imitate the voice of a particular person, it is necessary to add some fixed resonances.

8

Talking Computers

8.1 How Writing Must Be Pronounced

How do we get a computer to talk? My mother-in-law was nearly blind for many years at the end of her life. What she needed was a way of turning anything that could be written into good spoken English. She wanted to be able to put a book in front of a computer, sit back, and enjoy it. (How the computer was going to turn the pages was not her concern.)

Computers have been able to synthesize speech for many years. We saw in chapter 7 that a computer can make sounds like English sentences. But the quality of most synthetic speech is still not high enough to make enjoyable listening. One might think that all we need are the values of the formant frequencies and amplitudes, and the other parameters in table 7.4. But there are many steps in this process that are still not fully understood. So let us see why computers don't yet sound like you and me.

We want to have a system that will turn any kind of written text into synthesized speech, forming what is called a Text-To-Speech (TTS) system. The first step in turning a text into speech is to find all the abbreviations and symbols. They have to be converted into their full forms. Abbreviations have to be distinguished so that the sentence 'Dr. Smith lives at 10 Sunset Dr.' is pronounced as *Doctor Smith lives at ten Sunset Drive,* and 'St. Paul's church is on Church St.' as *Saint Paul's church is on Church Street.* Symbols have to be interpreted so that '$14.22' becomes *Fourteen dollars and twenty-two cents,* and '£1.40' becomes *One pound forty.* Most good TTS systems can deal with all these examples.

We also have to deal with acronyms, spelling out 'TTS' as *text to speech* and turning 'HE' into *His Excellency* or *high explosive,* whichever seems more suitable in the context. Some acronyms are normally not spelled out, but are pronounced just as a sequence of letters (like USA or UK). Others are pronounced as if they were words (like UNESCO). New acronyms (like TTS) are continually being devised, making this a difficult problem.

Numbers are pronounced in several different ways. Think how you would say *The year 1999* as compared with *1999 cars*. If you are talking about the year it has to be *nineteen ninety nine* or *nineteen hundred and ninety nine*, but the number of cars could be *one thousand nine hundred and ninety nine*. Telephone numbers are pronounced in different ways in different countries. Americans might pronounce 404 5911 as *Four zero four, five nine one one*, whereas British speakers might say *Four nought four, five nine double one*.

Once we have a text that contains only words, we have to take the written words and change them so that they are spelled phonetically. This may be quite straightforward. A written sentence like 'Black cats bring good luck' becomes, in a phonetic transcription, **blæk kæts brɪŋ gʊd lʌk**. Even if you don't remember the phonetic symbols for the vowels given in tables 4.1 and 4.2, you can still see the relationship between the letters and the phonetic symbols. But that was an easy sentence. We all know how difficult it is to spell some English words. The computer has similar difficulties in turning written English into a phonetic transcription. We will consider how it does this first for consonants and then for vowels.

Consonants are fairly easy to deal with. Each letter often corresponds to a phonetic symbol, as in the sentence 'Black cats bring good luck'. In this sentence, the only consonants that have to be changed from two letters into one symbol are the 'ck' at the end of 'black' and 'luck' and the 'ng' at the end of 'bring'. A general rule changing 'ng' at the end of a word into the phonetic symbol ŋ will work very well. Another example of a combination of letters that has to be regarded as a single sound is 'sh'. The computer has to know that this is not a sequence of the sound *s* followed by *h*, but a single sound of the kind that we earlier called a fricative. It gets a little more complicated in the case of the letters 'th', which can stand for either the fricative in *thin* or the one in *this*, in which the fricative noise is accompanied by vocal fold vibrations. A rough rule is that if the word is a noun, adjective, or adverb, then 'th' represents the voiceless sound in *thin*, otherwise it represents a voiced sound, as in words such as *the*, *this*, and *that*. Similarly, the computer has to have a general rule making 'ph' into the phonetic symbol **f** in words such as *photo* and *siphon*. Of course all the rules have problems and don't always work. When the computer comes to 'haphazard' it has to know that this word is an exception to the rule, and is not pronounced as if it were *hafazard*.

Vowels are a little more complex. When you were learning to read you had to deal with the problem of the silent 'e' at the ends of words. Each vowel letter can have at least two pronunciations. For example, the vowel 'o' is pronounced as a so-called long vowel when it is followed by a silent 'e' as in *note*, or when it is separated by a single consonant from another vowel in the same word, as in *notable*. It has a so-called short vowel sound when there are two or more consonants after it as in *bottle*, or when there is a single consonant and a word boundary after it, as in *not*. But these rules are far from foolproof. The first vowel in *nothing* has neither the sound of *not* nor that of *note*. We simply have to regard this and many other words as exceptions to the rules. Computer systems working only in terms of spelling rules with no exceptions soon get into difficulties. They cannot deal with the six different pronunciations of 'ough' in American English: *tough, though, bought, bough, cough, through* – to which the British add a seventh: *thorough*, which has ə in the last syllable.

If we have a computer with a large enough memory, we do not have to bother so much with spelling rules. We can store a large dictionary so that every word can be changed into its phonetic form simply by looking it up. The only problem with this form of synthesis is that it fails completely whenever it comes to a new word that is not in its dictionary, such as the previously little-used name *Clinton*. Most text-to-speech systems now rely on a mixed system, using a dictionary look-up for many words, but having spelling rules available for new words.

Phonetic rules and dictionaries will not be enough in some cases. In the sentence *The dog's lead was made of lead*, only a very smart computer could tell that the two forms of *lead* should be pronounced differently. A sophisticated speech synthesizer could manage by understanding the sentence in much the same way as we do. We know that the spelling 'l e a d' represents two different words. We also know that dogs have leads, and that they can be made of metal. In this way we know that the first 'lead' refers to the one word, and the second to the other. A human like you reading this page can appreciate the difference simply from the information in the text. A sufficiently powerful computer could do the same.

But the main problem remains. Computers reading long passages nearly always sound very machine-like because they can't get the correct intonation. They don't know which words should be emphasized and how the different tunes demonstrated in chapter 2 should be produced. They can handle simple sentences, and even use the punctuation to produce the intonation difference between 'He likes cats – and dogs with long hair', and 'He likes cats and dogs with long hair'. But other differences in phrasing are more subtle. When we speak, we know where to put the emphasis because we know the meaning and the grammatical structure of different sentences. If I asked you to name some liquids, you might say *Water is a liquid*, with the emphasis on *Water*. But if I asked you to name some properties of water, you might say *Water is a liquid*, with the emphasis on *liquid*. It is simple for you to make these differences. But computers have to learn a lot about language before they can manage such subtleties.

Early speech synthesis systems could say simple sentences, and distinguish between statements and questions appropriately. Now they are able to produce a wider variety of intonations, and they are very good at conveying straightforward information. But they use smoother pitch changes without the small ups and downs that occur in the real human intonation curves that we saw in chapter 2. Nor do they have the variety of intonations that any of us produce in everyday conversations. And when it comes to reading anything dramatic, they fail hopelessly. It will be a long time before a computer can give a good performance of *Hamlet* that my mother-in-law would have enjoyed.

8.2   Words and Sounds in Sentences

In discussing the problems of synthesizing speech, we have so far skipped over one point that deserves a section all to itself. When we talk we do not say each word separately. There are no pauses between the words in a phrase. That's why there is virtually no difference between phrases like *A name* and *An aim*.

One result of running the words together is that the pronunciation shown in the dictionary is seldom the way many common words are pronounced in a sentence. The end of one word will be changed because of the influence of the following word. When you talk about a hand gun you may well pronounce it as something like *hang gun*, without the **d** being fully formed. If a hand gun ever becomes an everyday item (what an awful thought) it will certainly be pronounced as if it began with *hang*, just as has happened in the case of the familiar word 'handkerchief'.

Combinations of words are continually changing so that they are easier to pronounce. Sometimes there are even semi-recognized spellings such as 'gonna' and 'wanna' for 'going to' and 'want to'. But the effects of talking in a standard colloquial style are not limited to just a few words. I've often heard a phrase like 'this shop' pronounced as *thish shop*, and 'in play' as *im play*.

Some people think that those who say things like this are not talking as precisely as they should. They consider such pronunciations to be sloppy speech. But this is something that everybody does. If you try to pronounce each word separately and distinctly, you will sound most unnatural. When somebody tells you that you should say *going to* instead of *gonna*, just tell them that you are talking more efficiently. You are conveying the same meaning with less effort.

Some speech synthesizers sound unnatural because they produce sentences that are too stilted. They do not take sufficient account of the way words run into one another. Sometimes they also fail because they do not allow for the ways in which many of the little words in speech become much abbreviated. When said in isolation the words *two* and *to* are the same. But they differ in the sentences *I have two fish* and *I have to fish*. The same is true for *but* and *butt* in *The goat will butt you, but it won't hurt much*. Nearly all the small grammatical words such as *but, and, for, to, from, a, the* are pronounced in a very reduced form in conversational speech. Speech synthesizers normally get most of these words right because they typically use the reduced forms. Problems arise in the failure to use the full form when it is required, as in a sentence like *He went to and from London*. In this sentence, the words *to* and *from* are pronounced in their full forms, and not in the reduced forms that occur in a sentence such as *He went to London from Paris*.

Although there are no pauses between most words in a spoken phrase, the white spaces between the words on a page certainly affect the way a phrase is pronounced. We can all hear the difference between *a stray tissue* and *a straight issue*, even though the sequence of phonetic symbols in a transcription is exactly the same. This is because when a **t** occurs at the beginning of a word (as in *tissue*) it has a burst of noise followed by a short period during which the vocal folds are not vibrating. During this period there is a semi-random noise centered at the frequencies of the formants. At the end of a word there is usually no burst of noise, and the clue to the presence of a **t** is in the vowel before it, and the movements of the formants as the **t** is formed. In addition, a word such as *straight* with a **t** at the end has a much shorter vowel than a word such as *stray* with no final consonant. We will return to this point below.

Similar differences are shown by the white spaces in the sentences *I'm gonna get my lamp repaired* and *I'm gonna get my lamb prepared*. When a computer makes a phonetic transcription of these two sentences, the sequence of sounds is the same in both. But when you say them they are easily distinguishable. This is because a **p** (like a **t**) has a burst of noise when it occurs at the beginning of a word such as *prepared*, but not when it occurs at the end of *lamp*. The burst of noise may be sufficient to cover up much of the *re* in *pre(pared)*. In each case the sound can be transcribed as a **p**. But a speech synthesizer needs to know that it has to produce a different waveform for a **p** or a **t** when it occurs at the beginning of a word as opposed to the end. In addition, as in the case of *straight issue* as compared with *stray tissue*, it has to know that the sequence *am* in *lamp* is shorter than the corresponding sequence in *lamb*.

There are differences between virtually all initial and final consonants. Sometimes they are only small differences in length, as in the case of **m** in *m u m*. When this word is said in isolation, the final **m** is much longer than the initial **m**. Sometimes there are more distinct changes in quality, as in the case of **l** in *leaf* and *feel*. You can hear these differences more plainly when you listen to a recording played in reverse. You might expect *leaf* played backwards would sound like *feel*. But when you listen to recording 8.1 you will hear that (at least in my British English) it does not.

A number of other variants of sounds have to be taken into account in speech synthesis (or, indeed, on any occasion when we require a full account of the way a language is pronounced). Many sounds have different forms when they occur in different circumstances. For example, **t** is not only different when it occurs at the end as opposed to the beginning of a word. In American English it is very different when it occurs within a word, before an unstressed vowel as in *pretty* or *better*. In these words it sounds more like a very short **d**. In these circumstances **t** is often called a voiced flap – a sound in which the tongue tip flaps very quickly against the roof of the mouth, rather than making full contact as in the pronunciation of word-initial **t**.

The sound **t** has at least one other variant that is important for high-quality speech synthesis. In a word such as *button* it is replaced by a glottal stop in most varieties of both British and American English. A glottal stop is the sound (or lack of it) caused by bringing the vocal folds tightly together, cutting off all air from the lungs. The phonetic symbol for a glottal stop is **ʔ**, so *button* can be transcribed as **bʌʔn**. You make a glottal stop when you cough or hold your breath. British English speakers (particularly those from big cities) tend to use glottal stops instead of **t** after a vowel. Cockney speakers are well known for pronouncing *butter* as **bʌʔə**.

Finally in this section, there is the matter of the length of each sound, which we mentioned briefly in comparing the words *stray* and *straight*, and *lamb* and *lamp*. The length of a vowel depends on a number of things. Firstly, each vowel has its own natural length; for example, the vowel **i** as in *heed* is longer than the vowel **ɪ** as in *hid*. Next, there is the question of whether the vowel is stressed or not. The first vowel in *personal* is stressed and is longer than the corresponding vowel in *personify*, which is unstressed. Third, vowel length depends on the number of syllables in a word. The vowel in *wit* is longer than the vowel in the first syllable of *witty*, and this in turn is longer than the vowel in the first syllable of *wittily*. Fourth, the length is very much affected by the way the syllable ends. We noted that the vowel in *stray* was longer than that in *straight*. The vowel in *strayed* is intermediate between these two. Long, medium, and short vowel lengths occur in *sigh*, *side*, *sight*, and in *Ben*, *bend*, *bent*. All these variations in vowel length can be described in terms of rules that a synthesizer can use. There are also similar complex rules governing consonant length that must be included in any high-quality synthesis system.

Variations in vowel and consonant length affect the rhythm of a sentence. Because speech synthesizers seldom pay sufficient attention to the small adjustments in length that are needed, they produce speech that is distinctly inhuman. We have already noted how the failure to produce natural pitch changes makes synthesized speech sound artificial. Mistakes in rhythm are equally responsible for the unnatural quality of synthetic speech.

8.3 Synthesizing Sounds from a Phonetic Transcription

Once we have a proper phonetic transcription of the text we wish to synthesize, we can go about making the corresponding sounds. There are two approaches to this problem. We can get a computer to calculate the waveform from information about the formants and other properties of each sound, much as I did when synthesizing the phrase *A bird in the hand is worth two in the bush*, in chapter 7. Alternatively, we can get a computer to join small pieces of stored sound so that they make new sentences.

In the first approach, which is called parametric synthesis, the target values for each sound (the frequencies of the formants, their intensities, and so on) are stored in a table. Part of the table describes the basic duration of the sound, and the durations of the transitions to the next sound. I didn't use a table of values when synthesizing *A bird in the hand is worth two in the bush*. I just looked at spectrograms of my own voice, saw where the formants were, and put the appropriate numbers into the computer. This wasn't really speech synthesis from text. It was just a demonstration that speech could be synthesized from a set of parameters.

The problem with going from a text to a set of target values is that we don't know all the rules for joining one sound to another. We can state the values of the formants for each vowel. We can also describe the parameters that vary in each consonant. But it is very hard to state rules that give all the details of how the parameters vary in continuous speech when joining sounds together.

The more common approach to speech synthesis involves storing larger sections of speech and then joining them up. This is known as concatenative synthesis. The sections can be as large as whole words or phrases. When you dial your telephone company and ask them to tell you somebody's number, you may hear something like *The number is, 421 3682*. The first part of the number is said as a group of three digits, *four two one*, in which the *one* is lengthened and ends with a rising pitch. The second part has four digits, *three six eight two*, with a slightly rising pitch on the *three six* and a large fall on the final *two*. In order to reproduce telephone numbers nicely, the telephone company has to have recordings of each digit said as it occurs in each of these positions with appropriate rising and falling pitches. Producing speech by joining recordings like this is a very simple example of concatenative synthesis.

In theory, if we wanted to synthesize a sentence such as *Black cats bring good luck*, we could do it by joining together stored versions of whole words and somehow adding the correct intonation. This is an impractical method of handling sentences that could contain not only any word in the language but also new words such as names that become important. The next politician of importance may be called 'Trinful Spalindic', and we are unlikely to have that stored. It could even be a relative of mine, and nobody knows how to pronounce *Ladefoged*. (In case you are interested, I pronounce it with the stress on the first syllable, which has the same vowel as in *lad*. The first two syllables, actually, are exactly the same as the diminutive *laddie*. The third syllable is just like *foe* and the final syllable is pronounced with the vowel in *did*. So the whole thing is **'lædɪfəʊgɪd**. It's just two Danish words put together, 'lade', which means 'barn' (the same root as in English 'larder'), and 'foged' which means 'steward'. So I'm really Mr. Barnkeeper.)

An alternative form of synthesis would be to store much smaller pieces, such as a recording of each separate sound. When we want to synthesize *Black cats bring good luck* or *Trinful Spalindic* we could simply take recordings of the sounds **b l æ k k æ t s** etc., and reproduce them one after another. But this would sound terrible because the pieces wouldn't be joined together properly.

Most speech synthesis systems use some stored whole words, some syllables, and some smaller units, which are usually not segments like **b l æ k**. A common technique is to use what is called 'diphone synthesis', in which a computer stores all possible sequences of two sounds in a language. There are 37 sounds in many forms of General American English (15 vowels and 22 consonants). Most of these can be followed by any one of the other sounds or a pause, so there are almost $38 \times 38 = 1{,}444$ possible combinations. Nearly every sound could occur at the end of one word and be followed by any other sound at the beginning of the next. There are a few exceptions; for example, no word can end in **h** and no word can begin with **ŋ** ('ng'). But we also have to add special variants of some sounds. We need, for example, the special form of **t** that occurs in *pretty* and *better*. We also need the form of **t** that is realized as a glottal stop in *button*. Altogether we need to store about 1,500 diphones for synthesizing English.

A diphone speech synthesizer uses a section of speech going from the middle of one sound to the middle of the next. In order to synthesize *Black cats bring good luck* it would use the stored sequences silence+**b**, **b**+**l**, **l**+**æ**, **æ**+**k**, **k**+**k**, and so on. So the first part of building a synthesizer consists of making a recording of someone saying a set of phrases from which these sequences can be cut. For the synthesis we are considering, the original recording might have included the phrases *cub luck, my lap, my back*, as illustrated in the spectrograms in figure 8.1. Each diphone sequence must be cut out of the recording, usually keeping just the last half of the first sound and the first half of the second sound, as indicated by the dotted lines on the spectrograms.

We need to store all the acoustic information about the diphones in a way that will allow us to modify the pitch on which they were said; and we also want the length to be adjustable. There are several ways of doing this. One involves a mathematical technique called LPC analysis. It produces a set of numbers called Linear Predictor Coefficients (LPCs) that represent everything about a waveform except its fundamental frequency (its pitch) and some of the elements that correspond to voice quality. We need not worry about the details of the technique. All that is important for us to note is that if you have a set of LPCs for every one-hundredth of a second (10 ms) throughout a changing sound, you can reproduce the complex sound at any pitch. (If you want to find out more about LPC analysis without getting too deeply involved in mathematics, you can read my book *Elements of Acoustic Phonetics*, University of Chicago Press, 2nd edn, 1996.) One way of creating a speech synthesizer is to store sets of LPCs for every diphone.

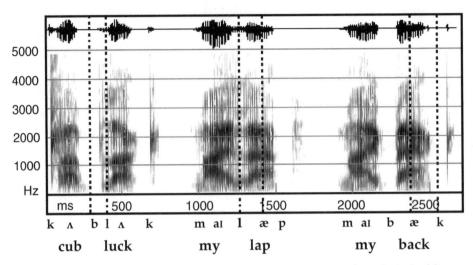

Figure 8.1 A spectrogram of the phrases *cub luck, my lap, my back,* with dashed lines marking the boundaries of the diphones **b+l**, **l+æ**, and **æ+k**.

An alternative, and more widely used, technique is to store the actual waveform of each diphone or other length of recorded speech. In this way we preserve all the naturalness of the original voice. We deal with the problem of varying the pitch along the lines that we used in synthesizing speech in chapter 7. As the computer can determine where each cycle of the complex wave begins and ends, it can stretch these points out if it wants to make a lower pitch than that in the original recording, or push them together if it wants to make a higher pitch. The fewer complex waves there are in a given interval, the lower the pitch, and vice versa. Altering the pitch in this way will alter the duration of that part of the utterance. If there has been too much compression in order to produce a higher pitch, then additional cycles of the complex wave will have to be added. If the pitch has been lowered by lengthening the interval between the starts of adjacent waves, then periods may have to be cut out. Any other variations that we make so that the diphones will have the correct length can be dealt with in the same way, by adding or deleting cycles of the complex waveform.

We have now seen all the elements of a Text-To-Speech (TTS) system. We begin with a written text, which is turned into an appropriate set of phonetic characters. From this the computer makes a list of the diphones and any syllables or whole words that are stored. (Larger computer systems are now storing several thousand words and syllables.) Variations in the normal lengths of the stored items are noted. The intonation pattern of the sentence is calculated, based on the punctuation and whatever else can be discerned about where the pitch should be modified, and the required pitch of each item is also noted in the list of items to be reproduced. Having devised a list of items with the right lengths and pitches, the computer reaches into its store of recorded items, modifies them appropriately, and produces sounds that are something like natural speech.

One of the best speech synthesizers available at the moment is the Fonix Acuvoice system. I must admit that I may be biased in favor of this system, as the scientist in charge, Caroline Henton, is a former colleague, and the voice that is modeled is that of Victoria Anderson, one of my former students. But they and the Fonix team have produced a state-of-the-art Text-To-Speech system, as you can hear in recording 8.2. This synthetic speech sounds like a natural human voice, but at times it is somewhat unintelligible. There is a trade-off in TTS systems between naturalness and intelligibility. Nobody has yet made a system that can be clearly understood and also sounds perfectly natural.

8.4   Summary

Computers can produce good speech, but it sounds far from perfect. The first step in turning a document into synthetic speech is to change it into a phonetic transcription. This includes making sure that all the abbreviations and numbers are properly transcribed. Sounds in connected speech are very much affected by the neighboring sounds, and the sequence of segments to be synthesized must be modified to take this into account. Many speech synthesis systems use an approach in which diphones – the last half of one segment and the first half of the next – are stored and used as the building blocks for complete utterances. About 1,500 diphones are needed for synthesizing English. Major problems still present include getting the right rhythm by the correct adjustment of the durations of the segments, and the right intonation, through consideration of the punctuation, the syntax, and, if possible, the meaning. We do not yet have enough information to be able to create the sound of a lively, intelligent conversation.

9

Listening Computers

9.1 Identifying Sounds

In many ways it is more difficult to get a computer to listen than it is to get it to talk. Talking involves producing just a few voices, but listening involves sorting out the jumble of thousands of words that might have been spoken by hundreds of different people.

Getting a computer to recognize words is mainly a matter of pattern recognition. The computer has to store the phonetic transcriptions of a large number of words and the acoustic patterns of all the different sounds in these words. The recognition task is one of matching the incoming sounds to these stored patterns. The way in which the pattern is stored involves complex signal-processing of the sound wave, but to simplify the process we can think of the patterns as being components of spectrograms.

The upper part of figure 9.1 shows a spectrogram of the word *August*. White lines have been drawn through the first three formants. As you can see, the first and second formants are very close together in the first syllable. The second and third formants move towards one another for the **g** in *August*, and then come apart as this consonant is released. The second vowel, which has formants near 500, 1,500 and 2,500 Hz, is followed by the fricative **s**, with most of the energy in the high frequencies. The final burst of high-frequency noise for the **t** is also clearly visible.

In order to regard the spectrogram of this word as a pattern that can be stored on a computer, we have to reduce it to a set of numbers. We could do this by taking little slices, each one-hundredth of a second long, and finding the energy in the different frequencies present in each slice. Three such slices are shown in the lower part of the figure. In each slice there are 32 bars representing the frequencies below 5,000 Hz. The length of each bar shows the energy in the different groups of frequencies. In the first slice the third and sixth bars show the energy corresponding to the first and second formants, which are very close together in the first vowel of *August*. The eighteenth bar in the vicinity of 2,500 Hz represents the energy in the third formant. The second slice shown is in the second vowel, in which all three formants are further apart. The second and third formants are still diverging after having been together at the release of the **g**. The final slice shown is during the **s** (remember there are actually many more slices not shown, each one-hundredth of a second). In this section most of the energy is in the higher frequencies.

The word *August* is about 0.75 seconds long, so in this scheme its pattern would be represented by 75 sets of 32 numbers (one set for every one-hundredth of a second). The task of a speech recognition system is to break the incoming stream of speech into pieces one-hundredth of a second long, and then to see if any set of these pieces is a match for part of the stored example of *August*. (A reminder: what is actually stored in a computer speech recognition system is not a spectrographic record, but a mathematically more complex representation of each of the slices.) If a match is found, then the computer tests the next one-hundredth of a second, and sees if it matches the next stored section, and so on. Of course, none of the matches needs to be exact. All the system needs to find out is whether there is a high probability of a match. The incoming word might not be exactly like the stored version. It might lack the final **t** for example. Try saying the months *July, August, September*. The normal thing to do is to run the word *August* into the word *September*, without pronouncing the final **t**.

When I first began working on a speech recognition project in the early 1970s, we all thought that we could get a computer to recognize speech in much the same way as we had learned to read spectrograms. We had (and still have) regular sessions sitting around the lunch table trying to interpret spectrograms that someone brings in. Given a little bit of context, we can usually work out what the spectrogram represents. We knew a number of rough rules, such as that the first two formants of **i** in *see* are as far apart as possible, those for **a** in *father* are close together and with a high first formant, and other aspects of spectrograms as discussed in chapter 7. We were hoping to program rules like these into a computer and get it to work in the same way.

You can get some feel for the way we thought a speech recognition system might work by looking at the spectrogram in figure 9.2. It is a spectrogram of my saying one of the days of the week. Can you say which it is? You might need to look back at chapter 7 so that you can see spectrograms of all the English consonants. Try to work it out for yourself before you read on. Look at the first sound, which has a lot of energy scattered over the higher frequencies, rather than having regular bands of the kind that are characteristic of formants. A guess about this sound will help you say which day it is.

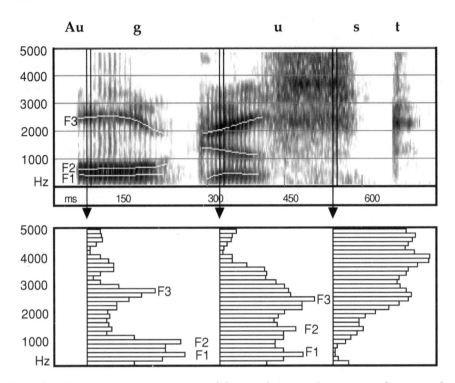

Figure 9.1 Upper part: a spectrogram of the word *August*. Lower part: three out of a possible 75 graphs representing the energy in a one-hundredth of a second section of this word.

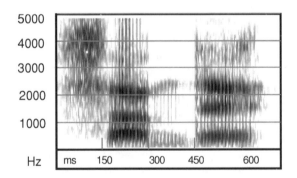

Figure 9.2 A spectrogram of one of the days of the week.

The sound at the beginning of the word is a fricative, as illustrated in figure 7.5. When it was shown in that figure, the frequency scale went up to 10,000 Hz, as we were considering as much detail about each sound as possible. But figure 9.2 is limited to 5,000 Hz, because that is the range that many speech recognition systems use. The major energy in this first sound is around 4,000 Hz with some energy going down to just above 2,000 Hz. This makes it **s** (or

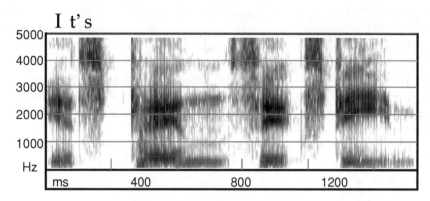

I t' s

5000

4000

3000

2000

1000

Hz

ms   400   800   1200

Figure 9.3   A spectrogram beginning with *It's*, announcing the time.

conceivably ʃ ('sh'), but no day of the week begins with 'Sh'). Now think how that limits your choices. There are only two days of the week beginning with **s**. Your task is simply to decide whether it is *Saturday* or *Sunday*. You can do this by considering how many vowels there are in the word. There are only two areas containing dark bands of energy that look like the formants of vowels, so it is a two-syllable word, *Sunday* not *Saturday*. You can also check this by looking at what happens after the first vowel. There are the fainter formants that characterize a nasal such as **n** or **m**, rather than the gap in the pattern that would be typical of some form of **t**. So, if a speech recognition system is trying to identify just one of the days of the week, you can see how easy it is.

If you want to try a slightly harder task, imagine yourself to be a speech recognition system trying to find out what I said when I told you the time. I might have said *It's three forty three* or *It's nine eighteen*. Figure 9.3 is a spectrogram of my saying a phrase like this. You know that the first word is *It's*, so I have filled that in. The next word must be a number between 1 and 12. Try to say what it is before reading on.

The first thing to note is that the word after *It's* begins with a stop – there is a gap in the pattern around time 400 ms, after the high-frequency noise for the **s**. The only appropriate numbers that begin with a stop are *two*, *ten*, and *twelve*. If it were *two* the formants after the stop would be for the vowel **u**, in which the first formant is low and the second descends. Instead, the formants are more in position for **ɛ**, as in *ten*. They are certainly not like those for **w** as in *twelve*, which would have the second formant rising from a very low position. So at the moment it looks as if the first number is probably *ten*. This becomes even more likely when we look at the consonant at the end of this syllable (between times 800 and 1,100 ms). It is one of those consonants in which there are steady-state formants that are not as loud – as dark – as they are in vowels. Possible consonants in this class are **m, n, ŋ,** and **l**, and in this case it must be **n**. Now, if you have not worked it out already, try to see what number comes after *ten*.

The next number begins with a sound with a great deal of high-frequency energy. It is followed by a vowel in which the first two formants are further apart than in the vowel in *ten*, which would make it **i** as in *three* or ɪ as in *six*. Considering the high frequency in the first sound in this word, which is similar to that in *It's*, this syllable probably begins *si-*. After the vowel there is a voiceless stop – the gap in the pattern just before 1,600 ms, which is followed by a second **s** pattern. So this syllable is **sɪks**, *six*. Now, what can follow it?

Given that this is a sentence of the form *It's ten six . . .* , the only possibility is the syllable *-teen*. Look at the spectrogram and you will see that at about 1,700 ms there is a voiceless stop that could well be **t**. The following vowel has the first and second formants as far apart as possible, making it **i** as in *-teen*, and at the end there are the faint formants of **n**, *It's ten sixteen*.

With only a basic knowledge of the acoustics of speech we can get quite a lot of information from a spectrogram. After looking at hundreds of them it was easy for those of us working with speech to imagine that we could build a speech recognition system that used our knowledge of the language and phonetics. But it turns out that the way we organize our knowledge is not very suitable for automatic speech recognition. Computers and humans 'think' differently. Humans express their knowledge in a manner that is difficult for computers to use, and computers lay out their knowledge in a way that humans can seldom understand.

This does not mean that humans and computers use different facts to recognize speech. It is sometimes said that current speech recognition systems do not use phonetic knowledge, but this is not correct. Speech recognizers use enormous amounts of phonetic knowledge that they build up and store in their own way. All of the examples of phonetic knowledge we have been considering, such as the high-frequency energy of **s** and the low-frequency energy in **n**, are learned and used by a speech recognizer. But the data are not stored in the way in which they appear on a spectrogram. It was worth showing you that you can learn a lot about describing speech sounds – the object of this book – by studying spectrograms. But it is not what speech recognition systems do.

The rules that a speech recognizer uses are not easy to relate to the knowledge we use when interpreting spectrograms. In this book I've said things like "the final **t** in *August* might be missing", but I've given no indication how often this is true (because I don't know). I've also said that the vowel **i** has first and second formants that are as far apart as possible. This is not precise enough for a computer recognition system; but if I had given precise formant frequencies then they would have applied only to particular utterances by particular speakers. The computer needs to develop some fuzzy boundaries, showing what is likely to happen.

Computer speech recognition systems also have to deal with the problems that occur when there is a match for some of the conditions for a given sound but there are conflicting cues indicating the possibility of another sound. I might, for example, have said the word *fit* with a big grin on my face, which would result in a vowel that might be like that in *feet*. An experienced spectrogram reader has no trouble judging the relative strength of each cue, checking the phonetic context, and combining all of this information to make a decision. Humans are natural pattern-recognizers – it's an important evolutionary advantage. Computers have no such advantage. If you want a computer to use rule-based reasoning correctly with ambiguous tokens, you need to specify a new rule for every possible degree and kind of ambiguity, and that's usually not a practical solution.

9.2   The Basis of Computer Speech Recognition

Current speech recognition systems rely more on computer science techniques than on information provided by phoneticians and linguists. Fred Jelanek, the computer scientist who led IBM's work in this field for many years, was fond of remarking: "Every time I fire a linguist we get along much faster." Or, as he once said looking at me: "Whenever I hire a linguist it sets the whole project back many months." Instead he and his team worked on techniques for getting computers to identify speech sounds using patterns identified by computational techniques.

The patterns representing the different speech sounds are formed from sets of numbers representing every one-hundredth of a second of a speech waveform. (If you would like to know more about these numbers, see the last section of this chapter.) The speech recognition system has to know how likely it is that a given set of numbers corresponds to a part of a particular speech sound. It needs to know this for every set of numbers that it will encounter with respect to every speech sound in its set of words – a very large task. It builds up a model of each speech sound in terms of the probabilities of the different acoustic patterns.

Speech recognition systems form these models by a training process. A system is trained by making a recording of a long list of sentences. All the computer knows to start with is where each sentence begins and ends, and the speech sounds that are present in a phonetic transcription of the sentence. The computer breaks the sentence up into strings of numbers representing each one-hundredth of a second slice. Knowing that a certain speech sound is present in many different sentences, the computer searches all those sentences for bits that might represent this sound. After churning away for a considerable time it comes up with a model that describes all the possible ways speakers might produce a particular speech sound, and the probability of each of these occurring. Speech recognition systems work in terms of probabilities rather than absolutes. For their pattern-matching they decide that a certain pattern has one chance in a thousand of being a given sound, another pattern has one chance in two, and so on.

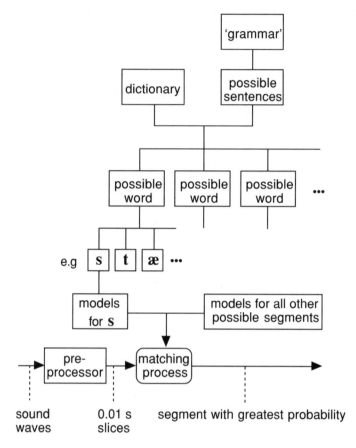

Figure 9.4   Stages in a speech recognition system.

When you talk into a general speech recognition system, the system analyzes the speech wave and matches sections of it with the models it has stored. An overall view of the process is shown in figure 9.4. At the top is a dictionary containing all the possible words. There is also what I have called a 'grammar'. In most speech recognition systems this would be nothing like what a linguist would call a grammar (which is why I put the word in quotes), but simply a statement of the probability of finding one word, given the preceding words. To begin with, the system has to consider the complete set of words in the dictionary as possible matches for the incoming signal. As recognition proceeds the 'grammar' may play a larger role in limiting the set of possible words to be matched. In any case, each word is considered as consisting of a number of phonetic segments (the figure illustrates a word beginning with the segments **stæ**), for each of which the training process has provided a model that represents all the different possibilities that the segment might have.

At the left in figure 9.4 is the pre-processing component of the system, sometimes referred to as the front end. This component takes the incoming sound wave and breaks it into one-hundredth of a second slices, which it characterizes by sets of numbers. These numbers are one input to the matching process, the other input being the set of models for the different sounds that are possible at that moment. Each of the models is evaluated as a potential match to the incoming speech.

Let's suppose that at some point the incoming slices were identified as **s** with a very high degree of probability. The next set of incoming slices might be considered to be **t** with a 50 percent probability, or **k** with a 30 percent probability, or **p** with a 20 percent probability. (This is simplifying things quite a bit, as other sounds would also have some probability.) At this point the possibilities would be limited to words like *step, stamp, scamp, speck, span* (and many more). The 'grammar' would also make its contribution to determining what the word might be. In this case, if the preceding words were *The first*, then the 'grammar' might assign a higher probability to *step* than to *stamp*, on the grounds that *The first step* is more likely than *The first stamp*. Of course, a lower-probability sentence such as *The first stamp was the British penny black* would also have to be taken into account.

The speech recognizer steps through all the sets of numbers representing each one-hundredth of a second of the incoming sound, and determines for each of them the most likely match. It combines successive sets of numbers to match whatever segments are most likely at that particular moment, given the likelihood of the different words in the most likely sentences. As you can see, the consideration of probabilities is a major part of speech recognition.

9.3 Special Context Speech Recognizers

When a computer is trying to recognize speech, the degree of accuracy for finding a match depends on the number of other words that are being represented by stored patterns. As we have seen, if we, or a computer, know that a speaker is going to say one of the months, then all that is needed is to recognize the first vowel to separate August from all the other possibilities. Different speakers may pronounce this vowel in different ways, but recognition systems can get round this by storing several examples of each word.

The simplest, and most effective, speech recognition systems are those that control the possible responses so that they are choosing among a very small number of possibilities. It is a trivial task for a telephone answering system to recognize the answer after it has said: *If you want the sales office, say one. If you want the repair department, say two.* When there is only a handful of words to be recognized, it is easy to sort out the patterns, as I hope you found out for yourself when trying to identify one of the days of the week. In these cases the whole word, and not the individual sounds, can be taken as the piece to be matched.

A computer can limit the possible answers to a reasonable number by taking charge of the conversation. This is what it does in a slightly more complex task such as an airline travel reservation system. It might start by asking: *From which airport do you wish to fly?* There are a large number of possible answers, but it is still a manageable pattern recognition task. If the speech recognition system gives similar probability scores to two different possibilities, it can always clarify the situation by asking a follow-up question such as: *Did you say 'Austin' or 'Boston'?*

Special purpose dictation systems can be very effective. Doctors can make good use of a system for providing reports on X-rays. In response to the queries: *Patient's number?* and *Region?* a radiologist examining an X-ray might answer: *One four eight two* and *Abdomen.* The computer can then use its stored information to type out: "This is a report on a radiological examination of patient number 1,482, Mr. John Smith, who was admitted with severe abdominal pains on August 5, 2000. X-rays were taken of the abdominal region." All that from a two-phrase response.

9.4   Recognizing Running Speech

When a computer is trying to interpret any possible sentence that might be said, it has a much more difficult task. But even with a completely unknown input from an author dictating a story the computer can use some stored knowledge. On hearing *Once upon a,* it can guess that the next word is more likely to be *time* than *tomato.* On hearing *Three times five equals* the likely next word is *fifteen.* Of course the speaker might be a trickster or a poor mathematician, but, provided it has been trained by looking at a number of possible sentences like these, the computer can look for these words first.

In any sequence of words the probability of each of the possible following words can be calculated. Given the sequence: *I gave my* the probability of a noun such as *dog, friend, wife, son, daughter* is much higher than that of a noun such as *climate* (although it could be *I gave my climate a high recommendation*). Given a sentence starting *The,* the probability of the next word also being *the* is almost zero. There are, however, notorious sentences in which words are repeated, such as the one containing five consecutive examples of the word 'that': *He said that that 'that' that that man used should be replaced by 'which'.* Even more horrific is the sequence of 11 consecutive examples of 'had' in a comment about the use of the word 'had' in comparison with the phrase 'had had': *Jones, where Smith had had 'had', had had 'had had'. 'Had had' had had the approval of the teacher.*

Fortunately, sentences of this kind are very rare, and, if people are talking sensibly, we can often make good predictions about what the next word might be, and what it is most unlikely to be. At any point in a sentence the next word is not a random choice from all the possible words in the speaker's vocabulary. There is an easy indirect way of showing the relatedness of successive words when you are using a word processor. Take a fairly long piece of text (I used the first five chapters of this book, about 10,000 words). Start with a random word (by chance I picked on the word 'note'). Now search for the next occurrence of this word. See what the word after it is (it was 'that'). Repeat this process: search for the next occurrence of the word that has just been found (i.e. 'that'), and see what word follows (it was 'is'). After I had done this a few times, taking the newly found word and then finding what comes after it when it next occurred, I came up with the sequence: 'note that is the speaker's lips together with two groups of a vowel in the air becomes too difficult when lamenting'. It's almost English, although it was generated by a completely mechanical process, depending simply on possible sequences. You can often produce quite long bits of nonsense like this before you have to stop, as I did, because the last word ('lamenting') occurs only once in the text. Each word does, to some extent, constrain the possibilities for the following word. In contrast, a random list of words (the last word in every twentieth line) produced 'same the without vocal but air as itself repetition higher distinctiveness meaning major at standard absolute can the consider', which is far from English.

You can use a similar process to demonstrate the relatedness of successive sounds. If, for the sake of this demonstration, we take letters as equivalent to sounds, we can search for sequences of letters. I started with a random number, 19, and picked the nineteenth letter in a randomly chosen paragraph. The letter was 'n'. Then I looked for the next 'n' and noted the letter after it, which was 'a'. From then on I worked in terms of sequences of two letters (counting a space as a letter), looking for the following letter, noting it, and then going on to find out what next followed this new sequence of two letters. After a while I came up with: 'nall eakerany of the oplexactrograt ust cas' – again not English, but not far from it, and actually including two real words: 'of the'. In contrast, a random selection of letters (the fifth letter or space in 40 sentences) produces: 'cfae ro ul anloo un s fs miehi soo ei'.

Like words, some speech sounds are more frequent than others. The left side of figure 9.5 shows the relative number of occurrences of each symbol in a transcription of American English totaling about 50,000 symbols. My colleagues, Ed Carterette and Peggy Jones, who supervised this transcription, describe the speech as conversational English as produced by adults. It is interesting to note that the consonants made with the tip of the tongue, d, s, l, t, r, n, are the most common. By far the most common vowel is ə, the sound in small words such as *a, the, to, at, from,* and, in the style of transcription they were using, in words such as *bud* and *but*.

Noting these probabilities is important for a speech recognition system. But at any point in a word the probability of the next sound is also dependent on what the previous sounds were. The right side of figure 9.5 shows the number of occurrences of each of these sounds after t. The most frequent sound in this

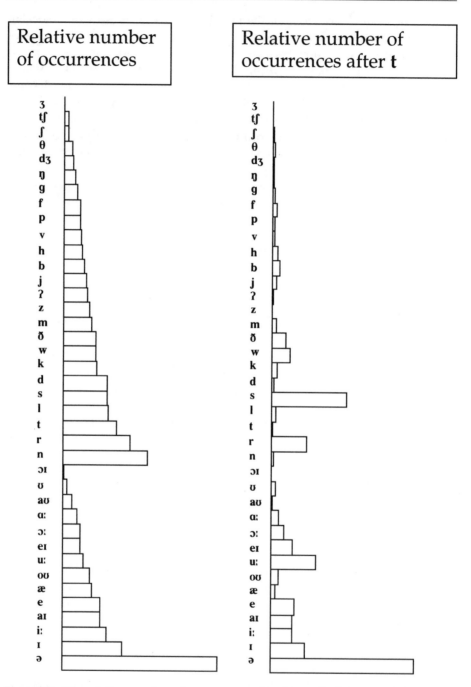

Figure 9.5 The relative number of occurrences of each sound of American English in a transcription including approximately 50,000 symbols (left side), and the relative number of occurrences of each of those sounds after **t** (right side).

position is still ə, but the other sounds have very different probabilities of occurrence. The consonants **s** and **r** and the vowel **u** as in *two* come out ahead. Some consonants, such as ʒ as in *vision* and ʧ as in *church* never occur after **t** in this text. Speech recognition systems have learned these kinds of facts as a result of their training.

Computers are good at taking all the possible matches and holding them in their memory while they search for thousands of likely words that might come next. Of course, they may get into difficulties, just as human listeners do. There are some well-known so-called 'garden path sentences', in which the computer is led 'up the garden path' to expect some kind of conclusion to a sentence, although the actual sentence has another form. For example, given a sentence: *The man pushed against the door . . .* , you may not expect the next words to be *fell over backwards,* as in the meaning 'The man (who was) pushed against the door fell over backwards'. Even worse are the ambiguous sentences that people produce, such as *Doctor Brown will talk about the nurse who was killed in an interview with our medical correspondent.*

Computers are sometimes helped and sometimes hindered by being able to find many more possibilities than may occur to human listeners. We have no trouble understanding a sentence such as *Time flies*, but it takes us a bit longer to grasp the meaning of *Time flies with a stopwatch* – something that one might say to biology students, telling them how to time the speed of some flies they are observing. Computers will come up with this interpretation very easily. Human beings are often very limited by their expectations. When you hear a sentence beginning *Rudolph the red nosed . . .* , you expect it to go on *. . . reindeer.* But it might be *Rudolph the Red-Nosed reigned here*, or even *Rudolph the Red knows rain, dear.* Computers can find all these possibilities very quickly.

Many problems arise through the difficulty of separating the words in a continuous stream of speech. When you know a language it is quite easy to decide where one word ends and another begins. But to a computer the situation is similar to ours when listening to a foreign language. The words all run together, and it is difficult to sort anything out. Figure 9.6 is a spectrogram of my saying *We were away when you called.* As you can see, there are no gaps between the words. With some knowledge of spectrogram reading it is possible to say where one word begins and another ends. Knowing what the words were, I could add dashed lines indicating the word boundaries. But without that knowledge a speech recognition system has a hard task. There are only very small differences between phrases such as *I can recognize speech* and *I can wreck a nice beach.*

The most difficult task in recognizing running speech is dealing with the little words like *a, the, of, to, at,* etc. Many of these words, some of which may be important, are difficult for a computer to recognize. There is not much difference between *This is toxic* and *This isn't toxic.* We can only hope that doctors dictating instructions will remember to speak precisely, without mumbling, and say *This is not toxic* rather than *This isn't toxic.*

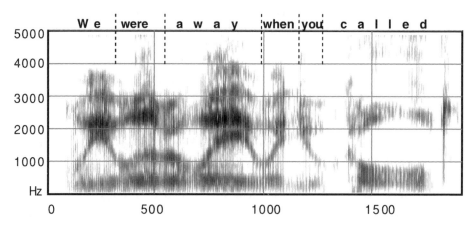

Figure 9.6   A spectrogram of *We were away when you called*, with dashed lines indicating the word boundaries.

Finally, problems with homophones – words that sound the same but have different meanings – can lead to bizarre possibilities. Consider, for example, *The sun's rays meet*. This might have been said of a farmer, whose daughters see to the vegetables while *The sons raise meat*. If the computer understood the topic of the conversation well enough, it might be able to do as well as a human, and decide which meaning was intended. We have some way to go before this will happen, but a computer can come up with this interpretation of the spoken sentence more easily than most humans.

9.5   Different Accents and Different Voices

Now that English is spoken in many different countries, there is no world-wide standard variety. Even within Britain or America there are differences that will cause problems for speech recognition systems. Within Britain, a Cockney English speaker might be heard as saying *light* when actually saying *late* (although a Cockney pronunciation of *late* or *fate* is actually different from BBC English *light* or *fight*). Many speakers of different kinds of American English might get a *pin* when asking for a *pen*. Between the different countries the situation is much worse. The Scots who pronounce *pearl* with an **r** before the **l** will say this word in a way that sounds to many Americans like *petal*. The American English pronunciation of *petal* will differ from that of a BBC English speaker, who will have a definite **t** sound in this word.

Differences in dialects are usually solved by recognition systems having a separate set of stored representations of the sounds and words for each dialect. Just as they can store the word *August* with and without a final **t**, so they can also store it with a General American pronunciation of the first vowel (which, at least for younger speakers, is the same as in *odd*) and a BBC English first vowel (which is the same as in *awed*, a very different sound from that in *odd* for most British English speakers).

Even without considering differences of accent, the range of human voices is enormous. The sounds of speech convey much more than the meanings of the words, as we saw in chapter 1. They convey who you are, your attitude – whether you are happy or sad – as well as your local accent, and much more that is irrelevant to the task of identifying the words. Of course it helps if the stored patterns were produced by someone with the same accent, or at least of the same sex. As we saw in chapter 6, the formants of men's and women's voices differ considerably. It is even better if the computer has been trained on a set of words you have produced yourself. Many systems urge you to correct the errors they make when taking dictation. They ask you to say the word again so that they can learn how you pronounce that particular word. The most successful systems are those that are used by only a single person, so that over time the system can learn just how that person speaks.

Speech recognition systems are improving all the time. In some ways they have an easier task than speech synthesis systems, in that they have to disregard, rather than put in, all the things that make one voice different from another. They have to recognize the words but disregard the subtle differences in intonation that are necessary to make a voice sound natural. When we consider the enormous differences in sound that can occur between voices, it is remarkable that anyone – human or computer – can recognize speech. My Californian granddaughter and I can converse despite differences in accent and large physical differences. The pitch of her voice is around 320 Hz (compared with my 100 Hz), and her formant frequencies are sometimes double mine. The upper part of figure 9.7 is a spectrogram of her voice recorded in a conversation with me. The lower part is my repetition of the same phrase. Even at just under four years old she can identify what is in common between the sounds of her words and the sounds of mine. We can talk together because humans are skilled pattern matchers. Computers are catching up with us.

9.6 More for the Computationally Curious

Here is a little more than many readers will want to know about how speech recognition systems work. The upper part of figure 9.7 shows the three one-hundredth of a second slices that were in the lower part of figure 9.1. The technical name for each of these slices is a spectrum. The computer does not store the spectrum itself; instead it stores a set of numbers that represent the shape of the spectrum. In one way of doing this the first number is a measure of the overall tilt, the degree to which the spectrum is rising or falling. This is

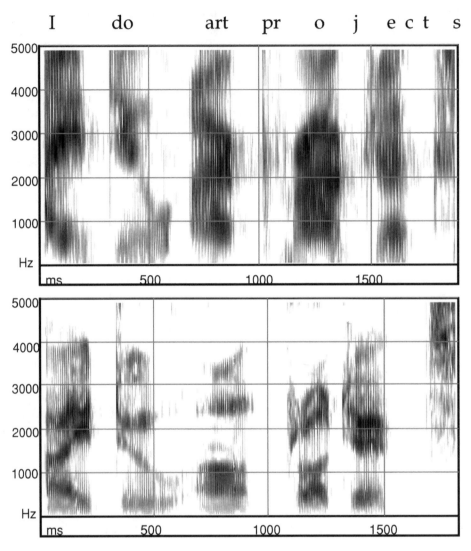

Figure 9.7 Upper part: spectrogram of a child saying *I do art projects*. Lower part: my repetition of the same phrase.

called the first spectral component. The easiest way to think about this is to say that this measure reflects how much the spectrum is like the first curve shown immediately below the three spectra in figure 9.8. The first slice is almost the opposite of the curve representing the first spectral component and therefore has a fairly high negative value on this measure. The middle slice is neither very like the first curve nor like its opposite, so it has a value nearer zero. The last slice has a high positive value, as most of the energy is in the higher frequencies, giving it a general shape very like this curve.

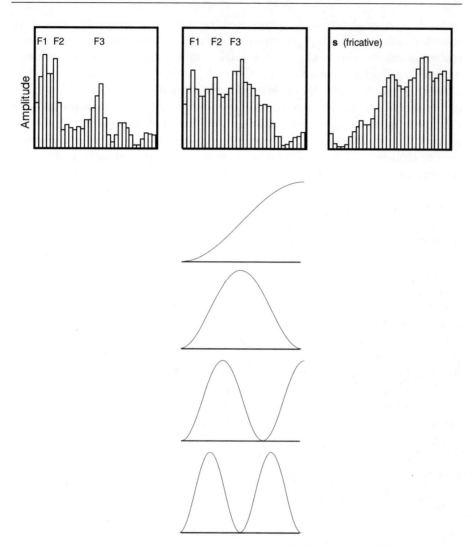

Figure 9.8   Upper part: the three spectra (one-hundredth of a second slices) that were shown in figure 9.1. Lower part: graphs that can be compared with each of these spectra so as to determine the relative amounts of the first four spectral components.

The second measure, the second spectral component, reflects the degree to which the energy is in the middle of the spectrum – the degree to which it is like the second curve below the three spectra in figure 9.8. The second spectrum shown comes out highest on this measure. The third measure reflects the extent to which the shape of each spectrum is like the next curve in figure 9.8 – the degree to which much of the energy is in the lower part of the spectrum, but there is also some in the higher frequencies. The final curve in figure 9.8 represents energy in two regions, one in the lower half of the spectrum and one in the upper. Additional measures of the spectrum can specify even more complex aspects of its shape, but it turns out that somewhere between five and twelve numbers of this kind are usually sufficient to give a fairly accurate representation of each spectral slice.

There is another point that I skipped over in the general presentation in the earlier sections of this chapter. In most speech recognition systems the training process is more complicated than the way in which it was previously described. We saw that training a speech recognition system involves determining the acoustic properties of a large number of examples of each element in a transcription. The system may actually regard each element in the transcription as having three states, perhaps corresponding to its beginning, middle, and end. The computer works out the probabilities relating each of these states to the numbers representing each hundredth of a second. When recognizing incoming speech signals, it refers to the models that it has developed in the training process and determines which of these are the most likely matches to the incoming sets of numbers. This kind of model is known as a Hidden Markov Model (HMM).

A Markov model is a representation of a sequence of events in which the probability of one event depends upon the previous events. I used a kind of Markov model to generate the sequence I produced earlier showing that the probability of one word in a sequence depends on the preceding words. Similarly, a Markov model of the probabilities of different sequences of letters produced: 'nall eakerany of the oplexactrograt ust cas'. The sequences of sets of numbers that the computer found in the course of the training procedures can also be regarded as produced by a Markov model. These sequences form models of possible speech sounds that are stored in the computer but not otherwise revealed, making this a Hidden Markov Model. Speech recognition systems using HMM techniques are widely used.

9.7   Summary

Computers recognize speech by storing the patterns of each of a large number of words. The patterns are stored as sequences of numbers representing a complex transformation of the original waveform which can be likened to (but is far from the same as) a spectrogram. Speech recognition systems find the patterns corresponding to a sound by a training process, in which they match acoustic representations with the corresponding speech sounds.

It is comparatively easy to recognize a word when it must be one out of a limited set. When the computer structures the interchange so that the speaker is answering a set of questions, very good speech recognition can be achieved. Recognizing the words in running speech is more difficult. Computers have to use built-in knowledge, such as which words are most likely to follow a given word. Much of a speech recognizer's task goes far beyond 'speech' in the sense that I have been using it, and demands knowledge of the language and the world. Differences in regional accent and personal quality can be overcome by matching the incoming speech with words previously recorded by someone with a similar accent, or (better still) by the actual person being recognized. My personal bet is that we will have almost perfect speech recognition systems before we have completely natural-sounding speech synthesis.

10

Making English Consonants

10.1   Acoustics and Articulations

Some years ago I tried to build a model that would talk. It looked much like me – we'd made a plaster cast of my face, and from that formed a mold for a rubber face and lips. We had good measurements of my mouth and throat, so we were able to make a rubber tongue that fitted into a more solid upper and lower jaw. And we had a special kind of loudspeaker that produced puffs of air like those produced by the vibrating vocal folds. It wasn't too bad at making steady-state vowels. But it couldn't produce a single consonant.

Part of the problem was that we didn't have a good way of mechanically moving the tongue and lips. Later we solved this by doing everything on a computer. Instead of moving an actual tongue and lips, we moved diagrams of them, and then calculated how the air in the tube would vibrate. But it still didn't produce good speech because we didn't know how to specify the movements. We could base our descriptions on X-ray movies that showed how the center of the tongue moved, and we had full-face movies that showed the lips. But we couldn't describe the movements in a way that a computer could interpret. We could do better now, but we are still a long way from being able to go from a written text to a three-dimensional model of the movements of the vocal organs.

We know far more about the acoustics of speech than about the movements of the tongue and lips. A spectrogram gives us more information about a sound than any present-day account in terms of the vocal organs. As we have seen, we can describe and synthesize natural-sounding speech by giving the values of about a dozen acoustic components. There is no way that we can describe all the movements of the tongue and lips equally accurately in terms of numbers. But in this chapter we will see what can be said about how speech sounds are made. We will describe them in terms of the articulations involved. An articulation is simply a movement of the vocal organs, perhaps better thought of as a gesture – a controlled movement made for a particular purpose.

10.2   The Vocal Organs

The lips and part of the tongue are the only vocal organs that we can readily see. It takes some form of X-ray to make the full complexity of the vocal tract visible. Figure 10.1 is a side view of the head, made using an imaging technique called MRI, which is similar to X-rays. The lips, tongue, teeth, and roof of the mouth are clearly visible, but the teeth do not show up so well in this view, and have been outlined in white. The vocal folds are also not readily distinguishable. Their location has been indicated by a line. Below them is the air passage into the lungs (the trachea).

None of the vocal organs were meant for talking. The lips are there to keep the mouth sealed off when we are not eating. The tongue and the teeth are for making food more digestible. The prime purpose of the vocal folds is to stop foreign matter entering the lungs. And the lungs are for breathing, not for pushing air out to make noises.

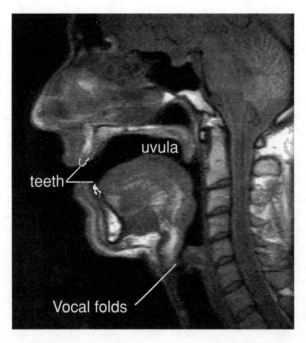

Figure 10.1   An MRI view of the head. The teeth have been outlined in white.

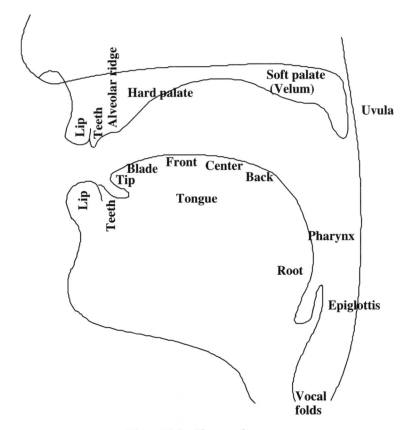

Figure 10.2   The vocal organs.

Most animals with comparable features make sounds that they use for communicating. Among mammals, only the giraffe is silent. But no animal can produce the wide range of sounds that any human can produce. Parrots and other birds can mimic many human speech sounds. But even they cannot produce all the sounds that occur in languages. As animals evolved, the vocal organs adapted so that they could take on the role of controlling sounds. By the time humans came along the larynx had lowered so that the vocal tract could make vowels with a wide range of formant frequencies – something that no other mammal can do – and all the possibilities of speech developed.

An outline of the vocal tract is shown in diagrammatic form in figure 10.2. This figure also shows the names for the different parts of the tongue and the roof of the mouth. The tip and blade form the part of the tongue that you can stick out. Behind them is the body of the tongue, which is divided into the front, center, and back. This makes the center of the tongue immediately below the highest part of the roof of the mouth. The pharynx is the part of the vocal tract behind and below the back of the tongue. The root of the tongue is just above the epiglottis, the small flap that is used to direct food into the esophagus, or food passage, which leads down to the stomach. It is one of the oddities of nature that the air passage from the nose to the lungs crosses the food passage from the mouth to the stomach. Animals evolved in this way because it provides a good means of increasing the air supply rapidly. By making the two passages connect, we can simply open our mouths and take in more air when we need to run fast.

We can divide the roof of the mouth into various parts. Behind the upper front teeth there is a small ridge which you can feel with a finger or the tip of your tongue. This is called the alveolar ridge. You can also feel that the front of the roof of the mouth has a fairly hard surface. Further back it is softer, and you may gag if you put your finger too far back. The front part is called the hard palate, and the back part the soft palate. A more technical term for the soft palate is the velum. The velum can be moved up and down so that air can be blocked from going out of the nose or allowed to escape that way, forming a nasal sound. Try saying a long **m**, followed by **ba**, so that you say **mmmbaa**, You probably can't feel your velum go up at the beginning of the **b**, but this is what happens to stop air going out through the nose. The uvula hangs down from the soft palate.

10.3 Places and Manners of Articulation

When you make a consonant you usually have to obstruct the air that is being pushed out of the lungs in some way. Consonants can be made by closing or narrowing the vocal tract at various places. Some of the technical terms that are used for the different places are shown in table 10.1. The definitions given

Table 10.1 Some places of articulation: regions of the vocal tract particularly associated with a particular gesture of the tongue or lips

Place	Description
Bilabial	The two lips coming together
Labiodental	The lower lip near the upper lip
Dental	The tip of the tongue near the upper front teeth
Alveolar	The tip or blade of the tongue touching or near the alveolar ridge
Post-alveolar	The blade of the tongue near the forward part of the hard palate just behind the alveolar ridge
Palatal	The front of the tongue near the hard palate
Velar	The back of the tongue touching the soft palate (the velum)
Labiovelar	The two lips approaching one another, and the back of the tongue raised towards the soft palate

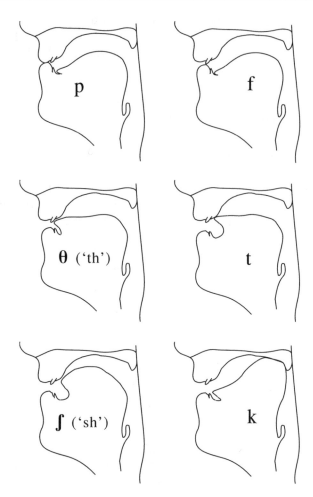

Figure 10.3 The positions of the vocal organs in the first consonant in each of the words *pie, fie, thigh, tie, shy, kite.*

are appropriate for English consonants. When describing other languages these terms may be used in slightly different ways.

Figure 10.3 illustrates the positions of the vocal organs in some English consonants at these different places of articulation. Although a particular position is shown, you should always remember that an articulation is really a gesture involving a movement. Try saying each of the words shown, and see if your vocal organs look and feel as if they move through these positions. If you have a mirror handy you can see the movements of the lips and the tip of the tongue. For other aspects of the articulations you will have to rely on what you can feel.

In chapter 6 we grouped the sounds of English into stops, approximants, nasals, fricatives, and affricates. We can now re-order these terms, add the

Table 10.2   Some manners of articulation

Manner	Description
Stop	Complete closure of the vocal tract. Air is blocked from going out through the nose and the mouth
Nasal	Closure of the vocal tract such that air can go out through the nose, but not through the mouth
Fricative	Constriction of the vocal tract so that a noisy airstream is formed
Affricate	A stop followed by a fricative made at the same place of articulation
Approximant	Constriction of the vocal tract to a smaller extent than that required for a noisy airstream
Lateral	The tongue touching the roof of the mouth but without contacting the teeth at the sides

term 'lateral', and define what we will call manners of articulation as in table 10.2.

The airstream is like water flowing through a garden hose. You can squeeze the hose at many different points and alter the flow of water. If you squeeze it tightly so that no water can flow, it will be like a stop. Producing a nasal would be like attaching a side tube to the stopped hose. Squeezing the hose so that only a small jet of water comes through corresponds to a fricative. A more gentle squeeze allowing water to flow fairly freely corresponds to an approximant. If you can manage to press the middle of the tube and allow water to escape around the sides, that will correspond to a lateral.

10.4   Describing Consonants

Consonants are nearly always movements at the beginning or end of a vowel. As we have noted, they are best thought of as gestures of the tongue and lips, like the gestures one makes with one's hand when writing, fluid movements that produce particular shapes. Gestures are difficult to describe and it is easier to associate a consonant with what one might think of as the target of the gesture – the positions of the vocal organs that characterize the sound. These positions can be described fairly well by considering only three questions: First, what are the vocal folds doing? As we saw in chapter 3, the air from the lungs can set the vocal folds vibrating, in which case the sound is said to be voiced, or it can pass freely between the vocal folds so that the sound is voiceless. Sounds such as **b** and **n** are voiced, and sounds such as **p** and **s** are voiceless. Second, where in the mouth is the sound made? Is it at the lips (making it bilabial, like **p** and **b**), or on the teeth ridge (making it alveolar like **n**) or elsewhere as described by the terms in table 10.1? Third, what

Table 10.3 A chart showing the IPA symbols for the consonants of English

	Bilabial	Labiodental	Dental	Alveolar	Post-alveolar	Palatal	Velar
Stop	p b			t d	ʧ ʤ		k g
Nasal	m			n			ŋ
Fricative		f v	θ ð	s z	ʃ ʒ		
Approximant	(w)			r		j	w
Lateral				l			

happens to the stream of air from the lungs? Is it completely stopped (as for **p** and **b**), or does it come out through the nose (like **m** and **n**), or what other kind of articulation, as shown in table 10.2, does it use? By answering these three questions we can, for example, describe **p** as a voiceless bilabial stop, **b** as a voiced bilabial stop, **n** as a voiced alveolar nasal, and so on.

Using this three-term approach, we can represent the symbols for the consonants on a chart as in table 10.3. The places of articulation are shown across the top of the chart, the manners down the side, and the symbols for voiceless consonants are on the left while those for voiced consonants are on the right. Table 10.3 is an abbreviated version of the full IPA consonant chart given earlier.

Say a long **z** as in *zoo*, **zzzz**. If you put your fingers on your throat you can feel the vocal folds vibrating. This is a voiced sound, so **z** is on the right-hand side in its column. You can feel that the tip of your tongue is near your alveolar ridge, so it is in the alveolar column. There is a noisy airstream, so it is in the fricative row. Each of the symbols in the chart can be interpreted in this way, though in some cases it is more difficult to feel what is happening. You can't make a very long **d**, so you may not be able to feel the vocal folds vibrating. But you can feel that the tongue comes up to touch the alveolar ridge, so that it is in the alveolar column. And you can tell that the airstream is completely stopped (which is what prevents you from making a very long **d**), so it is in the stop row.

I have simplified the chart a little, by not having a separate row for affricates. As we saw in chapter 7, they can be regarded as stops followed by fricatives. I have also not put the labiovelar approximant **w** in a separate column, showing it instead in parentheses in the bilabial column, as well as in the velar column. One consonant, **h**, has been left out altogether, as it does not have any particular place of articulation. On the IPA chart it is regarded as a glottal fricative, because most of the noisy airstream in **h** is produced just above the vocal folds. But this is not a very good description of the way this sound is made. It is usually just a voiceless version of the adjacent sounds. At the beginning of the words *heed, hid, head*, for example, it is the voiceless counterpart of **i** as in *heed*, ɪ as in *hid*, or ɛ as in *head*.

There are several gaps in the consonant chart. Some are because English does not happen to use a possible combination of place and manner of articulation. In the bilabial column, for example, there is a gap in the fricative row because English does not have a fricative made by bringing the upper and lower lips close to one another (though some speakers do make the sounds **f** and **v** in this way). Other languages, as we will see in chapter 14, have both labiodental fricatives **f** and **v**, and bilabial fricatives (for which the symbols are ɸ and β, to be found on the full IPA chart which will be discussed later). Some of the gaps in the consonant chart in table 10.3 are because the combination of that particular place and manner cannot be made. The bilabial column has a gap in the last row because it is not possible to make a distinct bilabial lateral. You can close one side of your lips or possibly even close your lips in the middle and let air escape at the sides, but the sound you produce won't differ from a regular bilabial.

It is generally quite easy to describe the consonants in an English word. Try saying *cling* slowly. You can feel the back of your tongue touching the roof of the mouth for the initial velar stop consonant, **k**. Next, the tip of your tongue comes up to touch the roof of the mouth on the alveolar ridge for the alveolar lateral, **l**. After the vowel (for which the symbol is ɪ), the back of the tongue comes up again for the velar nasal, **ŋ**. The English spelling 'ng' at the end of a word is nearly always **ŋ**, and not a sequence of a nasal **n** followed by a velar stop, **ɡ**.

Sometimes it's not so easy to feel what the tongue and lips are doing when producing a consonant. This is particularly true of the approximants in words such as *what, yacht, rot*. You can see the rounding of the lips in **w**, but it is difficult to realize that the back of the tongue is raised. The **j** ('y') at the beginning of *yacht* has the front of the tongue raised. You may not realize this if you try to pronounce this sound by itself, but you can probably feel the way the tongue moves down and back as you pronounce the whole word.

The **r** at the beginning of *rot* is difficult to describe for two reasons. Firstly, it is pronounced in different ways in different dialects of English, and secondly, in most forms of General American and BBC English, all that you can readily feel is the contact between the sides of the tongue and the molar teeth. There is usually no contact between the tongue and the roof of the mouth. Many BBC English speakers have the tip of the tongue raised towards the roof of the mouth in the general location of the alveolar ridge, but many American English speakers simply bunch the body of the tongue up so that it is hard to say where the articulation is. Somewhat by convention, **r** is placed on the consonant chart in the voiced alveolar approximant cell, which is all right for speakers such as myself, but is not a good description of most forms of American English **r**.

English has one lateral sound, **l**, in which the tip of the tongue touches the alveolar ridge just behind the upper front teeth, but does not make contact with the roof of the mouth anywhere else. As a result air can escape over the sides of the tongue. You can probably feel the tip of the tongue against the alveolar ridge if you try to make a long l sound. While holding that position, try breathing in. You can feel the cold air coming in over one or both sides of the tongue.

The terms in tables 10.1 and 10.2 are generally sufficient, but they are not precise enough to distinguish some notable dialect differences. For example, think about the movements of your tongue when you say the first sound in the word *thick*. This is clearly a voiceless dental fricative, θ, but where exactly is the tip of the tongue? Most speakers of American English, particularly those from the West Coast or the Midwest, put the tip of the tongue between the teeth, resting on the lower teeth and nearly touching the upper incisors. But speakers of most forms of British English have the tip of the tongue inside the mouth, behind the upper front teeth. (It's as if the British think it rude to stick their tongues out.) The difference between the two tongue movements can be described by adding terms to table 10.1, describing the American pronunciation as 'interdental' (between the teeth) and the British as just 'dental'.

The consonants in a word often overlap. When you say *plan* you will find that the tip of your tongue is already touching the alveolar ridge while the lips are closed for the bilabial stop, p. The consonants and vowels also overlap. In *pan* the soft palate lowers during the vowel so as to let air out of the nose for the final nasal, n. In *pit* and *pat* the tongue moves into position for the following vowel while the lips are closed. Even when the back of the tongue is raised for the velar stop, k, in *key* or in *car*, the rest of the tongue is approaching the position required for the different vowels in these words. As a result there is a subtle difference in the place of articulation of the two k sounds. You may be able to feel that the tongue is further forward in the mouth when making k in *key* than when making k in *car*.

We commented on the tendency for sounds to be influenced by the neighboring sounds in chapter 9, when we were discussing speech synthesis. We can now see how this happens in terms of the movements of the tongue and lips. In a word like *input*, the two lips have to be closed to make the p. Very often they begin closing during the vowel of the first syllable, *in-*. Some people pronounce this word as if it were *imput*. I have even seen people spell it this way, like lots of other words such as *import*, where the spelling has come to reflect the pronunciation.

10.5   Summary

Speech sounds have been traditionally described in terms of states of the vocal organs, although they are better thought of as movements. The more active of the vocal organs are the lips, and the tongue, which can be divided into the tip, blade, front, center, back, and root. The upper surface of the vocal tract consists of the upper lip, the upper front teeth, the alveolar ridge, the hard palate, and the soft palate or velum. The active vocal organs can approach or contact the upper surface of the vocal tract in various regions, producing bilabial, labiodental, dental, alveolar, palatoalveolar, palatal, velar, and labiovelar articulations. The manner of articulation of English consonants can be described as stop, nasal, fricative, approximant, or lateral. Symbols for consonants can be placed on a chart showing whether they are voiced or voiceless, and which place and which manner of articulation is represented. Consonant articulations are affected by the movements required for adjacent sounds.

11

Making English Vowels

11.1 Movements of the Tongue and Lips for Vowels

The vowels of English differ in the movements of the tongue and lips. But it is difficult to say what the tongue is doing except in the case of a few vowels. When you say **ɑ** as in *father*, you can see that the tongue is low and at the back of your mouth. This is the vowel that doctors ask you to say when trying to look at your throat. But the movements of the tongue in other vowels are harder to discover.

Look in a mirror while you say *heed, hid, head, had*. You can see that the mouth becomes more open as these words are said. The tongue is higher in the mouth and the jaw more raised for **i** as in *heed*, than it is for **ɪ** as in *hid*. The latter vowel has a higher tongue position than **ɛ** as in *head*, which has, in turn, a higher tongue position than **æ** as in *had*. As we noted in chapter 5, when giving a rough description of the tongue positions in vowels, we can say that these four vowels differ in tongue height.

The tongue positions for these four vowels are shown in figure 11.1. The diagram represents the average of X-ray pictures of five speakers of General American English. Only one representation of the lower front teeth has been shown, as the positions of the jaw differed markedly among the speakers. Some speakers moved the jaw (and the lower lip) considerably, while others did not. You can produce these vowels with or without jaw movements yourself. Put a thin pencil between your teeth so that you hold the jaw in a fixed position. You will find that you can say *heed, hid, head, had* without any problems. You can still say them perfectly well with a much larger object such as your thumb between your teeth holding your jaw further apart. What matters most for these vowels is the position of the tongue.

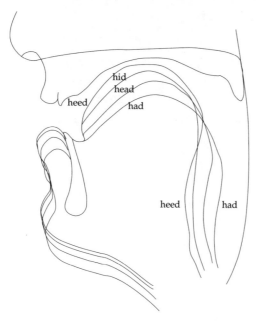

Figure 11.1 The mean tongue position in the vowels in *heed, hid, head, had* as produced by five speakers of General American English. The epiglottis has not been shown, so as to make the movements of the root of the tongue clearer. The position of the lower teeth is that in *heed*.

Figure 11.1 shows that the tongue gets further away from the roof of the mouth as each of these vowels is produced. In addition, the root of the tongue moves considerably. It is pulled forward for **i** (*heed*), making a large cavity in the back of the mouth. This large body of air is the source of the low pitch resonance, the low first formant that we noted in chapter 5 when discussing the acoustic structure of vowels. (Remember that large objects, be they organ pipes or strings on a double bass, or enclosed bodies of air, vibrate more slowly and have a lower pitch.) The tongue root moves further back for each of the vowels ɪ (*hid*), **ɛ** (*head*), and **æ** (*had*), making the body of air in the throat smaller. Because this smaller body of air vibrates more rapidly, the first formant goes up in pitch as this sequence of vowels is said.

The converse changes occur in the size of the body of air in the front of the mouth. In **i** (*heed*) there is only a small cavity behind the front teeth, giving rise to a second formant with a high frequency. As each of the other vowels is said, the body of air in the front of the mouth gets larger, and the pitch of the second formant gets lower.

You can easily see the most important change that occurs when you say the vowels in *hod, hood, who'd*. The lips become closer together. You can hold a pen between your lips and fix the jaw position when saying these vowels, but it is difficult to make them sound right without moving your lips. The tongue

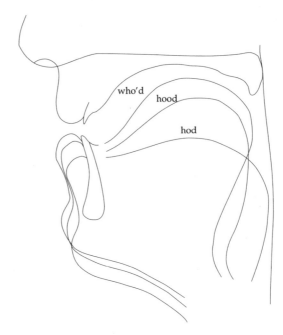

Figure 11.2 The mean tongue position in the vowels in *hod, hood, who'd* as produced by five speakers of General American English. The epiglottis has not been shown, so as to make the movements of the root of the tongue clearer. The position of the lower teeth is that in *who'd*.

positions are harder to discover. You can see that the tongue is pulled way down and back for the vowel **a** in *hod*, but the positions for **ʊ** (*hood*) and **u** (*who'd*) are difficult to determine without X-rays. Figure 11.2 shows the average shapes of the tongue for the same five speakers as in figure 11.1.

The tongue shapes for the vowels **a** (*hod*), **ʊ** (*hood*), and **u** (*who'd*) are very different from those of the vowels in *heed, hid, head, had*. But they also differ in the height of the tongue, and can be said to form two bodies of air, one in the throat and another in the front of the mouth. It is, however, more difficult to describe the relation between the sizes of the different bodies of air and the pitches of the formants in these vowels. The narrowing of the lip opening has a significant effect on the way the air vibrates.

In general, we can say that the tongue shapes for the vowels **a** (*hod*), **ʊ** (*hood*), and **u** (*who'd*) are in the back of the mouth when compared with the tongue shapes for **i** (*heed*), **ɪ** (*hid*), **ɛ** (*head*), and **æ** (*had*). The vowels **a, ʊ, u** can be called back vowels, as opposed to **i, ɪ, ɛ, æ**, which are called front vowels. We can call **a** a low back vowel, **ʊ** a mid back vowel, and **u** a high back vowel. Among the front vowels, **i** is a high front vowel, **ɪ** a mid-high front vowel, **ɛ** a mid-low front vowel, and **æ** a low front vowel.

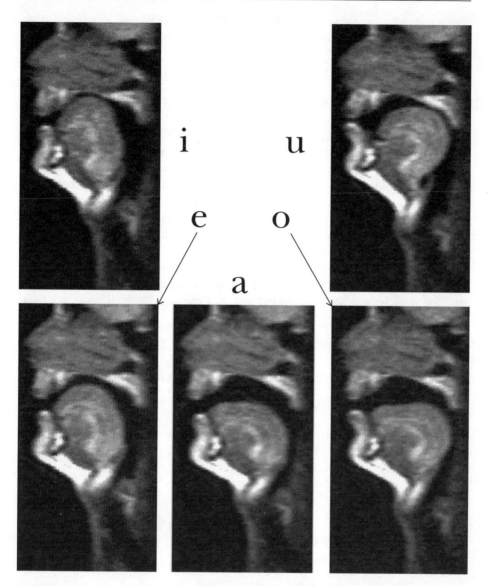

Figure 11.3 Images of the five vowels **i**, **e**, **a**, **o**, **u** as produced by the Belgian phonetician Didier Demolin.

These notions are also evident in the images of the five vowels **i, e, a, o, u** as produced by the Belgian phonetician Didier Demolin, and shown in figure 11.3. You can see these images as videos in the items for this chapter on the CD. There are three versions, one called 'tongue video', which lets you concentrate on the tongue movements, a second called 'jaw video', which points out the movements of the jaw, and the third called 'larynx video', which indicates the movements of the larynx. As you can see, even producing these five vowels involves many complex coordinated movements of the vocal organs.

11.2   Muscles Controlling the Tongue and Lips

The tongue is just a bunch of muscles. If you want to see what these muscles look like, the easiest way is to go down to the market and buy a sheep's tongue. Sheep have fairly similar tongues to ours. (Buying an ox tongue is not so useful. Cows have developed long tongues that they use to pull grass out of the ground, and put it in their mouths. Sheep eat more like we do. They are polite enough to nibble grass without sticking their tongues out.) Buy a cooked tongue if you can. Otherwise just boil it for about an hour and let it cool before you examine it.

If you slice a tongue (human or sheep) from front to back and then again from side to side, you can see the fibers of the muscles. Figure 11.4 shows how the muscles are attached to the jaw and the skull (which you won't see

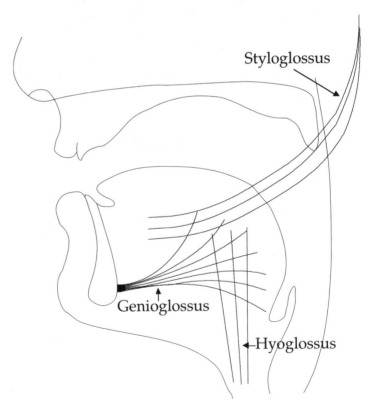

Figure 11.4   The principal muscles controlling the movements of the tongue.

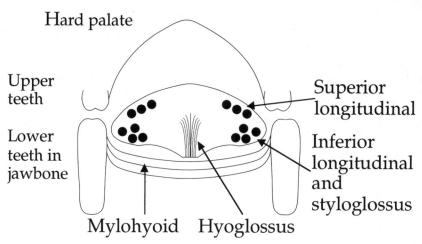

Figure 11.5 A view of the tongue from the front, showing some additional muscles controlling its movements.

without buying a whole sheep's head). The principal muscle of the tongue is the genioglossus, which pulls the back and root of the tongue towards the front of the mandible (the jawbone). The net effect of contracting the genioglossus muscle is that the tongue gets compressed within the jaw. The tongue is like a balloon filled with water. As the root is pulled forward the front has to go somewhere and so it moves up towards the hard palate. This is essentially what happens when you say **i** as in *heed*. You contract your genioglossus so that the body of the tongue gets squeezed within the jawbone, and part of it is pushed upwards. Producing the tongue shapes for the vowels in *hid, head, had* requires less activity of the genioglossus muscle, and also usually lowering of the jaw by means of muscles not shown in figure 11.4.

The styloglossus muscle, which is attached to a point on the skull just below the ear, pulls the tongue upwards and backwards. The hyoglossus muscle, which is attached to the hyoid bone in the neck, pulls the tongue back and down. These are the two muscles that are largely responsible for the tongue movements in *hod, hood, who'd*. But, as with all tongue gestures, there are many ways to make similar movements.

You can also control the height of the tongue within the jaw by contracting the mylohyoid muscle, which is shown in figure 11.5, a view of the tongue cut from side to side at the level of the back teeth. The mylohyoid muscle is like a sling going from one side of the jaw to the other. Tightening the sling raises the body of the tongue. Some people vary the height of the tongue in *heed, hid, head, had* mainly by using the genioglossus muscle, others make more use of the mylohyoid muscle, and yet others control tongue position more by raising and lowering the jaw. You can produce the required tongue shape in several different ways.

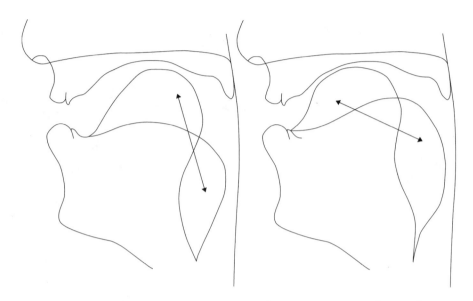

Figure 11.6   The two main components of tongue movements in vowels.

The muscles that are primarily responsible for moving the tip of the tongue are the superior longitudinals. These muscles lie just under the surface on either side of the tongue. When they contract they shorten the upper surface of the tongue, and thus cause the tip to curl upwards. The inferior longitudinal muscles run along the underside of the tongue, near the styloglossus. When they contract they bunch the tongue up.

The tongue is a very intricate mass of muscles – there are many more than we will consider here – so it is worth remembering that it is always difficult to be sure which muscles caused a particular speech movement. What matters most is the shape of the tongue rather than the particular muscles used. The muscles combine together in various ways to form particular shapes.

The principal muscle of the lips is the orbicularis oris, which circles round the lips. When this muscle contracts the corners of the lips are pulled together, producing lip rounding. The degree of lip opening is also controlled by the raising and lowering of the jaw (using muscles not shown here), which affects the position of the lower lip.

Analyses of X-rays have shown that the tongue shapes in most vowels can be described as different combinations of the two basic movements shown in figure 11.6. One of these movements determines the degree of raising of the tongue. The other is more associated with the backward movement of the tongue. The tongue shapes required for nearly all the vowels of English can be made by using different combinations of these two movements. The exception is the vowel in American English *bird*, which requires some bunching of the tongue using the inferior longitudinal muscles.

Table 11.1 Bell's symbols for vowels, as given in his book *Visible Speech* (1867), with keywords added

	Back	Mixed	Front
High	**ꓶ** 'boo'	**Ꞇ**	**ſ** 'bee'
Mid	**Ɔ** 'bow'	**ꓶ** 'bird'	**C** 'bay'
Low	**J** 'bad'	**Ꞁ** 'bud'	**ꓶ** 'father'

11.3 Traditional Descriptions of Vowels

The basic movements shown in figure 11.6 might be thought of as controlling the height of the highest point of the tongue and the degree of backness of this same point. As you can see, they don't exactly do this. The two components of tongue movements are not at right angles to one another and are not directly related to moving the tongue in the vertical and horizontal directions. But if we neglect this for the moment, we can think of vowels as differing in three ways: tongue height, tongue backness, and lip opening. This technique for describing vowels was started by the British speech teacher, Alexander Melville Bell, the father of the inventor of the telephone, Alexander Graham Bell. Both father and son were excellent phoneticians, and used to give public demonstrations of their skill. Alexander Graham would leave the room while his father interviewed a speaker of some foreign language. Melville Bell would then write down what was said in a phonetic transcription. Contemporary reports say that when Alexander came back into the room he would astound the audience by reading back his father's transcription and pronouncing the foreign language 'perfectly', often despite the fact that he did not know a word of it. I've put the 'perfectly' in quotes because I know that people are sometimes full of praise when I repeat, very imperfectly, phrases that they don't expect foreigners to be able to say. I've put my phonetic ability to work a number of times when I have been asked to make a speech in a foreign country. I begin with a few phrases in the appropriate language that I have carefully learned from a phonetic transcription of a native speaker – and then I lapse into English. As a fellow phonetician once remarked to me: "I can pronounce French perfectly, but I can't speak it. I know all the sounds of French, but unfortunately I don't know any words."

Melville Bell used a form of phonetic transcription that he called 'Visible Speech'. He made the position of the tongue in a vowel visible by placing a hook on a vertical line, as shown in table 11.1. If the tongue was high and in the front of the mouth, the hook was at the top and on the right, if high and

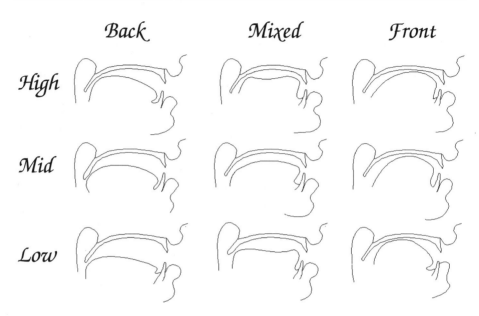

Figure 11.7 Bell's drawing of the tongue shapes of the vowels in table 11.1 (redrawn from his book *Visible Speech*, 1867).

back, then it was to the left. Low tongue positions had hooks at the bottom of the vertical line, and intermediate positions were in the middle. He called vowels with the tongue in the center of the mouth 'mixed' vowels, and put a hook on each side of the vertical line. Table 11.1 shows his basic set of vowel symbols, exemplified by some BBC English vowels.

You can see some examples of Visible Speech in the film *My Fair Lady*. I was a technical consultant on the film, and wrote the transcriptions that can be seen in Professor Higgins's notebook. You can also see a chart of the vowels written in Visible Speech, which Professor Higgins uses when demonstrating the different vowels to Colonel Pickering. It is actually my voice that you hear saying the vowels, not Rex Harrison's.

Melville Bell was a great phonetician, but unfortunately he was not all that accurate in his understanding of the tongue positions in vowels. He had to rely on what he could see and what he could feel, and, as I am sure you have realized, it is difficult to feel where one's tongue is. Bell imagined that the movement of the back of the tongue in going from **ɑ** as in *father* to **u** as in *food* was the same size as the movement of the front of the tongue in going from **æ** as in *bad* to **i** as in *see*. He also underestimated the importance of the position of the lips in producing the changing qualities in the back vowels in *hod*, *hood*, *who'd*. Figure 11.7 shows his diagram of the nine tongue shapes for the vowels in Table 11.1. As you can see they are somewhat different from the shapes of the tongue as we now know them from X-rays, as shown in figures 11.1, 11.2, and 11.3.

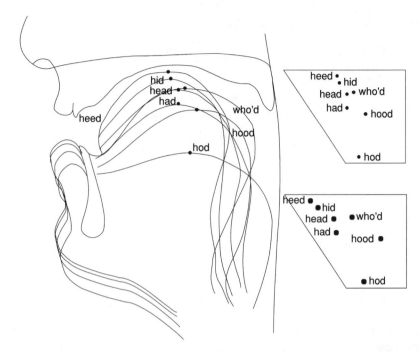

Figure 11.8 The position of the highest point of the tongue in General American English vowels. The lip positions are those for the vowels in figure 11.1. The lower quadrilateral on the right has the horizontal scale expanded.

Bell's work was very much admired by later phoneticians. They developed his notion of tongue height and backness, and plotted vowels on charts showing the supposed position of the highest point of the tongue. The vertical axis represented what they thought of as tongue height and the horizontal axis tongue backness or frontness.

These early phoneticians were much like astronomers before Galileo. The ancient astronomers could predict the positions of the heavenly bodies with reasonable accuracy. They thought that the sun went round the earth every 24 hours, and that most stars did the same. In their view the planets like Venus, Mars, and Jupiter went a bit faster or slower so that they were in slightly different positions every night. The observations of the early astronomers were wonderful. They could predict the apparent movements of the planets fairly well. These astronomers were certain they were describing how the stars and planets went around the earth. But they were not. The same is true of phoneticians. They thought they were describing the highest point of the tongue, but they were not. They were actually describing formant frequencies.

The position of the highest point of the tongue in each of the General American vowels is shown in figure 11.8. The diagram on the left in this figure is a combination of the X-ray data shown in figures 11.1 and 11.2. The solid points

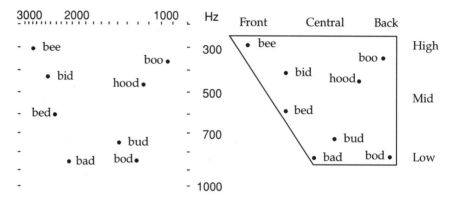

Figure 11.9   The quadrilateral on the right is a traditional representation of what is taken to be the relative position of the highest point of the tongue in some American English vowels. The corresponding acoustic data (taken from figure 6.5) are shown on the left.

on these tongue shapes are at the highest points. These points are shown by themselves in the upper diagram on the right, so that you can see exactly how high or low, and how back or front they really are. We can get a better impression of the difference between front and back vowels if we expand the horizontal scale and contract the vertical scale as in the lower diagram on the right.

When phoneticians draw diagrams to represent tongue height, they do not make them look like the diagram on the lower right of figure 11.8. Instead they place the dots as shown on the right in figure 11.9. This diagram is very like the one on the left in figure 11.9, which represents the acoustic qualities of vowels. The diagram on the left is identical to part of figure 5.5 in chapter 5. Traditional phoneticians (whether they know it or not) take the first formant as indicative of what they call tongue height and the second formant as indicative of some combination of lip rounding and tongue backness. Oscar Russell, a scientist who studied X-rays of vowels in the 1930s, suggested that traditional vowel diagrams express acoustic facts in terms of physiological fantasies.

The X-rays of English vowels show that the tongue shapes are very different from the shapes that Bell imagined. But we should consider Bell's descriptions in the context of his time. Before Bell proposed his three-dimensional scheme for categorizing vowels, it was thought that vowels varied in only two ways, jaw opening, which distinguished the vowels in *see, head,* and *father,* and lip rounding, which distinguished those in *father, boat,* and *boot.* Bell realized that vowels differed in three ways, tongue height, the part of the tongue that was varying in height, and lip opening. As you can see from the X-rays in figures 11.1 and 11.2, there is more than a grain of truth in Bell's idea, although the tongue shapes are very different from those he imagined.

Finally, we should consider the position of the lips. The English front vowels have a fairly neutral lip position. The lips become more open as the jaw lowers, but there is no lip rounding. The back vowel **ɑ** as in *father* is also pronounced with a neutral lip position. In going from **ɑ** as in *father* towards **u** as in *who* the lip rounding steadily increases. In my grandfather's day, **u** *(who)* had a considerable amount of lip rounding, but nowadays younger speakers have comparatively spread lips in this vowel. Nevertheless, in general, lip rounding increases in back vowels as they become higher.

11.4 Summary

The movements of the tongue in forming vowels are best described in terms of two components: (1) a raising component associated principally with the actions of the genioglossus and mylohyoid muscles, together with the muscles controlling the jaw height; and (2) a backing component largely associated with the styloglossus and hyoglossus muscles. But many different muscular actions can be used to produce similar tongue shapes.

The traditional way of describing how vowels differ is in terms of the height and backness of the highest point of the tongue, and the degree of lip opening. This form of description had its roots in the work of the nineteenth-century speech teacher Alexander Melville Bell. Although Bell was mistaken in his views on tongue shapes, his approach has dominated vowel descriptions. Phoneticians who were actually describing variations in formant frequencies phrased their descriptions in terms of tongue positions.

English vowels also differ in lip position. The lips are usually in a neutral position for front vowels, and in an increasingly rounded shape as back vowels become higher.

12

Actions of the Larynx

12.1   Voiced and Voiceless Sounds

When we first looked at the vocal folds, in chapter 3, we considered them mainly as ways of making sounds that differed in pitch. Later, in chapter 7, we saw that their actions also distinguish voiceless sounds such as **f** and **s** in *fat* and *seal* from their voiced counterparts **v** and **z** in *vat* and *zeal*. Most languages have sounds that differ only in that one is voiced and the other is voiceless (although, as we will see later, Hawaiian does not). Many languages have more pairs of sounds than those found in English. Burmese has voiceless versions of nasal and lateral sounds that occur only as voiced sounds in English, as shown in table 12.1 and recording 12.1. Voiceless versions of voiced sounds are indicated by a small open circle under or over the voiced symbol, m̥, n̥, ŋ̊, l̥. The accents above the vowels indicate the tones, which affect the meanings of the words, just as the tones affect the meanings of the Chinese words discussed in chapter 3.

Table 12.1   Words illustrating contrasts in voicing and aspiration in Burmese

Nasals	Bilabial	Dental	Palatal	Velar	Alveolar lateral
Voiceless	m̥â 'from'	n̥ă: 'nasal'	ɲ̊ă: 'considerate'	ŋ̊â 'borrow'	l̥â 'beautiful'
Voiced	mâ 'lift up'	nă: 'pain'	ɲă: 'right'	ŋâ 'fish'	lâ 'moon'

Welsh is another language that has voiceless versions of sounds that are always voiced in English. The Welsh spelling 'll' indicates a voiceless alveolar lateral, which is usually fricative and has the symbol ɬ. It appears at the beginning of the word ɬan, *llan* 'church', and in the name of the Welsh captain in Shakespeare's *Henry V*, ɬuɛlɪn *Llwelyn*.

12.2 Voicing and Aspiration

The sound of English **b** is not quite the same as Spanish **b**. English **p** is also not the same as Spanish **p**. Table 12.2 shows some words illustrating these sounds. The first syllables of each of these words are similar in the two languages, but if you listen to recording 12.2 you will hear that there is a difference between them. Spanish *pe(sos)* sounds more like English *ba(sis)* than English *pa(ces)*.

You can see why this is so by comparing the waveforms of these words, which are shown in figure 12.1. The first line shows the **b** at the beginning of the Spanish word *besos*, which has a waveform with a very small amplitude. The vocal folds are vibrating, but the lips are closed, so the sound is not very loud. What you hear comes mainly through the walls of the neck. When the lips come apart and the vowel is produced, the waveform becomes much larger. The Spanish **p** in *pesos* in the second line of the figure is voiceless, and so there is nothing to be seen during the lip closure. As soon as the lips come apart the waveform of the sound indicates that there are vocal fold vibrations.

Now look at English **b** in the third line. In this utterance, which is typical of my pronunciation of words beginning with **b** said in isolation, the waveform is virtually identical with the Spanish **p**. The last line shows the English **p**, which is distinguished from **b** by a small burst of noise when the lips open, followed by a slightly noisy interval of about 30 ms before the vowel starts.

English **b, d, g** often do not have voicing throughout the closure. When they are at the beginning of an utterance, the voicing may start just before the release of the stop, but on many occasions (as in figure 12.1) they may be

Table 12.2 A comparison of English **b, p** and Spanish **b, p**

	b	p
Spanish	*besos* **besos** 'kisses'	*pesos* **pesos** 'pesos' (money)
English	*bases* **besɪz**	*paces* **pʰesɪz**

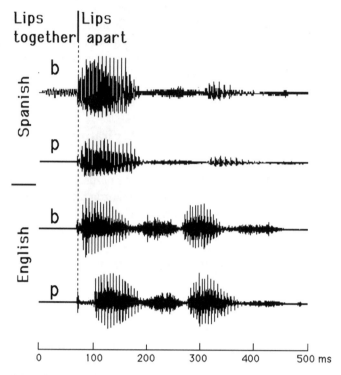

Figure 12.1 Waveforms of the Spanish words *besos* 'kisses', *pesos* 'pesos' (money), and the English words *bases, paces*.

completely voiceless. Between vowels, as in *abbey, adder, leggy,* they will be voiced throughout, but after a silence or a voiceless sound, as in *this boy, this day, this guy,* there will be little or no voicing during the stop. In Spanish, however, **b, d, g** are virtually always fully voiced.

In English the vocal folds are apart and not vibrating while the lips are closed for **p,** and while the tongue is touching the roof of the mouth for **t** or **k.** They do not come together and start vibrating immediately after the closure is released. There is a small delay before the following vowel in which the air rushes out, forming what is known as aspiration. The English stops **p, t, k** are said to be aspirated. After Spanish **p, t, k,** the vowel starts immediately, and the stops are unaspirated.

The interval between the release of a stop and the start of a following vowel is called the Voice Onset Time (VOT). In English, the VOT is 50–60 ms for **k,** and slightly less for **t** and **p.** In Spanish the VOT for **k** is about 20 ms, and even less for **p.**

In general, Germanic languages like English, German, and Danish have comparatively long aspiration intervals (i.e. long VOTs), contrasting voiceless or only weakly voiced stops with aspirated stops. In Romance languages like

Table 12.3 Words illustrating a three-way contrast in stop voicing in Thai. The accents above the vowels indicate the tones

	Bilabial	Dental
Voiced	**bâː** 'crazy'	**dàː** 'curse'
Voiceless unaspirated	**pâː** 'aunt'	**taː** 'eye'
Voiceless aspirated	**pʰâaː** 'cloth'	**tʰâː** 'landing place'

French and Spanish, the voiceless stops have virtually no aspiration, and the contrast is between fully voiced stops and voiceless unaspirated stops. Although they are typically voiceless, English (and other Germanic languages) are commonly said to have voiced stops that contrast with voiceless stops.

Some languages contrast three kinds of stops. They have fully voiced and voiceless unaspirated stops as in French and Spanish, and in addition they have aspirated stops somewhat like those in English and German. Table 12.3 and recording 12.3 provide Thai illustrations. When there is a three-way contrast of this kind the aspirated stops may be symbolized by using a small raised **h**, e.g. **pʰ**.

Figure 12.2 shows the waveforms of the three Thai words in the bilabial column. In the first word, **bâː** 'crazy', there are vibrations of the vocal folds during the lip closure, much as there were in Spanish *besos*. In the second word, **pâː** 'aunt', the vibrations begin within a few milliseconds of the lips opening, as they did in Spanish *pesos*. The last word, **pʰâaː** 'cloth', has a long period of aspiration, about 100 ms, after the lips open and before the vibrations of the vocal folds begin. This is more like the English **p** in *paces*, but with an even longer interval after the opening of the lips before the vocal folds start vibrating.

12.3 Glottal Stops

There are several states of the vocal folds other than simply vibrating for voiced sounds or being apart for voiceless and aspirated sounds. They can, for instance, be held tightly together, forming a glottal stop. You bring the vocal folds tightly together when you cough, or when you take a deep breath and hold it.

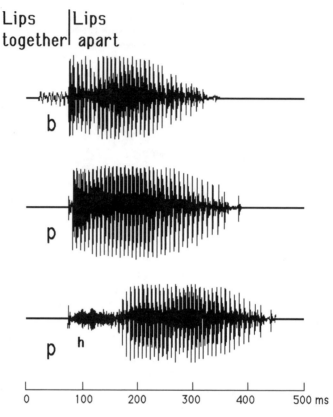

Figure 12.2   Waveforms of the three Thai words **bâː** 'crazy', **pâː** 'aunt', **pʰâaː** 'cloth'.

Glottal stops are used quite regularly in most forms of English. Nearly everybody makes a glottal stop instead of at least part of the **t** in words such as *button*. The symbol for this sound is **ʔ**, so button would be transcribed as **bʌʔn**, or perhaps **bʌʔtn**. Nowadays younger speakers of many forms of British English have glottal stops at the ends of words such as *cap*, *cat*, and *back*. A generation or so ago speakers of BBC English would have regarded such a pronunciation as improper, almost as bad as producing a glottal stop between vowels as in the London Cockney pronunciation of *butter* as **bʌʔə**. If you are a really old-fashioned speaker of British English, you may still be glottal-stop-free, but there are not many such people left. Glottal stops are spreading fast. In America nearly everybody has a glottal stop in *button* and *bitten*, although most speakers of American English have not progressed as far as the British in substituting **ʔ** for **t** at the ends of many words.

Some languages, such as Hawaiian, have a glottal stop as a regular part of their consonant system. Hawaiian has eight consonants, as shown in table 12.4 and recording 12.4. In some senses the glottal stop replaces **t** in Hawaiian (although historically this is not exactly what happened).

Table 12.4 Hawaiian words illustrating the eight consonants in the language in initial position

	Bilabial	Alveolar	Velar	Glottal
Stop	**paka** 'to remove the dregs'		**kaka** 'to rinse, to clean'	**ʔaka** 'to laugh'
Nasal	**maka** 'eye'	**naka** 'to quiver, to shake'		
Approximant	**waka** 'sharp, protruding'	**laka** 'tame, gentle'		**haka** 'shelf, perch'

12.4 Breathy Voice

If the vocal folds are held together only loosely, a breathy voice will be produced. There are many variations of breathy voice. It is sometimes made with the vocal folds fairly far apart, so that it sounds like a voice produced while sighing. It is as if the vocal folds were flapping in the breeze, as one phonetician has put it. At other times the vocal folds are only slightly further apart than in ordinary voice, producing a kind of murmured sound.

Many speakers of English have a form of breathy voice when **h** occurs between vowels in words such as *ahead* and *behind*. Figure 12.3 shows my vocal folds when producing a sound similar to a very breathy **ɦ** of this kind. (The hook at the top of the h-like symbol indicates that this is a breathy-voiced 'h'.) The vocal folds are far apart, and the one on the right of the picture (which is actually the left vocal fold) is definitely flapping in the breeze, somewhat irregularly. As with all the pictures of the vocal folds in this book, a color version of this photograph is on the CD.

Most of the Indo-European languages spoken in northern India use a form of breathy voice to distinguish a set of stop consonants. These breathy-voiced consonants are often called voiced aspirated stops, because of their similarities with the (voiceless) aspirated stops. Examples from Hindi, the principal language of India, are given in table 12.5 and recording 12.5. There are some unfamiliar symbols in this table, because Hindi has, loosely speaking, two kinds of **d** in the first row, **ḍ** and **ḍ**, and two kinds of **t** in other rows, **ṭ** and **ṭ**. We will discuss these sounds in the next chapter. Here we are just interested in the actions of the vocal folds, noting that Hindi has four kinds of stops, voiced, voiceless unaspirated, voiceless aspirated, and voiced aspirated (breathy-voiced).

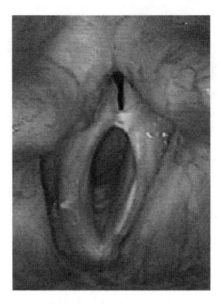

Figure 12.3 The vocal folds during breathy voice.

Table 12.5 Words illustrating Hindi stops

	Bilabial	Dental	Post-alveolar	Palatoalveolar	Velar
Voiced	bal 'hair'	ḍal 'lentil'	ḍal 'branch'	dʒal 'net'	gal 'cheek'
Voiceless unaspirated	pal 'take care of'	ṭal 'beat'	ʈal 'postpone'	ʧal 'turn'	kal 'era'
Voiceless aspirated	pʰal 'knife blade'	t̪ʰal 'plate'	ʈʰal 'wood shop'	ʧʰal 'bark'	kʰal 'skin'
Voiced aspirated	bʱal 'forehead'	d̪ʱar 'knife'	ɖʱal 'shield'	dʒʱal 'cymbals'	gʱal 'confusion'

Figure 12.4 shows the waveforms of the four Hindi words in the bilabial column. The first three are much the same as the waveforms of the three Thai words shown in figure 12.2. During **b** there is voicing while the lips are closed. In **p** the vibrations start at the beginning of the vowel, almost immediately after the lips open. In **pʰ** there is an interval of about 100 ms before vibrations start. The fourth word, **bʱal**, has a voiced aspirated (breathy-voiced) stop. There are vibrations during the lip closure, but they are smaller than in the regularly voiced **b**. Breathy voice is not so loud. The vibrations continue with

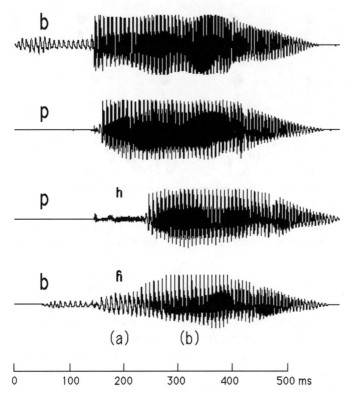

Figure 12.4   The waveforms of the Hindi words **bal** 'hair', **pal** 'take care of', **pʰal** 'knife blade', **bʱal** 'forehead'. In the last word (a) indicates the breathy-voiced portion as compared with (b) which marks a part of the vowel with regular voicing.

a slightly greater amplitude after the lips open, and after about 80–100 ms increase to the full amplitude of the vowel.

The difference between breathy voice and regular voicing becomes clearer when we look at parts of the waveform for the last word, **bʱal**, more closely. Figure 12.5 shows the parts of the wave marked as (a), shortly after the lips open, and (b), during the vowel, in figure 12.4 on an expanded time scale. The sound in (b) has regular voicing, and is like the wave of my saying **a** as in *father*, in the very first figure in this book, figure 1.1. You can see not only the onset of each wave produced by a vocal fold pulse (marked by a solid point) but also the prominent peaks within each pulse (marked by open circles) that correspond to one of the resonances of the vocal tract – the first formant.

The breathy-voiced wave in (a) has a slightly lower amplitude and far less well-defined structure within each repetition. The vocal fold pulses are still visible (a little bit further apart because this section of the wave is on a slightly lower pitch), but the waves corresponding to the formants are not so obvious. This is because the resonances of the vocal tract are less well excited by breathy

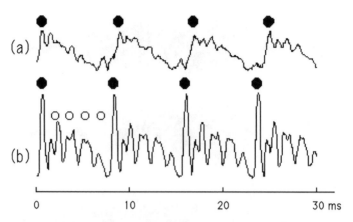

Figure 12.5 The waveforms (a) of the breathy-voiced part of **bʱal** shortly after the lips open in figure 12.4, and (b) of the part of the vowel with regular voice in the same word.

voice. To get well-defined formants, which can be seen as the subsidiary waves within each major peak in (b), you need sharp pulses from the vocal folds. Breathy-voiced waveforms often show little more than the fundamental frequency with a few extra variations in air pressure superimposed.

Finally, while considering northern Indian languages, we will look at Gujarati. In this language there are breathy-voiced vowels resulting from the loss of **h** between two syllables. The IPA symbol for breathy-voiced vowels is the symbol for the corresponding voiced sound with two dots below, e.g. **a̤**. Gujarati also has voiceless aspirated stops and voiced aspirated stops, leading to some interesting three-way contrasts, as shown in table 12.6 and recording 12.6.

Table 12.6 Words illustrating breathy-voiced vowels in Gujarati

Voiced vowel	Breathy vowel	Aspirated stop
pɔr 'last year'	**pɔ̤r** 'dawn'	**pʰɔdz** 'army'
bar 'twelve'	**ba̤r** 'outside'	**bʰar** 'burden'
kan 'ear'	**ka̤n** 'Krishna'	
veɳ 'current'	**ve̤ɳ** 'speech'	
mɛl 'dirt'	**mɛ̤l** 'palace'	

All the words in the second column in table 12.6 were originally two-syllable words containing **h**. They are now pronounced with breathy-voiced vowels – at least in normally spoken conversational Gujarati. If you ask Gujarati speakers to read the words in table 12.6 to you, they will probably read them as they are spelled, with two syllables. Educated Indians have a long tradition of literacy. They had a written language for centuries before English speakers.

12.5   Creaky Voice

Some languages have sounds in which the vocal folds are held more tightly together than in regular voicing. This produces what is called creaky voice, the sound that often occurs at the beginning of a sentence beginning with a vowel, or at the end of a sentence when a speaker goes down into a very low pitch. Creaky voice is not used in English except as part of the intonation, and perhaps as an indicator of a particular accent. Elderly upper-class speakers of BBC English are particularly likely to use it. Figure 12.6 shows my vocal folds during creaky voice. It is difficult to see the vocal folds during creaky voice, as there is a great deal of constriction, not only at the larynx, but also in the part of the vocal tract immediately above it. The vocal folds are pressed together, and only a short length of them vibrates.

Creaky voice distinguishes one sound from another in some languages. Table 12.7 and recording 12.7 illustrate creaky-voiced vowels (sometimes called laryngealized or glottalized vowels) in Jalapa Mazatec, a language spoken in

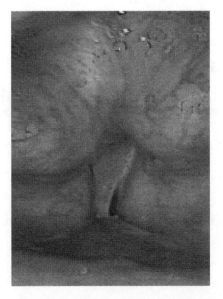

Figure 12.6   The vocal folds during creaky voice.

Table 12.7   Words illustrating vowels with different voice qualities in Jalapa Mazatec

Voiced	Creaky-voiced	Breathy-voiced
tha	nda	nda
tʰǽ	ndǽ̰	ndǽ̤
'seed'	'buttocks'	'horse'

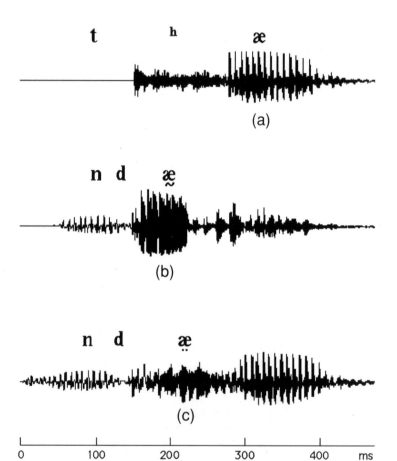

(a)

(b)

(c)

0   100   200   300   400   ms

Figure 12.7   Waveforms of the three Mazatec words **tʰǽ** 'seed', **ndǽ̰** 'buttocks', **ndǽ̤** 'horse': (a), (b), and (c) indicate parts of the waveform that are shown on an expanded time scale in figure 12.8.

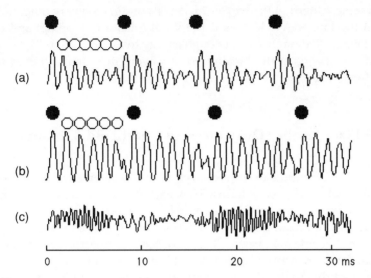

Figure 12.8 Parts of the three Mazatec words shown in figure 12.7 with the time scale expanded: (a) regular voice, (b) creaky voice, (c) breathy voice.

Mexico. As you can see from the table, this language also has breathy-voiced vowels. Creaky-voiced sounds are marked by a wavy line (a tilde) underneath the symbol.

Waveforms of the three Mazatec words are shown in figure 12.7. The first word has a long aspirated tʰ (the VOT is over 100 ms) followed by a vowel with regular voicing. You can see the pulses of the vocal folds in the part of the vowel marked (a). The second word illustrates a creaky-voiced vowel. This word begins with low-pitched voicing in the **nd**, and, when the vowel begins, very large pulses of the vocal folds (above the part marked (b)). The third word has breathy voice of a slightly different kind to that found in Hindi or Gujarati. Above the part marked (c) there is the waveform of a very breathy æ̤, with no regular pulses visible.

The differences between the three types of voicing are more evident when the time scale is expanded, as in figure 12.8. Regular voice in the first row has vocal fold pulses (marked with solid points) and, within them, a wave corresponding to the first formant (marked with open circles). The second row shows creaky voice. The vocal fold pulses are slightly further apart. Within each pulse the wave corresponding to the first formant has a greater amplitude than in regular voicing. As we noted in chapter 4 with reference to recording 4.2, the first formant becomes more evident when a vowel is said with a creaky voice.

Breathy voice is illustrated in the last row. In this language very little of the breathy voice waveform shows evidence of vocal fold vibrations, although there is some pattern in the waveform corresponding to every other vocal fold pulse in the line above. It is as if the vocal folds are flapping, and only on every other oscillation produce enough energy to excite vocal tract resonances. Most of the energy in the breathy voice waveform is semi-random noise at higher frequencies.

12.6   Further Differences in Vocal Fold Vibrations

As you can see from the examples given in this chapter, neither breathy voice nor creaky voice are precise terms. They each cover a range of voice qualities. As a final example of a subtle difference of this kind, table 12.8 and recording 12.8 illustrate contrasting vocal fold actions in Mpi, a language spoken by a few hundred people in Northern Thailand. Mpi has one set of vowels in which the vocal folds are vibrating in a normal manner, and another set in which they are slightly stiffer, although they are not held as tightly together as in creaky voice in Mazatec. There is also a stiffening of the walls of the pharynx, the part of the throat just above the vocal folds, all of which contributes to making the voice have a harsher, slightly tense, quality. We will refer to this quality as tense voice. As Mpi also distinguishes words by tones, a single consonant and vowel combination such as **si** may have 12 different meanings, as shown in the table. Listening to these sounds is an interesting experience for speakers of European languages, who do not use pitch or voice quality to distinguish words. As an Italian friend of mine said on hearing the 12 versions of **si**, "They all sound like 'yes' to me."

The subtle adjustments of the vocal folds required for the various kinds of breathy voice and creaky voice need greater articulatory precision than that required for regular voiced sounds. They are also hard for listeners to distinguish, particularly as a breathy or creaky voice quality may be simply the person's normal way of speaking. Most of us can think of individuals who have a Marilyn Monroe breathy voice quality or a Louis Armstrong creaky

Table 12.8   Words illustrating vowels with different voice qualities and different tones in Mpi

Tone (pitch)	Regular voice	English	Tense voice	English
Low rising	si	'to be putrid'	si	'to be dried up'
Low level	si	'blood'	si	'seven'
Mid rising	si	'to roll rope'	si	'to smoke'
Mid level	si	(a color)	si	(classifier)
High falling	si	'to die'	si	(name)
High level	si	'four'	si	(name)

voice quality. As a result these voice qualities are used by a comparatively small number of languages.

12.7   Ejectives

We have seen that the vocal folds can be held together and produce a glottal stop, as in English **bʌʔn**, *button*. In some languages the glottal stop action can be used in another way. Speakers pull the closed vocal folds upwards, and compress the air in the mouth. Try saying a glottal stop at the end of a word such as *sock*. Take a deep breath, say **ak**, and then hold your breath. After a second or so, release the **k** closure, while still holding your breath. You should be able to hear a faint popping sound. Sounds of this type are called ejectives. With a little practice you can make a vowel after an ejective. Take a deep breath, say **ak**, hold your breath, release the **k** closure, and say **a** as you release your breath. The IPA symbol for ejective sounds is a raised comma after the regular symbol, so you will be producing the sequence **ak'a**. Once you get the feel for making a glottal stop and a **k** closure, you will be able to leave out the preliminary maneuvers and say **k'a**, with an ejective at the beginning of a syllable.

If you feel ambitious you can try making an ejective **p'** with a bilabial closure. Take a deep breath, hold it with a glottal stop, and then open and close your lips fairly forcibly a few times (while still holding your breath). You can hear a faint popping sound, which is a weak ejective. Ejective **p'** is not as strong as ejective **k'**. Join a vowel on, and you will be saying **p'a**. You can go on to make a **t** closure with a glottal stop (perhaps starting from a **t** in *button*) and say **t'a** as well.

The mechanism for producing a velar ejective **k'** is shown in diagrammatic form in figure 12.9. The muscles of the pharynx contract, making the walls stiff, and the closed vocal folds move upwards and compress the air behind the **k** closure. While they are still closed the **k** closure is released, producing a louder sound than that in a regular **k**.

Ejectives occur in many American Indian and African languages. Table 12.9 and recording 12.9 give examples from Quechua, the language of the people who live in the Inca regions of Peru and Bolivia. Note that Quechua also has a contrast between voiceless (unaspirated) and (voiceless) aspirated stops.

Ejectives occur in only about 20 percent of the world's languages. As we saw in chapter 1, speakers and listeners like languages to have distinct sounds that are easy to hear, but they also want sounds that are easy to make. Ejectives are more difficult to make, and this outweighs any advantage they may have in being slightly louder.

The balance between these two forces – ease of articulation versus ease of hearing – is well illustrated by another fact about ejectives. Velar ejectives are

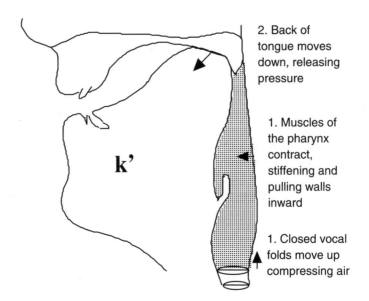

Figure 12.9 The mechanism used for making a velar ejective **k'**. The shaded area contains air that has been compressed by the upward movement of the closed vocal folds.

Table 12.9 Quechua words illustrating voiceless, aspirated, and ejective stops. The symbol **q** represents a uvular stop, a sound made with a closure at the back of the mouth, near the uvula

	Palatoalveolar	Velar	Uvular
Voiceless	ʧaka	kujui	qaʎu
	'bridge'	'to move'	'tongue'
Aspirated	ʧʰaka	kʰujui	qʰaʎu
	'large ant'	'to whistle'	'shawl'
Ejective	ʧ'aka	k'ujui	q'aʎu
	'hoarse'	'to twist'	'tomato sauce'

more common than alveolar or bilabial ejectives. This is because, as shown in figure 12.9, the body of air behind the closure for **k'** is comparatively small, and a small movement of the closed vocal folds will compress it considerably. When producing a **p'** the body of air involved is much larger and is bounded by the cheeks, which are more easily distended. As a result, the same movement of the closed vocal folds will produce a smaller increase of pressure. When the ejective **p'** is released it is not so different from a regular **p**. Each of the ejectives **p'**, **t'**, **k'**, **q'** is somewhat hard to produce, so they are all disfavored in the world's languages. But **k'**, which is no easier to produce than **t'** or **p'**, is a little more favored because it is auditorily more distinct.

While we are thinking about what we might call the ecology of languages, there is yet another point to note about ejectives. Once a language has some ejectives, the principle of gestural economy discussed in chapter 1 often comes into play. Ejective sounds will be made with the same articulatory gestures as those used in other sounds in the language. Thus Quechua has ejectives made at the same places of articulation as it has other stops.

12.8   Implosives

Just as the closed vocal folds can be raised so that they push air out of the mouth, so also they can be lowered so that they suck air in. Sounds made in this way are called implosives. Usually, when the vocal folds are pulled downwards lowering the pressure of the air in the mouth, they leak a bit, and get set into vibration by the air that is passing between them, producing a voiced sound. Most of the languages that have implosives produce them as voiced sounds, although it is possible to make them with the vocal folds tightly together, so that they are voiceless. In the next section we will discuss one language, Owerri Igbo, spoken in Nigeria, which has both voiced and voiceless implosives.

I don't know an easy way to teach people to make implosives. They are more difficult sounds to produce than ejectives, which is why they occur in only about 10 percent of the world's languages. Some children make them when imitating a frog noise, but most adults have lost the art of producing them spontaneously, and find them hard to make.

Unlike the ejectives, which are all symbolized by using a raised comma, ', the implosive at each place of articulation has its own special symbol, formed by adding a right hook to the basic symbol. The symbols corresponding to **b**, **d**, **g** are **ɓ**, **ɗ**, **ɠ**.

Sindhi, an Indo-European language spoken in India, has a series of voiced implosives. Like its neighbor Hindi, it also has stops at five places of articulation, and contrasts between voiced, voiceless unaspirated, voiceless aspirated, and voiced aspirated stops. Table 12.10 and recording 12.10 illustrate all these sounds.

12.9   Recording Data on Larynx Actions

One of the few languages that has both voiced and voiceless implosives is the Owerri dialect of Igbo, a Nigerian language. This language has six bilabial

Table 12.10   Words illustrating Sindhi stops

	Bilabial	Dental	Post-alveolar	Palatal	Velar
Voiced	bənʊ 'forest'	ḍərʊ 'door'	ɖorʊ 'you run'	ɟəʈʊ 'illiterate'	gʊɳʊ 'quality'
Voiceless unaspirated	pənʊ 'leaf'	t̪ərʊ 'bottom'	ʈənʊ 'ton'	cəʈʊ 'to destroy'	kənʊ 'ear'
Voiceless aspirated	pʰəɳu 'snake hood'	t̪ʰərʊ (district name)	ʈʰəɠʊ 'thug, cheat'	cʰəʈʊ 'crown'	kʰənʊ 'you lift'
Voiced aspirated	bʱaɳʊ 'manure'	d̪ʱərʊ 'trunk'	ɖʱəɠʊ 'bull'	ɟʱəʈʊ 'grab' (n.)	gʱəɳɪ 'excess'
Voiced implosive	ɓəni 'field'		ɗəɳʊ 'festival'	ʄəʈʊ 'illiterate'	ɠəɳʊ 'handle'

Table 12.11   Words illustrating the stops of Owerri Igbo.
The accents above the vowels indicate the tones

	Bilabial	Alveolar
Voiced	íba 'to get rich'	ída 'to cut'
Voiceless unaspirated	ípa 'to carry'	ńtà (name)
Aspirated	ípʰà 'to squeeze'	ítʰa 'to blame'
Breathy-voiced	íbʱa 'to peel'	ídʱa 'to fall'
Voiceless implosive	íɓ̥a 'to gather'	íɗ̥a 'to chew'
Voiced implosive	íɓa 'to dance'	

stops as shown in table 12.11 and recording 12.11. The voiced, voiceless unaspirated, and aspirated stops are similar to those in Thai. There is also a so-called breathy-voiced stop similar to that in Hindi and Sindhi. All these contrast with the voiced and voiceless implosives.

The sounds of Owerri Igbo are so unusual that it is worth examining them in more detail. This will also provide an opportunity to show how phoneticians get data on all these actions of the larynx. When I recorded these speakers in Nigeria I was able to observe exactly how each sound was made. I asked one of the speakers, Sister Mary Uwalaka, to say the words while she was holding a mask pressed against her face. In this way I was able to measure the flow of air as it went in and out of her mouth. I also asked her to place a small tube between her lips so that I could measure the air pressure in her mouth when her lips were closed. This is all simpler than it sounds, and she was able to speak quite naturally. (Being a linguistics student and practiced at doing this sort of thing probably helped her as well.) The sound was, of course, muffled by the airflow mask, but I had already made good recordings of her saying these words (which you can hear in recording 12.11), so I was not worried about the poor sound quality. However, I needed to know exactly when the vocal folds were vibrating, so I placed a small microphone on her neck, near her larynx.

Figure 12.10 shows the instrumental records for the bilabial stops in the first column in table 12.11. Note that in each case the stop is in the middle, between two vowels. For the voiced stop, **b**, in (1), there is no flow of air out of the mouth during the period between the arrows, when the lips are closed. In this period the pressure behind the lips is slightly above normal, and is varying considerably (the air pressure record is a very thick line) because the air in the mouth is vibrating. The larynx microphone record shows that the vocal folds were vibrating throughout. This is a fully voiced stop.

For the voiceless stop in (2) the pressure behind the lips goes up when the lips close. The larynx microphone record is a straight line when the pressure is high, showing that there is no voicing at that time. The voicing starts the instant the pressure falls. This is a voiceless unaspirated stop.

The pressure behind the lips goes up in (3) for **p^h**, much as it does for the **p** in (2). But this time it falls very rapidly when the lips open and the record of the airflow in the top line shows that a burst of air comes out of the mouth. This is an aspirated stop.

The breathy-voiced stop in (4) has some of the characteristics of the voiced stop in (1). The pressure record shows that the vocal folds are vibrating throughout the closure. But the pressure of the air in the mouth is increasing in a way that it does not do in the voiced stop. This is because more air is passing between the vocal folds. They are vibrating more loosely so that the pressure behind the lips rises until it is as high as the pressure in the aspirated stop in (3). As the lips open and the pressure is released, there is a rapid airflow with breathy voice.

The implosive ɓ in (5) is a voiceless sound, as is evident from the straight line in the larynx microphone record during the stop. The pressure of the air behind the lips is decreasing because the closed vocal folds are moving downwards. Towards the end of the closure the vocal folds are not held together so

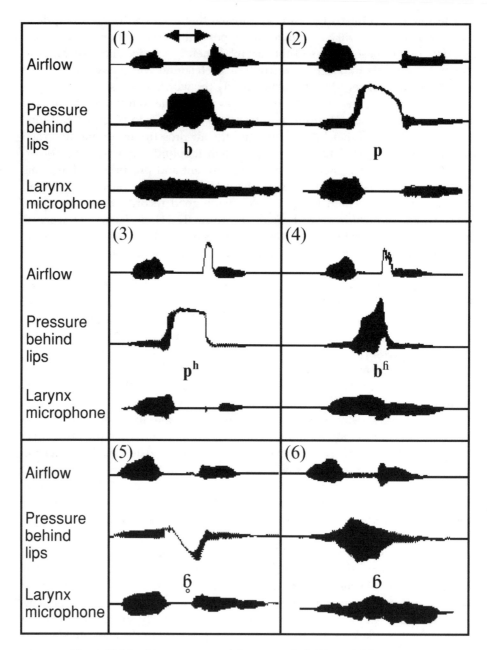

Figure 12.10   Air pressure and flow records in Owerri Igbo stops.

tightly, and air from the lungs passes between them, setting them vibrating. When this happens the pressure behind the lips starts increasing. By the time the lips open the pressure behind them has returned to zero and there is no airflow into the mouth. Nevertheless, because there is a suction effect from the descending vocal folds during the stop, this sound is regarded as an implosive.

The sound in (6) is also an implosive, but this time it is voiced. The average pressure behind the lips is only slightly negative because air from the lungs is flowing between the vibrating vocal folds into the mouth. This sound is regarded as an implosive because the larynx descends. If the larynx were not going down, the pressure behind the lips would go up, as it does in the voiced labial stop shown in (1).

12.10   Summary

Voicing can be continuous throughout an articulation such as the coming together of the lips for **b**, producing a voiced stop. Or the vocal folds can be apart during the closure, but start vibrating as the closure is released, producing a voiceless stop such as **p**. Or the vocal fold vibration can start some 40 or more milliseconds after the release of the closure, producing a (voiceless) aspirated stop such as **p**^{h}. These differences are known as differences in Voice Onset Time (VOT).

As well as vibrating or being apart (for voiced and voiceless sounds), the vocal folds can be tightly together for a glottal stop, **ʔ**. The vocal folds can vibrate loosely producing breathy voice, as in voiced aspirated stops in many languages spoken in India. The vocal folds vibrate more stiffly when they are held somewhat tightly together, producing creaky voice. Various kinds of breathy and creaky voice can be produced.

If the larynx is moved upwards while the folds are together, air will be pushed upwards. If there is a stop closure the air will be compressed. When the stop closure is released there will be the sharp sound of an ejective, such as **k'**. A downward movement of the closed vocal folds will decrease the pressure in the mouth and form an implosive. If (as is usually the case) air passes up through the descending vocal folds, setting them in vibration, a voiced implosive such as **ɓ** will be produced.

13

Consonants Around the World

13.1 Phonetic Fieldwork

I've spent much of my life searching for all the different sounds that occur in the world's languages. For the last eight years I have been working almost exclusively on recording the phonetic structures of endangered languages, languages that are likely to be no longer spoken 100 years from now. There are about 7,000 languages in the world today, and over half of them are spoken by less than 10,000 people – the size of a small town in many countries. Over a quarter of the languages of the world are spoken by fewer than 1,000 people.

If you are a speaker of a language with a small number of speakers, you probably speak another language as well. In Europe this is true even when the language, like Dutch or Danish, is spoken by a few million people. All over the world communities interact, and it is not at all unusual for people to be able to speak many languages. There are very few groups who are so completely isolated that they have virtually no contact with their neighbors. The only completely monolingual community I have ever known are the speakers of Pirahã, a small group of about 300 people who live in the Amazonian rain forest. They ignore strangers and have as little to do with the outside world as possible. You have to learn their language to speak to them, a tedious and difficult process involving hours of patient observation and trial and error. It was a long time before the missionaries, Keren and Dan Everett, who went to live with them could communicate fluently. With their help I learned about Pirahã. I've often had reason to be thankful for the dedicated work of missionary linguists, who don't seem to mind that I'm a member of Atheists for Jesus.

Even if a language is spoken by only a few people, it has all the capabilities of any other language. You can say anything you want in any language. There may be no word for something that is not known in the neighborhood, but every language has ways of dealing with this situation. The Hausa of Nigeria, for example, did not use forks. They had a word for spoon, 'cokali'. When they found they needed a word for a fork they simply called it 'cokali mai yatsu', a spoon that has fingers. Languages can always invent or borrow new words so that they can say anything. Remember that until recently we had no word for a machine with four wheels and an engine that can move along a road. Now we can call it a car, or an automobile, or use one of many slang terms.

The nearest I have come to finding a language that is limited in what it can express has been when a concept is missing. Many groups have little need to count things and have no words for numbers. Most Australian aboriginal languages have words equivalent to 'one, two, some, many', but nothing (until they borrowed them from English) for 'three, four, five', etc. One elderly speaker, when asked, in his own language, "How many spears do you have?" said something like "Well, I have my long throwing spear, a short throwing spear, a jabbing spear, a broad blade spear and my ceremonial spear." When it was pointed out that he had five spears (using the English word for five) he, being wise and knowing perfectly well what was happening, said, "Yes, if you say so." He was then asked, "If I took one away, how many spears would you have left?" He smiled and said, "That would depend on which one you took away, wouldn't it?" He might not be able to do arithmetic in his own language, but he could name and list things in a remarkable way. He could tell us all his ancestors for several generations back – which is something few of us could do in our languages.

The Australian aboriginal languages are disappearing, as are the languages of many small communities all over the world. Nowadays it is more difficult for a group to live on its own. Many small communities see benefits in becoming more like their prosperous neighbors. Standards of living are rising, and roads and communications are improving. More and more people go to a school where the regional language is used, and children no longer talk to their parents in their mother's tongue. People start using the languages they need to get a better job. They want to listen to TV and radio, and to be entertained at the cinema. Parents talk to their children in the language they have started using outside the home, and the old language begins to be used only by the elderly. When the elderly die, the language disappears and an important part of the tribal heritage is gone.

It is difficult for those of us who are native speakers of one of the larger languages to understand what this may mean to people who speak an endangered language. Our language is a tool, and most of us do not view it as in any sense sacred. It is not part of our religion. But, as one tribal elder put it to me: "The mysteries of our life are bound up in our language." For them it really is a holy thing. Their words were created by their God. There is also a feeling of tribal identity that goes with a language. A young man whose language had gone said to me sadly: "We can no longer keep in touch with our ancestors."

13.2   Well-known Consonants

There are about 600 consonants used in different languages. There is no way that I could describe all of them in this introductory book. This chapter is called 'Consonants Around the World' because the sounds it describes are largely those I've recorded while doing fieldwork in many different countries. But even without including the more obscure and endangered languages, people use a wide range of consonants. The ten most widely spoken languages are listed in table 13.1. These languages use about 100 different consonants (depending slightly on which dialect you choose as typical of the language) of which only 22 occur in English.

Some consonants occur more frequently than others. The most common are the voiceless stops. About 98 percent of the world's languages have the three voiceless stops **p, t, k**, and every known language has sounds similar to two of these three. The versions of **p, t, k**, that occur in other languages may not be exactly like the English sounds. They may be aspirated or unaspirated as we saw in the previous chapter, and the place of articulation may be slightly different. But the odds are strongly in favor of a language having sounds that are something like all three of the voiceless stops **p, t, k**. Moving the lips, or the tip of the tongue, or the back of the tongue are the easiest things to do. Over half the world's consonants are made with the tip or blade of the tongue.

English has stops made at a fourth place, in addition to **p, t, k**. The sound **ʧ** ('ch') and its voiced counterpart **ʤ** ('j') have the air blocked by the tongue contacting the roof of the mouth at a place slightly behind that used in the

Table 13.1   The ten most widely spoken languages

	Language	Number of speakers
1	Chinese, Mandarin	885,000,000
2	English	322,000,000
3	Spanish	266,000,000
4	Bengali	189,000,000
5	Hindi	182,000,000
=6	Portuguese	170,000,000
	Russian	170,000,000
8	Arabic (all forms)	161,000,000
9	Japanese	125,000,000
10	German	98,000,000

formation of **t** and **d**. Either the tip or the blade (the part of the tongue just behind the tip) can be used for these sounds. These four places of articulation are used by many languages.

There are also many other possible places of articulation. In this chapter we will expand our view of consonants by first considering these additional possibilities, which form one axis of the IPA chart. We will then consider the other main axis of the IPA consonant chart, the manner of articulation. Finally we will discuss some sounds that do not fit neatly into the chart, because they are not produced by pushing air out of the lungs.

13.3   More Places of Articulation

In chapter 10 I mentioned that some languages distinguish sounds made by squeezing the air passage between the two lips and sounds made by bringing the lower lip near the upper teeth – the usual way of producing **f** and **v**. Ewe, a language spoken in Ghana, uses these two places of articulation, so that it has bilabial fricatives, symbolized ɸ and β, as well as the more familiar fricatives **f** and **v**. Table 13.2 and recording 13.1 illustrate these sounds. These are fairly subtle distinctions that are not easy to hear.

When it comes to articulations made with the tongue there are many more subtle distinctions. As you can see from the IPA chart at the end of the book, the symbols **t**, **d**, **n** stand for stops made in the dental, alveolar, or post-alveolar region. This is a wide range of possibilities, and sometimes (as we saw in table 12.5 for Hindi and table 12.10 for Sindhi) it is necessary to distinguish different types of each of these sounds. We can do this by adding a diacritic, a small mark accompanying the symbol. A diacritic somewhat like a

Table 13.2   Words illustrating bilabial and labiodental fricatives in Ewe (a language spoken in Ghana)

	Bilabial	Labiodental
Voiceless	éɸá 'he polished'	éfá 'he was cold'
	éɸle 'he bought'	éflé 'he split off'
Voiced	èβè 'Ewe' (language)	èvè 'two'
	èβló 'mushroom'	évlo 'he is evil'

Table 13.3 Words illustrating different places of articulation in Nunggubuyu
(a language spoken in Australia)

Dental	Alveolar	Retroflex	Post-alveolar
t̪araɡ	tarawa	ʈakowa	tˢaro
'whiskers'	'greedy'	'prawn'	'needle'

tooth under the symbols, t̪, d̪, indicates a dental sound in which the tongue touches the upper front teeth. We used these symbols in both Hindi and Sindhi. An underline, t, d, shows that the tongue touches the roof of the mouth further back, behind the center of the alveolar ridge. We used these symbols in the Hindi words ʤal 'net', ʧal 'turn', ʧʰal 'bark', ʤʰal 'cymbals'. In each of these words the t or d is followed by a palatoalveolar fricative ʃ or ʒ. These affricates are very much like the English affricates in *chap* and *jam*, which we might well have transcribed ʧæp and ʤæm.

There is yet another type of t, d, n in which the tip of the tongue is curled up and back to touch the roof of the mouth behind the alveolar ridge. The symbols are a long ʈ, ɖ, and ɳ, with hooks to the right. These sounds, called retroflex sounds, also occur in Hindi and Sindhi; ʈ and ɖ were illustrated in tables 12.5 and 12.10.

A few languages spoken in Australia distinguish three different types of t. They have t̪, t, ʈ as well as having a palatoalveolar tˢ, somewhat similar to English ʧ ('ch'), but with a slightly less noticeable ʃ. When a sound is a less noticeable part of another sound it can be represented by a raised, smaller, symbol. Table 13.3 and recording 13.2 illustrate examples in Nunggubuyu, a language spoken by a few hundred people in the Northern Territory, Australia.

The differences between these four sounds can be seen in figure 13.1, which shows spectrograms of the first syllables of each of them. There are subtle differences in both the bursts of noise at the beginning of each syllable, and the movements of the formants. As indicated by the arrows, the most prominent peak in the burst has a slightly higher frequency in t̪ than in t. The difference between t and the retroflex ʈ is almost non-existent. In running speech the retroflex ʈ is most clearly marked by the effect of the tongue movements (which we discuss later) on the preceding word. The burst for the palatoalveolar tˢ is slightly lower in pitch, and also has a higher intensity for a longer period. The dark area by the arrow persists for almost 50 ms. This is definitely an affricated stop (a stop followed by a fricative noise due to the articulators coming apart comparatively slowly). It is similar to the English ʧ in *church*, but with a slightly less strong fricative portion. In addition the first formant begins at a lower frequency and the second formant begins at a higher frequency, showing that the tongue body is high and forward in the mouth.

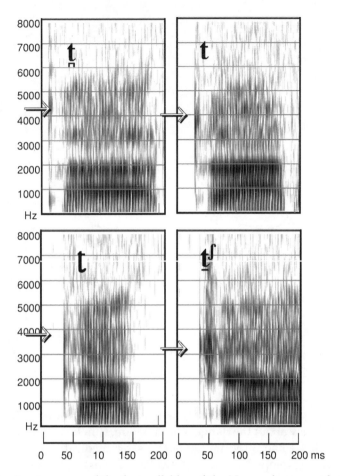

Figure 13.1 Spectrograms of the first syllables of the Nunggubuyu words in table 13.3. The arrows indicate the most evident parts of the burst, the noise that occurs as the stop closure is released.

Another way of thinking about these sounds is to consider how they are made. Figure 13.2 shows estimates of the positions of the tongue during the stop closures. These pictures are not as useful as the spectrograms for two reasons. First, even during the stop closures, the tongue is still moving. No static diagram can adequately represent the tongue gestures. Second, they may not be accurate. The only data I have on Nunggubuyu is from my own fieldwork in Australia. I could see the tip and blade of the speaker's tongue, and get some idea of where the tongue touched the roof of the mouth. I could also feel what my own tongue was doing while I tried to say each word in a way that the speaker accepted as a reasonable pronunciation. But to know exactly how the tongue was moving while saying these words, we would need X-ray motion pictures or other dynamic images that modern medical

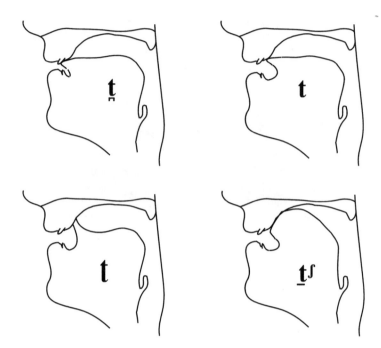

Figure 13.2   The positions of the tongue during the stop closures in the four Nunggubuyu words shown in table 13.3.

techniques can produce. X-rays are no longer permitted for research purposes, now that we know about the dangers of radiation. (I'm lucky that I've survived the amount that I had 30 years ago.) The safer medical imaging techniques that have been developed are not yet available for use in fieldwork situations, such as the Australian outback.

There is, however, a simple way of getting some useful information on the articulation of these sounds, using what is called palatography. So that you can see another of the investigative techniques that phoneticians use, we'll look at how palatography can be used to examine languages like Nunggubuyu. Palatography lets us make pictures of the roof of the mouth and the tongue, showing where the tongue has touched the roof of the mouth during the pronunciation of a word.

The tongue has to be painted with a suitable black mixture. We use olive oil and medicinal charcoal in about equal parts. Olive oil by itself does not taste too bad, and charcoal is tasteless (if you've ever had burnt food you've probably already eaten some). After the tongue has been painted, the speaker says a word. When the tongue comes up and touches the roof of the mouth it transfers some of the black mixture onto the upper surface of the mouth. If you put a mirror into the mouth, you can photograph the appropriate areas, as shown on the left in figure 13.3. At the top of the picture on the left you can see the speaker's upper front teeth, some of which are missing. Below them is

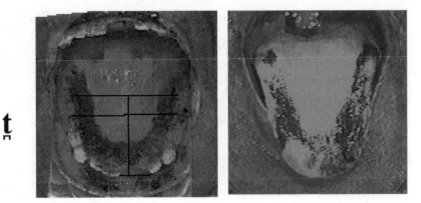

Figure 13.3 A palatogram (on the left) showing the roof of the speaker's mouth, and a linguagram (on the right) showing the tongue after producing a word with a dental t̪.

the mirror, which is reflecting a view of the roof of the mouth. In this reflected view the upper front teeth are at the bottom of the picture. You can see in this reflected view that some of the black mixture is on the upper front teeth and the alveolar ridge just behind them.

You can also see which part of the tongue did the touching by reversing the painting process. Paint the roof of the mouth with the olive oil and charcoal mixture. When the speaker says a word in which the tongue contacts the roof of the mouth, some of the mixture will come off on the tongue. You can then photograph the speaker's tongue, producing what is called a linguagram, as shown in the picture on the right in figure 13.3. You can see black marks on the tip and the blade (the part just behind the tip) of the tongue.

Victoria Anderson, a former student now at the University of Hawaii, made palatograms and linguagrams of some words in Arrernte, a language related to Nunggubuyu. Figure 13.3, which we have been using to illustrate the technique, is part of her work. (She drew the lines on the photographs in the course of making measurements of exactly where the tongue touched the roof of the mouth.) Using her data we can compare all four of the Arrernte counterparts of the sounds in Nunggubuyu.

The four sets of palatograms and linguagrams are shown in figures 13.3 to 13.6. They tell us a great deal about how the sounds are made. Figure 13.3, which we have been discussing, shows the dental t̪, which is made by the tip and blade of the tongue contacting the upper front teeth and the area behind them. A different kind of t, more like the most common variety of t in English, is shown in figure 13.4. As you can see from the picture on the right, it is the tip of the tongue that does the touching. There is none of the marking medium on the blade of the tongue, except at the sides. The picture on the left shows that the tongue did not touch the upper teeth at all, but made contact with a narrow area on the alveolar ridge, just behind the teeth.

t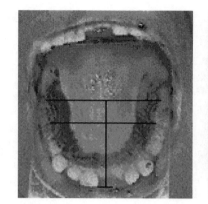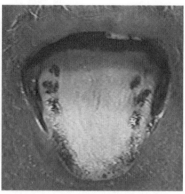

Figure 13.4   A palatogram and a linguagram showing the roof of the mouth and the tongue after producing a word with an alveolar **t**.

t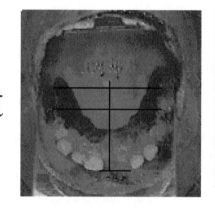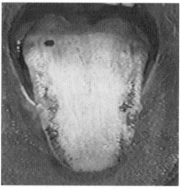

Figure 13.5   A palatogram and a linguagram showing the roof of the mouth and the tongue after producing a word with a retroflex **ʈ**.

The articulation of the retroflex **ʈ** is shown in figure 13.5. The contact on the roof of the mouth is even further back, and there is less of the black marking medium on the tip of the tongue than for the alveolar **t** in figure 13.4. This is because it is the underside of the tip of the tongue that touches the roof of the mouth. The inadequacy of static diagrams such as those in figure 13.2 is particularly applicable in the case of **ʈ**. Before the beginning of the syllable the tongue tip is curled up and back. This has a great effect on the formants in the preceding vowel (not shown in figure 13.1), in that the third formant is lowered as it is for most **r** sounds. When the tongue first contacts the roof of the mouth it is in the position shown in figure 13.2, but then the tip slides forward so that when it leaves the roof of the mouth it is more in the position for an alveolar **t**. As we saw in the discussion of figure 13.2, it produces a sound that is not very different.

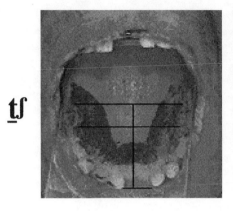
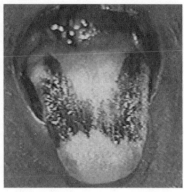

tʃ

Figure 13.6 A palatogram and a linguagram showing the roof of the mouth and the tongue after producing a word with a palatoalveolar t̪ʃ.

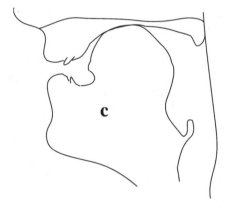

c

Figure 13.7 The articulations for a palatal stop.

The last articulation to be studied in this set is the palatoalveolar t̪ʃ, which we likened to English ʧ ('ch'). In this case, as you can see in figure 13.6, the contact area on the roof of the mouth is similar to that for the retroflex ʈ, but covering a slightly wider area. The part of the tongue involved is behind the tip and blade.

Another fairly unusual sound similar to t̪ʃ is c, a voiceless palatal stop, although in this case we do not have to go so far to find good examples, as it occurs in Hungarian. The articulation for this sound is shown in figure 13.7. As you can see, it is somewhat like that for t̪ʃ, which we have been discussing. It is difficult to get your tongue bunched up so that it touches just the forward part of the roof of the mouth – the hard palate – without also contacting the back part of the alveolar ridge, which is the gesture used for the ʧ sound. This is why more languages have ʧ ('ch') than have a true palatal c. The voiced counterpart of this sound is symbolized by ɟ, an inverted letter 'f', and the

Table 13.4   Palatals in Hungarian

	Voiceless stop	Voiced stop	Nasal
Initial	tyúk **cuːk** 'hen'	gyújt **ɟuit** 'he ignites'	nyújt **ɲuit** 'he reaches'
Between vowels	atya ɔcɔ 'gather'	agya ɔɟɔ 'his brain'	anya ɔɲɔ 'mother'

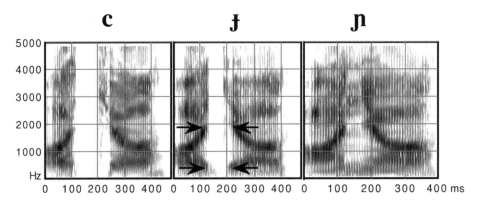

Figure 13.8 Spectrograms of the Hungarian words ɔcɔ 'gather', ɔɟɔ 'his brain', ɔɲɔ 'mother'. The arrows in the center panel show the location of the first and second formants as the closure is formed and released.

corresponding nasal is ɲ, a letter 'n' with the tail of a 'j' on its left-hand side. Palatal nasals are much more common than palatal stops. They occur in well-known languages, such as in Spanish *señor*, **seɲor** (sir), Italian *signore*, **siɲore** (sir), and French *agneau*, **aɲo** (lamb). Spanish and Italian also have palatal laterals, in which the central contact is similar to that in the nasals, but air passes over one or both sides of the tongue. The symbol for a palatal lateral is ʎ as in (European) Spanish *pollo*, **poʎo** (chicken) and Italian *figlio*, **fiʎo** (son).

    Examples of palatals in Hungarian are given in table 13.4 and recording 13.3. Spectrograms of these sounds between vowels (the lower part of table 13.4) are shown in figure 13.8. The distinguishing features of palatal sounds are the low first formant and the high second formant (marked by the arrows in the center panel, but also apparent in the other two panels). These formants are in much the same region as the first and second formants in a high front vowel i, which is not surprising as the tongue is raised and in the front of the mouth in all these sounds.

Table 13.5 Words illustrating contrasting stops and nasals in Malayalam (a Dravidian language spoken in India)

Bilabial	Dental	Alveolar	Retroflex	Palatal	Velar
kʌmmi	pʌn̪n̪i	kʌnni	kʌɳɳi	kʌɲɲi	mʌŋŋi
'shortage'	'pig'	'first'	'link in chain'	'boiled rice and water'	'faded'

Table 13.6 Words illustrating the voiceless stops of Aleut. The words are shown in the Aleut orthography, as well as in an IPA transcription

Dental	Velar	Uvular
tiistax̂	*kiikax̂*	*qiighax̂*
tiistaχ	**kiikaχ**	**qiiɣaχ**
'dough'	'cranberry bush'	'grass'
taangax̂	*kaangux̂*	*qaadan*
taangaχ	**kaanguχ**	**qaaðan**
'water'	'healthy'	'dolly varden' (fish)

Nearly every language has a velar stop, **k**, and most of them also have **g**. The nasal **ŋ** is also well known, although it occurs in fewer languages than **m** and **n**. However, there are also languages that have nasal consonants at all the places of articulation we have been considering. Malayalam, a language of southern India, has six nasal consonants, as shown in table 13.5. You can hear all these sounds in recording 13.4.

A few languages have another stop, **q**, in which the back of the tongue touches the roof of the mouth a little further back, nearer the uvula. Examples of this sound in Quechua were given in table 12.9 and recording 12.9. Aleut, the language of the people of the Aleutian Islands, also has uvular sounds, illustrated in table 13.6 and recording 13.5. Aleut is one of the few languages that have no bilabial stop, **p**. This sound occurs only in words recently borrowed from English or Russian. Table 13.6 illustrates not only the uvular stop **q**, but also the uvular fricative **χ** that occurs at the ends of some of these words.

13.4 More Manners of Articulation

Speech sounds depend not only on where in the mouth they are made, but also on what you do with your lips and tongue. So far in this chapter we have discussed only sounds that require a complete closure at some point – stops

Table 13.7 Words illustrating bilabial and alveolar trills in Kele and Titan

	Kele		Titan	
Bilabial	ᵐʙuɛŋkei?	ᵐʙulim	ᵐʙulei	ᵐʙutukei
	'fruit' (species)	'face'	'rat'	'wooden plate'
Alveolar	ⁿruwin	ⁿrikei	ⁿruli?	ⁿrakei?in
	'bone'	'leg'	'sand piper'	'girls'

and nasals. A bilabial trill, ʙ, occurs when the lips are set in vibration by the outgoing air. This sound is fairly rare, but it occurs in a number of different parts of the world. Table 13.7 and recording 13.6 provide examples from Kele and Titan, two related languages spoken on a small island just north of the Papua New Guinea mainland. These languages also have trills made with the tip of the tongue near the alveolar ridge, symbolized by r. In these languages both the bilabial and alveolar trills are combined with short preceding nasals, which are shown by small raised symbols.

Figure 13.9 shows the waveforms of the Kele words ᵐʙuɛŋkei?, a fruit of some kind (the speaker I recorded did not know what the English word was – or even if there was one) and ⁿruwin 'bone'. The arrows indicate the vibrations of the lips and the tongue tip. They are a little further apart in the upper diagram, indicating that the lips vibrated a little more slowly than the tongue tip.

There is another way in which it is possible to make a trill. The uvula, which hangs down at the back of the mouth, can be set into vibration, just like the tip of the tongue. Very few languages use a uvular trill. French, German, and Southern Swedish speakers use a sound made with the back of the tongue near the uvula for the sound of 'r', but it is seldom actually a uvular trill. Recording 13.7 illustrates a rather formal southern Swedish pronunciation of the words ʀatː 'ratt' (steering wheel) and ʀotː 'rått' (raw). The symbol for a uvular trill is ʀ, a small capital 'R'.

Sounds in which the airstream is forced through a narrow gap are called fricatives. They can be divided into two groups: the sibilants, like English s, ʃ ('sh'), and the non-sibilants, like English f, θ ('th'). Two things are necessary for a sibilant sound. First, there must be a fast-moving jet of air formed by the tongue making a narrow channel. Second, this jet of air must blow over some sharp obstacle such as the edge of the upper front teeth. The non-sibilant fricative noises are produced more simply. Turbulent eddies occur when there is a narrowing of the vocal tract and the air is pushed through a less severe obstruction.

Fricatives are far more common than trills, and only slightly less common than stops or nasals. Sibilants are more common than other fricatives, because

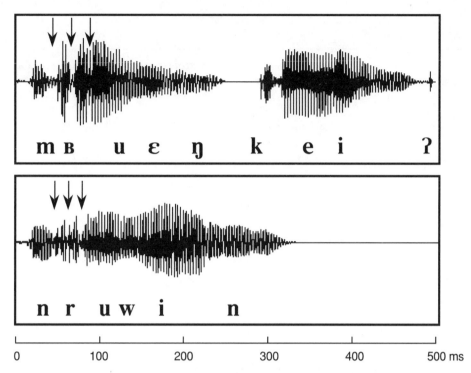

Figure 13.9 Waveforms of the Kele words ᵐʙuɛŋkeiʔ, 'fruit' (species) and ⁿruwin 'bone'. The arrows indicate the vibrations of the lips and the tongue tip.

they have more acoustic energy. They stand out from other sounds even in non-speech contexts. People go **sssss** to hiss villains and **ʃʃʃʃʃ** to quiet their children.

There are languages like Polish that have not only two sibilants rather like the English sounds, but also a third possibility, made with the tongue a little further back in the mouth. Table 13.8 and recording 13.8 illustrate the six sibilants of Polish, three voiced and three voiceless.

Phoneticians have discussed these sounds at length, as they are not easily classified in articulatory terms. The column headings in table 13.8 do not fully convey the positions of the articulators. I used the IPA symbols for retroflex sibilants, ʂ and ʐ, for the sounds in the second column, as these sounds have the tip of the tongue raised so that there is a space below it. They are made a little further back in the mouth than English ʃ ('sh') and ʒ, but they do not have the tongue tip curled up as much as in the retroflex sounds ʈ and ɖ in Hindi. The symbols ɕ and ʑ are used in the third column. These sounds are described by the IPA as 'alveolo-palatal fricatives', implying that they are made with the front of the tongue raised behind the alveolar region.

The Polish sibilants shown in table 13.8 vary in both the frequencies present in the fricative noise, and in the movements of the formants, as can be seen in

Table 13.8 Words illustrating the Polish sibilant sounds, word-initial and
in between vowels

	Alveolar	Retroflex	Alveolo-palatal
Voiceless initial	sali	szali	siali
	sali	**ʂali**	**ɕali**
	'room' (gen.)	'scale' (gen.)	'sown'
Voiced initial	zalew	zⱡali	ziali
	zalɛf	**ʐali**	**ʑali**
	'bay'	'complains'	'gasped'
Voiceless medial	kasa	kasza	kasiasz
	kasa	**kaʂa**	**kaɕaʂ**
	'case'	'groats'	'burglar'
Voiced medial	skaza	gazⱡa	kazia
	skaza	**gaʐa**	**kaʑa**
	'flaw'	'gauze'	(name, gen.)

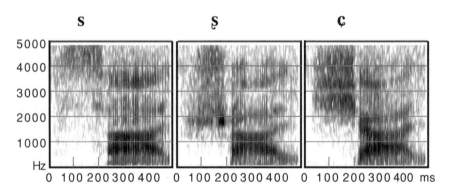

Figure 13.10 Spectrograms of the Polish fricatives.

figure 13.10. Most of the energy in **s** is very high pitched, above 4,000 Hz. The
energy in **ʂ** includes some low frequencies, below 2,000 Hz. The energy in **ɕ** is
between these two, in the region 2,500–3,500 Hz. This sound has the body of
the tongue raised and in the front of the mouth, much as in the vowel **i**. As a
result, the first formant is low and the second formant is high when the voicing begins for the following vowel.

You might think that three voiceless sibilants would be enough for any language, but it is possible to distinguish more. Toda, a language spoken in the
Nilgiri Hills in the south of India by a few hundred people, has four voiceless sibilants – one more than Polish – all of which can be used to distinguish

Table 13.9   Words illustrating the sibilant sounds at the ends of words in Toda (a Dravidian language spoken in the south of India)

Dental	Alveolar	Post-alveolar	Retroflex
kɔṣ	pɔsʸ	pɔʃ	pɔş
'money'	'milk'	'language'	(name of a clan)

Table 13.10   Laterals in Melpa

	Dental	Alveolar	Velar
Medial	kialţim	lola	paʟa
	'fingernail'	'speak improperly'	'fence'
Final (voiceless)	waⱡ	baɬ	ɹaⱡ
	'knitted bag'	'apron'	'two'

words. The four sibilants occur at the ends of words in Toda, as shown in table 13.9 and recording 13.9. The difference between the first two is that the ş at the end of kɔṣ is made on the teeth and has energy at an even higher pitch than the s at the end of pɔsʸ.

There are even more non-sibilant fricatives than sibilants. If you look at the IPA chart at the end of the book, you will see that the fricative row has more symbols in it than any other row. We have already seen some of the other symbols, such as χ for the uvular fricative at the end of the Aleut word **taangaχ** 'water' (table 13.6, recording 13.5). A complete account of all the possibilities would take us beyond what I can cover in this book.

We will end this section on manners of articulation by looking at some of the different lateral sounds that occur around the world. In lateral sounds the tongue forms an obstruction, so that air comes out over the sides. We used to think that the obstruction had to be in the front of the mouth, and it is certainly true that the most common laterals are formed by the tongue touching the teeth or the alveolar ridge as in English l. I once said in a lecture I was giving in Papua New Guinea that you couldn't make laterals with the back of the tongue. One of the students raised his hand and said "Perhaps you can't, but we can." In his language, Melpa, the whole body of the tongue is narrowed so that the back of the tongue can touch the roof of the mouth and air can come out around the sides. He opened his mouth and pronounced some words very slowly so that I could see him doing this. Unfortunately I did not have a camera with me, but I did make a recording, which you can hear in recording 13.10. The words are shown in table 13.10. To complicate matters still further, Melpa has two other l sounds, which are also shown in the table

Table 13.11   Laterals in Zulu. The words are shown in the Zulu orthography, as well as in an IPA transcription

	Alveolar	Nasal plus alveolar	Velar
Voiced lateral approximant	lala **lálà** 'sleep'		
Voiced lateral fricative	dlala **ɮálà** 'play' (imper.)	indlala **ínɮàlà** 'hunger'	
Voiceless lateral fricative/ejective	hlanza **ɬânzà** 'vomit'	inhlanhla **íntɬʼàntɬʼà** 'good luck'	tlina **kʟ̥ʼîná** 'be naughty'

and are on the recording. In the dental lateral the blade of the tongue touches the teeth, and in the alveolar lateral the tip of the tongue touches the alveolar ridge. The contrasts are illustrated in various positions. When they are at the ends of words the laterals are voiceless. We have already seen that the symbol for the voiceless counterpart of l is ɬ (in chapter 12). The symbol for a velar lateral is a small capital 'L', ʟ. There is no special symbol for its voiceless counterpart. As we saw in chapter 12, we can show the voiceless counterpart of a sound by putting a small circle under it, in this case forming ʟ̥.

Laterals can get even more complex. Usually the airstream passes out freely over the sides of the tongue, but it can be pushed through a narrow opening so that fricative noise is produced. This typically occurs in the voiceless sounds in Welsh words like ɬan (church), and in Melpa at the ends of words. But it can also occur for voiced laterals. The symbol for a voiced alveolar fricative lateral is ɮ. Zulu has voiced and voiceless laterals that are fricative, as shown in table 13.11 and recording 13.11. As a further complication, after a nasal, **n**, the voiceless lateral fricative ɬ becomes part of an ejective **ntɬ'**. There is also a velar ejective **k'** that may be followed by a voiceless velar lateral ʟ̥, although not all Zulu speakers pronounce this combination in this way. In the Zulu orthography, voiceless laterals are written as 'hl' and voiced laterals as 'dl'.

13.5   Clicks

Zulu is probably better known for the clicking sounds that it has than for its laterals. All of us can make clicks, but they occur as regular speech sounds only in languages spoken in Africa. English speakers use clicks as noises that are like signals, such as the sound that novelists write as 'tsk, tsk', used to express disapproval.

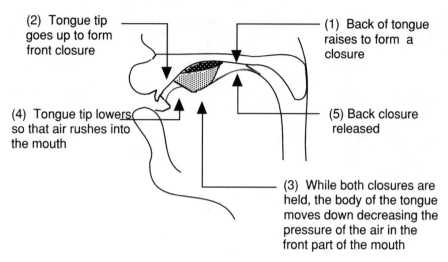

(2) Tongue tip goes up to form front closure

(1) Back of tongue raises to form a closure

(4) Tongue tip lowers so that air rushes into the mouth

(5) Back closure released

(3) While both closures are held, the body of the tongue moves down decreasing the pressure of the air in the front part of the mouth

Figure 13.11   The movements involved in making a click. The dark shaded area shows the cavity enclosed when the closures are formed. The light shaded area shows the cavity just before the release of the front closure. The dashed lines show the lowered tongue positions corresponding to steps 4 and 5.

All clicks involve sucking air into the mouth. If you close your lips and make a kiss-like sucking action, when you open your lips you will make a bilabial click. This sound actually occurs in !Xóõ, a Bushman language that we will discuss at the end of the next chapter. Drawing the tongue down and back so that it pulls air into the mouth will produce a click when any closure in front of the tongue is released. The front closure can be made by the lips, but most clicks are made by the tip or blade of the tongue against the teeth or the roof of the mouth. The sequence of movements is illustrated in figure 13.11. It looks more complicated than it is. Try: (1) Raising the back of the tongue. (2) Raising the tip of the tongue. (3) Making a click. You will be doing it by lowering the body of the tongue, and then (4) lowering the tip of the tongue. Finally (5) lower the back of the tongue. All just as shown in the figure.

You can tell that making a click involves just the air in the mouth, as it is possible to hum (or, as we can put it more technically, make a voiced velar nasal ŋ) while producing a click. Try humming while you make a kiss-like click. It's not difficult. If you want to make it a bit harder, try humming, making a click, and then adding a vowel after it. If you make the *tsk, tsk* sound, a dental click for which the IPA symbol is ǀ, you will soon be able to say ŋǀo, an actual word in a click language that you can see in table 13.12.

Table 13.12 and recording 13.12 illustrate the 20 clicks of Nama, a language spoken in Namibia. The four columns use the IPA symbols for the different types of clicks. The dental clicks in the first column are made with the tip and blade of the tongue against the upper teeth and teeth ridge. Try saying *tsk, tsk* (of course not the sounds **tsk, tsk**, but the click expressing disapproval). You

Table 13.12   Words illustrating contrasting clicks in Nama. All these words have a high tone

	Dental	Alveolar	Palatal	Alveolar lateral
Voiceless unaspirated	kǀoa 'put into'	kǃoas 'hollow'	kǂais 'calling'	kǁaros 'writing'
Voiceless aspirated	kǀʰo 'play music'	kǃʰoas 'belt'	kǂʰaris 'small one'	kǁʰaos 'strike'
Voiceless nasal	ŋ̊ǀʰo 'push into'	ŋ̊ǃʰoas 'narrating'	ŋ̊ǂʰais 'baboon's behind'	ŋ̊ǁʰaos 'cooking place'
Voiced nasal	ŋǀo 'measure'	ŋǃoras 'pluck maize'	ŋǂais 'turtle dove'	ŋǁaes 'pointing'
Glottal closure	kǀʔoa 'sound'	kǃʔoas 'meeting'	kǂʔais 'gold'	kǁʔaos 'reject a present'

can probably feel the tip and blade of your tongue on and just behind your upper front teeth. The clicks in the next column, headed alveolar, are made with the tip of the tongue touching the roof of the mouth somewhat further back, on the alveolar ridge or even behind it. Those in the third column have the tongue tip down behind the lower front teeth, and nearly the whole body of the tongue pressed against the roof of the mouth. The front of the tongue is in much the same position as in the palatal sounds that we considered earlier. The final column illustrates lateral clicks – sounds that are sometimes used to show approval. In these clicks the tongue tip is raised much as it is in the alveolar clicks, but it is the side of the tongue that is lowered to let the air rush in.

    As each click involves the back of the tongue making a closure against the roof of the mouth, there is always a k or ŋ accompanying each click symbol. Sometimes it is just a plain kǀ, as in the first row, and sometimes an aspirated symbol, kǀʰ, showing that a burst of air follows the release, as in the second row. Sometimes, as in the last row in the table, it is followed by a glottal stop that begins the following vowel, kǀʔ. The nasal can be voiceless and followed by aspiration, ŋ̊ǀʰ, as in the third row, or it can have regular voicing, ŋǀ, as in the fourth row. The distinctions between the columns (the different types of clicks) are fairly easy to hear, but the distinctions between the rows (the different click accompaniments) are fairly subtle.

    Clicks involve a sucking gesture that might seem difficult to integrate into the stream of speech. But this may not be true, as clicks have often been borrowed from one language into another. All the clicking sounds that now occur in the languages of southern Africa first developed among the ancestors of the people we now call the Bushmen. From there they spread to other tribes such as the Nama of Namibia. A few hundred years ago the Zulus, Xhosa, and other Bantu tribes swept southward from central Africa and conquered the Nama and the Bushmen, taking them as wives and servants. They also took some of their click sounds into their languages. We know for certain that clicks are borrowed sounds in Zulu and other Bantu languages, as these languages did not have any clicks a few hundred years ago. But clicks are now very much part of their regular sound systems, appearing in print with 'c' for the dental click, 'x' for the lateral click (as in the name of the language *Xhosa*), and 'q' for a click in which the tongue tip curls up as it makes contact with the roof of the mouth.

As a teacher of phonetics for many years, I have found it quite easy to get people to say words with clicks in them. Students find it much easier than, for example, learning to produce a trilled *r* sound, or making some of the sequences of consonants that occur in Polish. Clicks are also auditorily very distinct from other sounds, and, although the different accompaniments (the rows in table 13.11) are hard to distinguish, there seems no obvious reason why most languages should not have at least two or three different types of clicks. Perhaps eventually all languages will evolve so that they include some clicks among their consonants. The Bushmen, who have them already, may have the most evolved languages in the world so far; but maybe in two or three thousand years most languages will have a few clicks among their consonants.

13.6   Summary

Over half the 7,000 languages in the world are spoken by fewer than 10,000 people, and over a quarter of all languages have fewer than 1,000 speakers. As a result of increased communications many languages are now spoken only by elderly people. Many of the world's 600 different consonants will not be used 100 years hence, and phonetic fieldwork in out-of-the-way places is necessary to investigate them now.

Consonants can be made at additional places within the mouth that are not used in English. Nasals made with the tongue touching the upper front teeth are distinguished from those made on the alveolar ridge in Malayalam. Palatal stops (e.g. in Hungarian) and uvular stops (e.g. in Aleut) are distinguished from the more familiar English velar stops. The lips and the uvula can be trilled, and a wide range of fricatives and lateral sounds can be made. Click sounds are regular consonants in some languages spoken in Africa.

14

Vowels Around the World

14.1   Types of Vowels

How many different vowels are there in the world's languages? It was difficult enough to estimate how many distinct consonants there are, but it is far
harder to say how many vowels there are. We can make one vowel glide into
another. This is exactly what you do when you say a word like *react*. You pass
through a number of different vowel qualities. There is a kind of continuous
vowel space in which vowels can be described in terms of their formants or
tongue and lip gestures. This space does not provide distinct categories like
many of those used in descriptions of consonants.

   Listeners can distinguish vowels that have very small differences in their
formant frequencies. Diane Kewley-Port, a psychologist working on this
matter, has shown that listeners can distinguish vowels that have formant
frequencies differing by only 12 Hz in some regions of the vowel space. On the
basis of her work it seems that listeners might be able to distinguish about
40 vowel heights (variations in the first formant) and from 5 to 30 degrees of
vowel backness (variations in the second formant), depending on the height.
Of course in the rough and tumble of everyday speech, differences as small as
this are unlikely to be used for distinguishing words. They are, however,
probably sufficient to distinguish different accents.

   Languages differ greatly in the number of vowels that they use. Some languages, such as most of the aboriginal languages of Australia, have as few as
three vowels. This does not, of course, mean that these languages are in any
way simpler. Many Australian languages have complex consonant systems.
As we saw in table 13.3, Nunggubuyu has ʈ, t, t̪ and t̪ʲ, which are hard for

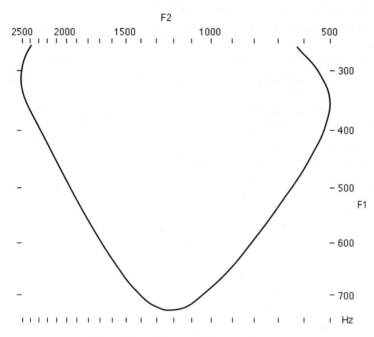

Figure 14.1 The possible vowel space.

speakers of languages like English to distinguish. In general, the number of vowels in a language is not a good predictor of the number of consonants. There are languages such as Hawaiian with 5 vowels and only 8 consonants, and others such as Zulu in which there are 5 vowels and 44 consonants.

Probably every language uses at least three distinct vowels. (Linguists argue about this, and there are claims that Kabardian, a Caucasian language spoken in Russia, has less than three vowels, but I am not convinced that this is so.) Languages that have only three vowels usually have sounds that can be symbolized **i, a, o** or **i, a, u**. The first of these vowels is somewhere between English **iː** as in *seat* and ɪ as in *sit*. The second is something like Spanish **a** as in *masa* (dough), between English **æ** as in *bat* and **ɑ** as in *father*. The third is often a back rounded vowel between **o** as in Spanish *mosca* (fly) and **u** as in Spanish *musa* (muse). Languages use these three vowels extensively because, as we saw earlier, they are far apart in the vowel space.

About 20 percent of the world's languages have five contrasting vowels. There seems to be a slight preference for an odd number of vowels, perhaps because the vowel space is triangular. If you construct a computer model of a male vocal tract and make it move through all the possible lip and tongue positions for vowels, it will produce sounds that all fall within the formant space shown in figure 14.1. Because of the complicated way lip and tongue movements interact in producing acoustic changes, the vowels are not evenly distributed in this space. There are more of them in the left-hand half, corresponding to vowels such as **i, e, a,** and comparatively few in the upper right, corresponding to vowels such as **u** and **o**. Even so, if there are only a small number of vowels, they will be most distinct from one another if one of them, **a**, is at the center at the bottom, and the others are distributed evenly on either side.

Another interesting fact that applies to most languages with five vowels is that the order of the letters in the Latin alphabet, **a, e, i, o, u**, is also the order of the frequency of occurrence of these sounds. The most common vowel in nearly all languages is **a**, and the least common vowel in languages with five vowels is usually **u**, with the other vowels falling in between in frequency.

We don't have to go far afield to find languages that have more than 7 vowels. The well-known forms of English have from 14 vowels (e.g. in Californian English) to 20 vowels (e.g. in BBC English). Other European languages such as German and Swedish have an even greater number of vowels, particularly among the more conservative, country dialects. The record for the greatest number of vowels (excluding those with special voice qualities, which we will discuss later) is probably held by the Dutch dialect of Weert, which has 28 different vowel sounds, 12 long, 10 short, and 6 diphthongs.

The vowels of English differ in what is usually called vowel height and vowel backness. They also differ in lip rounding (but there are no pairs of vowels that differ only in lip rounding). Many other European languages use lip rounding to contrast different vowels. In this chapter we will discuss some of these languages. We will also consider nasalized vowels, and further examples of vowels distinguished by voice quality.

14.2   Lip Rounding

We saw in chapter 11 that English front vowels are unrounded and the back vowels have a degree of lip rounding that generally increases with vowel height. Most of the world's languages follow a similar pattern, often with a greater increase in rounding for the high back vowels. But a number of European languages make greater use of lip rounding.

In chapter 5, when discussing the third formant, we mentioned that French distinguishes vowels by making a difference in lip rounding. French has words such as *lit* 'bed' – phonetically **li**, the written 't' is not pronounced – in which the lips are spread apart and the tongue is raised in the front of the mouth, somewhat as it is in English *lee*. French also has *lu* 'read (past participle)', in which the tongue is in much the same position as in **li** *lit*, but the lips are rounded. The phonetic symbol for a vowel of this type is **y**. If you want to make the French vowel **y**, try saying **i** as in *see*, and then simply round your lips. This vowel is not used in standard English, but some forms of Scottish

Table 14.1 A set of French words illustrating some of the
vowels that contrast in a conservative form of Parisian French

	Front		
Unrounded	Rounded	Back
lit	lu	loup
li	**ly**	**lu**
'bed'	'read' (p.p.)	'wolf'
les	le	lot
le	**lø**	**lo**
'the' (pl.)	'the' (m. sg.)	'prize'
laid	leur	lors
lɛ	**lœʀ**	**lɔʀ**
'ugly'	'their'	'during'
là		las
la		**lɑ**
'there'		'tired'

English have a vowel of this type in words such as *who* and *do* which are
pronounced as **hy** and **dy**.

The effect of closing the lips is to lower the frequencies of all three formants.
The first formant frequency is already low in **i** as in French *lit* or English *lee*.
The second formant is not much affected by lip rounding in the case of this
vowel. The principal difference between **i** and **y** is in the frequency of the third
formant, which is distinctly lower for **y**.

French has another pair of vowels in which the tongue positions are very
similar but the lips are rounded in the one vowel but not in the other. The lips
are rounded in *peu* 'little', but not in *paix* 'peace'. The symbol for this rounded
vowel is **ø**, so *peu* can be transcribed **pø** contrasting with **pe** *paix* (the written
'x' is again not pronounced). In this case both the second and third formants
have a lower frequency. A set of words illustrating some of the vowel contrasts in French is shown in table 14.1, and can be heard in recording 14.1.

Swedish, Danish, Norwegian, and German are among the other European
languages that contrast rounded and unrounded vowels. The Swedish vowel
system is shown in table 14.2 and illustrated in recording 14.2. The vowels
have been divided first into front and back vowels, and then the front vowels
have been further divided into rounded and unrounded. Lastly, the so-called
long and short versions of each vowel have been shown. These vowels differ
not only in length, but also in height and backness. The short vowels are lower

Table 14.2   A set of words illustrating Swedish vowels

	Front				Back	
	Unrounded		Rounded			
	Long	Short	Long	Short	Long	Short
High	rita	ritt	ryta	nytta	rota	rott
	riːta	**rɪtː**	**ryːta**	**nʏtːa**	**ruːta**	**rʊtː**
	'draw'	'ride' (n.)	'roar'	'use' (n.)	'root' (vb.)	'rowed'
Mid-high	reta	rätt	ruta	rutt	Råta	rått
	reːta	**rɛtː**	**rʉːta**	**rɵtː**	**roːta**	**rɔtː**
	'tease'	'correct'	'window pane'	'route'	(name of a valley)	'raw'
Mid-low	räta		röta	rött	rata	
	rɛːta		**røːta**	**rœtː**	**rʊːta**	
	'straighten'		'rot'	'red'	'refuse'	
Low	här		hör			ratt
	hæːr		**hœːr**			**ratː**
	'here'		'hear'			'steering wheel'

and more centralized. The table uses the IPA symbols for the vowels, and the IPA mark ː indicating that the previous segment is long. Swedish usually has a long consonant after a short vowel and a short consonant after a long vowel.

The German vowel system is shown in table 14.3 and illustrated in recording 14.3. Some of these words are in slightly unusual forms, such as the dative plural or the subjunctive, in order to show the contrasts more clearly. German also has a set of diphthongs – vowels that have a change in quality within a single syllable – that are shown separately at the bottom of the table.

A few languages have unrounded versions of the high back vowels that are normally rounded. Scottish Gaelic has two back unrounded vowels, as shown in table 14.4 and illustrated in recording 14.4. These vowels are comparatively rare in the languages of the world, and those that occur in Gaelic are not as common as the other Gaelic vowels. Because they occur in fewer words, it is not possible to find a good set of words that contrast only in the rounding or unrounding of the vowels. In table 14.4 the word illustrating the low vowel **a** has been placed in an undivided last row, as this vowel is neither front nor back, and has a neutral lip position.

Table 14.4 uses the appropriate IPA symbols for the vowels, and also illustrates some additional consonantal possibilities that we have not discussed.

Table 14.3 A set of words illustrating German vowels

| | Front | | | | Back | |
| | Unrounded | | Rounded | | | |
	Long	Short	Long	Short	Long	Short
High	bieten **biːtən** 'offer'	bitten **bɪtən** 'ask'	wüten **vyːtən** 'rage'	Bütten **bʏtən** 'tubs' (dat. pl.)	buhten **buːtən** 'booed'	Butten **bʊtən** 'flounders' (dat. pl.)
Mid-high	beten **beːtən** 'pray'		böten **bøːtən** 'offered' (subj.)		Booten **boːtən** 'boats' (dat. pl.)	
Mid-low	bäten **bɛːtən** 'asked' (subj.)	Betten **bɛtən** 'beds'		Böttingen **bœtɪŋən** (name of a town)		bottich **bɔtɪç** 'vat'
Low	baten **baːtən** 'asked'	Batten **batən** (name of a town)				
Diphthongs	weiten **vaɪtən** 'widen'		Beute **bɔʏtə** 'booty'		bauten **baʊtən** 'built'	

Table 14.4 A set of words illustrating Scottish Gaelic long vowels

	Front	Back rounded	Back unrounded
High	bìodach **piːtəx** 'tiny'	bùth **puːᵚ** 'shop'	baothair **pɯːhəðʲ** 'idiot'
Mid-high	beudach **peːtəx** 'harmful'	bò **poː** 'cow'	foghlam **fɤːlˠəm** 'education'
Mid-low	Gaidheal **kɛːəlˠ** 'Gael'	bòid **pɔːtʲ** 'oath'	
Low	bàidse **paːtʲə** 'musician's fee'		

The symbol **x** is used for a voiceless velar fricative – a kind of fricative form of **k**. This sound also occurs in German, as in the name of the composer *Bach* **bɑx**, or in the Scottish English pronunciation of *loch* **lɒx**. A slightly more complicated notion is that Gaelic has two forms of many consonants. In one the tongue is raised in the gesture for the vowel **i** while the consonant is being produced. The symbol for this so-called secondary articulation is a raised ⁱ as in **tʲ** in the last word in the table. The other form of some consonants has the back of the tongue raised. The symbol for this kind of secondary articulation is another raised character, ˠ, as in **lˠ** in the word meaning 'education'.

14.3   Nasalized Vowels

We all of us speak through our noses on some occasions. Whenever we say a word with an **m**, **n**, or **ŋ** the air comes out of the nose and not the mouth. Usually the nasal passages are blocked off during other sounds. But when there is a nasal consonant, **m**, **n**, or **ŋ**, after a vowel (as in *ram, ran, rang*), the soft palate may lower somewhat early, so that during the last part of the vowel air goes out through the nose. The result is a nasalized vowel.

Nasalized vowels are common in all dialects of English, particularly when there is a nasal consonant on either side of the vowel, as for example in the word *man*. In these circumstances nearly everybody makes a vowel that is nasalized throughout. In other words, such as *bad*, nasalization is usually considered inappropriate. "They talk through their noses" is a frequent characterization of the way another group speaks. Sometimes it is true, but often it just means that the other group speaks with a noticeable accent.

How you speak when you have a heavy cold is interesting. If your nose is completely stuffed up then, obviously, you cannot be producing sounds through your nose. All your nasal sounds will be superficially more like the corresponding stops. Writers wanting to show this effect will spell 'Good morning' as 'Good bordig'. But this is not completely accurate. There will still be a difference between **m**, **n**, **ŋ** and **b**, **d**, **g**. Try pinching your nose while saying *bad* and *mad*. The two words still sound different. Air does not actually have to come out of the nose for a sound to be nasal. It is just that the soft palate has to be down so that the resonances of the nasal cavities affect the sound. If you have a very heavy cold, then all your speech may sound nasalized, despite the fact that no air whatsoever is coming out of your nose. This is because the back of your throat may be sore and swollen, so that you can no longer close off the nasal passages. Whatever sound you are producing will be affected by the resonances of the nasal cavities.

The acoustic changes that occur are demonstrated in figure 14.2, which shows my pronunciation of the words *mean, min, men, man* with heavy nasalization in comparison with the words *bead, bid, bed, bad* with the soft palate raised and no

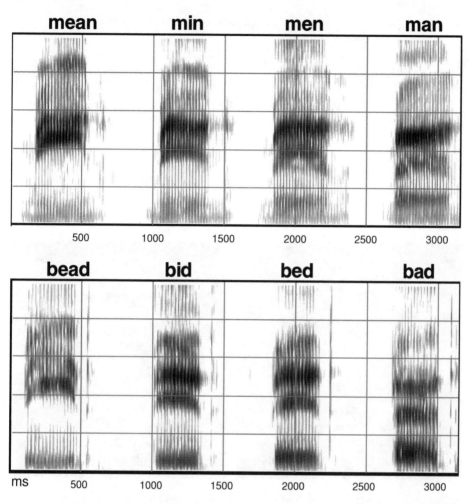

Figure 14.2   A comparison of words with nasalized vowels (upper part), and words with oral vowels (lower part).

nasalization. In the oral vowels in the lower spectrogram the first formant is well defined and has a greater amplitude (the first dark band is narrower and darker). Acousticians describe the change by saying that nasal vowels have a wider first formant bandwidth. This increase in bandwidth is also evident in the second formant of the vowels in the last two words. In these two vowels, the frequency of the first formant is increased. One of the problems in describing nasalization is that it does not affect each vowel in the same way.

It does not make a difference to the meaning of an English word if a vowel is nasalized or not. In French it matters a lot. Earlier in this chapter I carefully noted that table 14.1 and recording 14.1 illustrated only some of the French vowels. French also has a set of nasalized vowels. Contrasts in nasalization in

Table 14.5 Words illustrating contrasts between oral and nasal vowels in French

Oral	Nasal	Oral	Nasal
laid	lin	leur	lundi
lɛ	lɛ̃	lœʁ	lœ̃di
'ugly'	'flax'	'their'	'Monday'
las	lent	lot	long
lɑ	lɑ̃	lo	lõ
'tired'	'slow'	'prize'	'long'

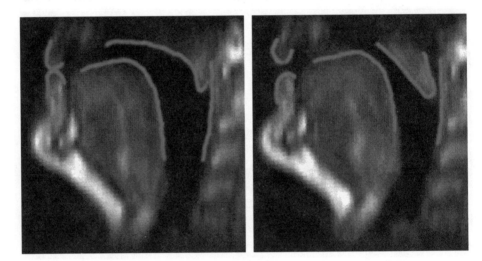

Figure 14.3 The soft palate raised during the stop **b**, and lowered during the nasalized vowel **ɛ̃** (frames from the video on the CD with added outlines of the lips, tongue, soft palate, and the back wall of the pharynx).

four pairs of vowels are illustrated in table 14.5 and recording 14.5. (Some French speakers do not have all these nasalized vowels. This is a rather conservative style of French.) The vowels in these words have similar tongue positions, but differ in that those in the second and fourth columns are nasalized. Nasalized vowels are marked by a wavy line, called a tilde, over the vowel, e.g. **ã**. The 'n' in the spelling reflects an older pronunciation when **n** was actually pronounced.

    The movements of the soft palate in forming nasalized vowels are illustrated in another video included on the CD, showing the same Belgian phonetician, Didier Demolin, producing the sequence **bɛbɛ̃**. Frames in the video corresponding to the **b** and **ɛ̃** sounds are shown in figure 14.3. The positions of the lips, tongue, soft palate, and the back wall of the pharynx have been outlined, as these MRI videos are not very clear. But what is evident is that the soft palate is raised during **b**, in the left-hand picture, and is lowered during the nasalized vowel on the right.

14.4 Voice Quality

In chapter 12 we saw that languages distinguish sets of vowels by using different voice qualities. Amongst other possibilities there are breathy-voiced vowels in Gujarati, creaky-voiced vowels in Mazatec, and tense-voice vowels in Mpi. If we add the range of possible voice qualities to the ranges of vowel height, backness, rounding, and nasalization that occur, you can see that the total set of possible vowels is very large. We will conclude this chapter – and our survey of unusual sounds – by looking at another language, !Xóõ, that uses an even wider set of voice qualities in vowels.

!Xóõ, a Bushman language spoken in the Kalahari Desert, has more phonetically interesting sounds than any other language that I have ever heard. I was taken into the desert by Tony Traill, a skilled linguist who had already fully described the sound system of this language. He showed me that over half the words in !Xóõ begin with a click of some sort. If we count sequences of clicks and other consonants as single sounds (which is not really a very good idea – it would be like counting **s**, **sp**, **spl** as single sounds in English), then there are 83 ways of beginning a word in !Xóõ with a click. There are also ejectives and other unusual sounds.

Even the name of this language, !Xóõ, is difficult for speakers of European languages. It begins with an alveolar click, !, which has the tip of the tongue and the back of the tongue raised for the click mechanism. After the tip of the tongue has come down and the click sound has been produced, the back of the tongue lowers slowly, so that there is a velar fricative of the kind we noted in Gaelic, and in German *Bach*, **bax**. (In writing the name of the language, '!Xóõ', a capital letter 'X' is used.) The complex click at the beginning of the word is followed by a long nasalized vowel on a high tone. The vowel is written with two letter 'o's, so that the high tone can be marked on one and the other can have the nasalization mark. It is, nevertheless, just one long, high-tone, nasalized vowel.

!Xóõ has such a rich array of consonants that one might naively expect a simple vowel system. But in fact there are not only nasalized vowels but also four different types of voice quality. The vowels **a, o, u** can be said much as a Spanish speaker might say them, with a regular voicing. They can also be said with a more constricted pharynx, forming what are called pharyngealized vowels. The third possibility involves a tightening of the lower part of the pharynx near the epiglottis, forming what are called strident vowels (there

Table 14.6 Words illustrating contrasting vowels in !Xóõ

Plain (voiced)	Pharyngealized	Strident (epiglottalized)	Breathy
kǁáa	qáˤa	k!ào	k!ạo
'camelthorn tree'	'long ago'	'base'	'slope'

is no IPA marking for this type of sound). Finally, they can also be said with a breathy voice, much like that in Gujarati. These possibilities are shown in table 14.6 and recording 14.6. As you can hear, some languages have both complex consonants and complex vowels.

14.5 Summary

The languages of the world have from 3 to 24 or more different vowel qualities that can be described in terms of vowel height, backness, and rounding. Some languages, e.g. French, Swedish, and German, have front rounded vowels. A few languages, e.g. Scottish Gaelic, have back unrounded vowels. In English, vowels are nasalized when next to nasal consonants. Some languages, e.g. French, contrast oral and nasal vowels. Vowels can also contrast in voice quality. In addition to breathy-voiced and creaky-voiced vowels, !Xóõ, a Bushman language, has pharyngealized and strident vowels.

15

Putting Vowels and Consonants Together

15.1   The Speed of Speech

All of us have enormous athletic ability in the way we can move our tongues and lips. We can make rapid, precise movements that are as skilled as the finger movements of a concert pianist. When you say the word *particular* the coordination between the lips, the tongue, and the vocal folds demands the timing of a trapeze artist. You can also repeat movements with the tip of the tongue very rapidly. Saying the word *deadheaded* with its four **d** sounds requires four contacts between the tongue tip and the roof of the mouth. Now, to extend this example as suggested by John Ohala, a professor of Linguistics at the University of California, Berkeley, imagine you have a stupid friend called Ed who is an editor. You can easily say *Deadheaded Ed had edited it*. There's no problem in saying it fairly quickly; it isn't even a tongue twister. Figure 15.1 is a spectrogram of my saying it in less than 1.5 seconds. The tip of my tongue was moving up and down at a rate of almost seven times a second. This is about the fastest rate at which most of us can tap with a single finger.

With a little practice you can learn to say tongue twisters fairly rapidly. Start by saying as separate words *She sells seashells on the seashore*. Slowly increase the pace, concentrating on the feel of what your tongue is doing. When you have become adept at saying this phrase, try moving on to the longer version: *She sells seashells on the seashore and the seashells that she sells are seashells I'm sure*. Figure 15.2 is a spectrogram of my saying this phrase fairly rapidly, at a rate of almost six syllables a second, as in recording 15.1. (Network newscasters speak at about half that rate.) There are 38 phonemes – vowels and consonants – in

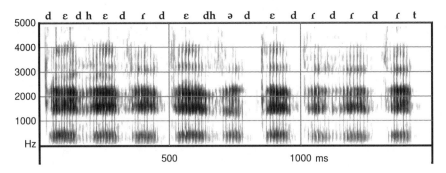

Figure 15.1 A spectrogram of my saying *Deadheaded Ed had edited it.*

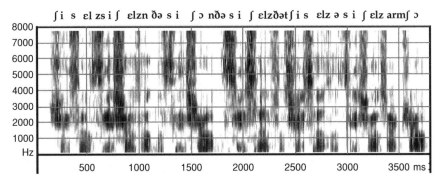

Figure 15.2 A spectrogram of my saying *She sells seashells on the seashore, and the seashells that she sells are seashells I'm sure.*

3,700ms, over 10 consonants and vowels per second. But are these syllables composed of consonants and vowels? Of course we can describe them that way, but does this mean that they are stored in the brain as a sequence of consonants and vowels? When we talk are we really joining consonants and vowels together?

The answer, I think, is no. When you talk you don't join vowels and consonants together for the simple reason that they are not stored separately. Talking involves pulling stored forms of words out of some part of the brain, but words are not stored as sequences of sounds. They are stored as wholes, or at least as whole syllables, in which the consonants and vowels are not separate items. We should even consider whether consonants and vowels exist except as devices for writing down words. This may seem an odd thought from someone who is writing a book called *Vowels and Consonants*. And I must warn you that most people who are working on speech do not agree with the views expressed in the next two sections. But I hope to show you that consonants and vowels are largely figments of our good scientific imaginations.

15.2   The Alphabet

The symbols of the alphabet represent segments of speech, and it is probably from thinking in terms of these symbolized segments that we get the idea that there are separable sounds. But it is worth looking a little more closely at the alphabet and the way that it came about. The earliest writing systems were of a very different kind.

All writing systems began by having symbols in the form of little pictures that represented words. One of the earliest systems was that of the Sumerians, who lived in what is now Iraq. They developed a set of picture symbols that eventually became stylized representations of words. There are two great steps in going from that stage to an alphabetic system. The first came when some symbols began to be used not just for particular words but also for other words that had the same sounds but different meanings. It was as if the sign for the word 'sun' became used for the word 'son' – a totally different word that happened to have the same sound. This is an enormous conceptual step. It means that a symbol now represents a particular sound and not a particular meaning.

The next great step was the recognition that syllables – the most commonly symbolized sounds – could be broken down into their component segments. This amazing idea arose from the lucky chance of the Greeks getting together with the Phoenicians, who lived on the shores of the Mediterranean and spoke a Semitic language similar to Hebrew. In the eighth century BC, the Greeks were trading with the Phoenicians. At the time, Greek had seven vowels and a fairly small number of consonants. Phoenician, like Hebrew, had a large number of consonants and only three vowels, none of which were represented in the writing system. Phoenician syllables were written down with symbols that depended only on the consonants. (At a later time Semitic languages developed ways of symbolizing the different vowels, but the vowels were never written in the early writing.)

The Greeks realized that they did not need all the symbols used by the Phoenicians. The symbol called aleph, for example, represented syllables beginning with a glottal stop. Greek did not have any syllables of this sort, but they did have a syllable that began with the vowel in the most common of these syllables, ʔa. The Greeks started using this spare symbol for the vowel **a** wherever it occurred. Over time they did the same with other Phoenician syllables that had sounds that did not occur in Greek. By the fifth century BC the Greek alphabet had 24 letters, 17 for consonants and 7 for vowel-like sounds. Breaking syllables up into vowels and consonants was an enormous scientific achievement. Speakers of other languages saw what could be done and started using alphabetic characters for writing their languages, forming many other alphabets. But the original notion that syllables could be split into vowels and consonants occurred only once in human history.

The Chinese also invented symbols for the words of their language. These symbols never got to represent the sounds of the syllables. They stood for the meanings. There are advantages in having a system in which you represent just the meaning and not the sound. The same symbol can be used for writing down words in different languages. This is true, for example, of Cantonese and Standard Chinese. These are two different languages, and speakers of one cannot understand speakers of the other. But the character 心 has the same meaning in both languages. In Standard Chinese it is pronounced as ɕin (the symbol ɕ is much like ʃ ('sh') so the Chinese word is similar to the English word *sheen*). In Cantonese this character is pronounced as səm, rather like the English word *sum*. People in China speak many different languages, but nearly all of them can read the same newspaper. When somebody in Shanghai reads a newspaper out loud, somebody from Beijing will not be able to understand what is being said, just as you could not understand if I were to say *sheen* instead of *sum*. But people all over China can get the meaning from the written characters. When people in China who speak different languages try to converse, they often resort to scribbling or even drawing characters in the air to convey their meaning.

Our European languages are written in a very different way. The letters stand for the sounds, not the meanings, of words. In former times there was a fairly good correspondence between the sounds and the letters, but as time passed and the languages changed, the letter-to-sound relation became less clear. The best matches between sounds and letters are in languages like Swahili that have been written down more recently.

The advantage of a system that represents the sounds is that we can write down any word using a limited set of letters, all of which we can put on a small keyboard. Typing Chinese is a much more complicated affair, requiring the writer to find the hidden locations of thousands of different characters. But we users of alphabetically spelled languages lose out in that we cannot, without learning another language, read newspapers published in Germany, France, and other countries.

We also lose out in that our thinking about words and sounds is strongly influenced by writing. We imagine that the letters of the alphabet represent separate sounds instead of being just clever ways of artificially breaking up syllables. It is noteworthy that alphabetic writing has almost certainly been invented only once, whereas there are many independent inventions of systems for writing down syllables. Early forms of syllabic writing include Assyrian cuneiform and Japanese hiragana. In the nineteenth century the Cherokee chief Sequoyah invented a system for writing down the syllables of his language.

The only possible exception to my statement that the alphabet was invented only once is the Korean writing system. There is a charming story about the origin of this system. In the fifteenth century, at a time when alphabets were fairly well known in other parts of the world (and were probably known to scholars in Korea), Korean was written with thousands of Chinese characters. The king of Korea, realizing the greater efficiency of an alphabetic system, devised an appropriate set of letters that represented the ways in which the sounds of Korean were made. His symbols had a phonetic basis. For example, all the sounds that were made with the lips had symbols that included a □ shape, reminiscent of the lips.

The king was worried that the people might not accept the new alphabet, and thought that it should appear to have a magical origin. So one evening he used some honey to paint large leaves with the shapes of the new letters. Next day he took a walk with his soothsayer, who saw the leaves. Just those parts of them that had been painted with honey had been eaten by insects, making it seem as if the letters had been etched into the leaves. The soothsayer thought that the letters were gifts from Heaven, and adopted the king's suggestion that they should be used for writing Korean. From that day on the Koreans have celebrated the invention of their alphabet. October 9th is a national holiday. As far as I know, Korea is the only country that has a national holiday celebrating a linguistic event. Perhaps we should all join in and make this an international linguists' festival. (My Christian friends have suggested that a possible contender for such an event might be Pentecost, the miraculous moment 40 days after Easter, when all the apostles were heard accurately pronouncing many different languages.)

The fact that the alphabet has been invented only once (assuming the king of Korea got the idea from the Indian scholars with whom he had been in contact) shows that the division of the syllable into vowels and consonants is not a natural one. Alphabets are scientific inventions, and not statements of real properties of words. There is additional evidence for this from the study of speech errors, as well as from various experiments on the perception of speech.

15.3   Slips of the Tongue and the Ear

We often make mistakes when we talk; and the interesting point is that the mistakes are not random segmental errors. One of the most common types of error is the spoonerism, the interchange of sounds as when, for example, *Our dear old queen* becomes a *Our queer old dean*. Dr. Spooner was an Oxford academic who was well known for making mistakes of this kind. When meaning to say *You have missed all my history lectures and wasted the whole term*, he is reputed to have told a student: *You have hissed all my mystery lectures and tasted the whole worm*. This is almost certainly an untrue story, but it is a good example of the most usual form of these errors. They are typically confusions involving consonants at the beginning of one syllable with consonants at the beginning of another. Mistakes involving consonants in different parts of the syllable do occur, but they are no more frequent than chance substitutions of one syllable for another.

Words must be stored in our brains in some way, but it is unlikely that a word such as *cat* is stored as instructions for making a **k** followed by **æ** followed by **t**. The evidence from speech errors is that larger units are involved. When talking we may make the mistake of pulling out one syllable that has a great similarity to another syllable, but we seldom simply misarrange the sounds within a syllable. I've never heard anyone mispronounce *cat* as *tack*, a mistake they could quite conceivably make if the sounds existed as separate items in the brain.

It seems probable that we organize our speech production in terms of units more like syllables than individual speech sounds. We could be storing smaller units, like the diphones we considered in speech synthesis, but it is unlikely that the words in our minds are made up of separate speech sounds. If it hadn't been for those Greeks and Phoenicians getting together to make an alphabet, probably nobody would ever have thought that possible.

Listening to speech also involves attending to the patterns of whole syllables or words rather than individual speech sounds. In many ways listening is like reading. When you read the words on a page, your eyes do not move steadily along the line, looking at each letter. Instead, you fixate on three or four points in a line, taking in whole groups of words at a time. Reading consists of looking at one point on a page for about a fifth of a second, and then making a rapid jump (a saccadic movement is the technical term) to another point where you look for the next fifth of a second.

It's possible that when listening you take in chunks of speech that last about a fifth of a second as well. This would be somewhere near the duration of a syllable. People have difficulty in analyzing the order of events in shorter sections. If you play someone a recording of a sentence on which a click has been superimposed, they usually cannot tell you very precisely where the click occurs. The same is true if it is a speech sound that has been superimposed, such as an *s* from another sentence. If people were listening to successive segments they should be able to say on which sound or between which sounds this segment occurred. But they can't, as you can try for yourself by listening to recording 15.2, which has an *s* superimposed on the sentence *They thought it was Jane who could be brave and in the team*. If you have the opportunity, listen to this sentence and make a note of your answer. We'll come back to this point after we have discussed another example of the difficulty of deciding what occurs before what.

This second example is illustrated in the perceptual tests making up recording 15.3. In these tests you are asked to listen to two complex sounds, each made up of two components, a buzzing noise and a hissing noise. Each of the complex sounds has the duration of a short syllable. People can usually separate the two possibilities – hiss first and buzz first – when one of the complex sounds is played by itself. But they find it very difficult to tell which bit comes first when the complex sounds are in the midst of a sequence of other sounds. Try listening to the recordings yourself.

The syllables of speech are complex sounds, usually consisting of two or more parts. We can tell which part comes first because we know how to make these sounds. We can say syllables slowly and work out how they are made. Whenever I am doing fieldwork and listening to a language I don't know, I always try to imitate what the speaker says, and then say it to myself slowly so that I can feel what I am doing. But when people listen to their own language, they don't normally do this. They recognize larger sequences such as syllables and relate them to the patterns of words stored in their brains without breaking them into smaller pieces.

If you have tried the perceptual experiments discussed in the preceding paragraphs, you might like to know the actual results of controlled experiments of this sort. I played a recording very similar to one in which an *s* is superimposed on a sentence to 121 students. When they heard the sentence *They thought it was Jane who could be brave and in the team*, most of the students thought the superimposed sound was on *who*. In the recording they heard, as in recording 15.2, the *s* was actually between *could* and *be*.

In the experiment involving listening to complex non-speech sounds, most people did slightly better than chance when listening to the sounds in isolation or when in well-separated pairs. They usually found it easier to say whether two sounds were different than to say which piece came first in the complex sounds. But they did no better than chance when listening to these sounds in the middle of a sequence of tones. It is clear that people are not very good at telling the order of a sequence of unfamiliar sounds.

The problem with the experiments that I have been describing is that there are other experiments that show that listeners can make use of extremely short lengths of speech. They can distinguish one vowel from another when the recording has been edited so that there is only a single glottal pulse producing a sound less than one-hundredth of a second long. They can also recognize parts of words corresponding to separate vowels and consonants very quickly. Many of my colleagues believe that experiments like these show that we do, in fact, hear and produce speech in terms of pieces the size of a consonant or vowel. But what one can do when pushed in a laboratory experiment may be different from what one normally does when listening to speech. There is little evidence against my own view that normal conversational speech is produced and perceived in terms of larger units. We can recognize syllables as having a number of parts, but this does not make these parts more than analytical devices. Vowels and consonants may be simply convenient fictions for use in describing speech. They are, however, invaluable aids for talking about the sounds of languages, and we will continue to use the symbols of the International Phonetic Alphabet for this purpose.

15.4   The International Phonetic Alphabet

At the beginning of the book we noted that there were three ways of describing speech sounds. In the first part of the book we described them in terms of their acoustic properties. In the second part we discussed the articulations involved, noting how the sounds are made. In addition, throughout the book we have been using the third method: we have been referring to sounds by using the symbols of the International Phonetic Alphabet.

A symbol is a shorthand way of representing something. Just as H₂O is a way of representing the combination of two atoms of hydrogen and one of oxygen to form water, so the symbol **i** is a way of representing the combination of vocal fold pulses and the formants that occur in the vowel in *bead*. Phonetic symbols are like chemical symbols in that they stand for the elements of a sound. We may not know what hydrogen and oxygen are, but we understand what it means to say that H₂O stands for water. Similarly, we need not know what formants are to appreciate that **i** is the symbol for the components of the vowel in *bead*. If we do have some understanding of formants, the position of the symbol on the IPA vowel chart will tell us something about what the first two formants will be. As we saw in chapter 5, the vowel **i** would be at the top left of a formant chart, which means that it is at a similar place on an IPA vowel chart. This means that it has a first formant with a low frequency and a second formant with a high frequency. In the case of consonants, the location of the symbol on the IPA chart provides a shorthand description of the way in which the sound is made. Thus **b** is on the right in its cell, which means that it is voiced. It is in the column for bilabial sounds, and the row for stops. So **b** symbolizes the combination of being voiced, being bilabial, and being a stop. Similarly ʃ ('sh') is a combination of being voiceless, being made in the post-alveolar region and being fricative.

At this point we should note another IPA principle concerning the use of symbols. The symbol for a tongue tip trill is **r**, and that for the approximant found in most forms of English is ɹ, an upside-down letter 'r'. If you are discussing the pronunciation of the word *red* as spoken by a Lowland Scot who has a trill and an Englishman who doesn't, you can describe the sound as **r** for the one speaker and ɹ for the other. But when you are not trying to make such precise distinctions, the IPA recommends that you always use the simplest possible symbol, which in this case is **r**, even for transcribing a BBC English pronunciation. Then, at the end of the transcription, you should simply say **r** = ɹ.

Other symbols on the IPA chart represent other forms of 'r'. All the symbols ɾ, ʈ, ʁ, and ʀ can be transcribed as **r** in cases where they are the only sound of this kind being discussed. The symbol ɾ represents a tap, often used by Scottish speakers of English in words with 'r' at the beginning or in the middle, such as *red* and *bury*. Speakers of General American English will use a tap ɾ for 't' in words such as *pity* and *Betty*, making *Betty* sound like Scottish *bury*. Many Scots will pronounce a tap ɾ even before l as in *pearl*, making this word sound like *petal* to many Americans.

The symbol ʈ represents a form of 'r' in which the tip of the tongue is curled up and back. The symbols ʁ and ʀ are used for 'r' sounds made in the back of the mouth as in French. These and all the other sounds on the IPA chart at the end of the book are demonstrated in recording 1.1.

15.5   Contrasting Sounds

The IPA chart has 113 symbols for segments (84 consonants and 29 vowels) and numerous diacritics for marking small differences in sounds. I am often asked "How many sounds are there in the world's languages?" The answer is that I don't know – and I doubt that it is possible to give a definitive answer. The problem is that there is no way of deciding whether a sound in one language is the same as a sound in another. All we can do is count how many sounds there are in any one language (and, in my view, even then we may be counting simply fictitious elements, the vowels and consonants that are used to describe words).

There are hundreds of thousands of words in a language such as English. Both the Oxford English Dictionary and Webster's Dictionary have nearly half a million words. But each language has only a small set of vowels and consonants. English has about 40 contrasting sounds altogether – as we have seen, the exact number depends on the dialect. All of the words that are part of the English language are made up of just a small set of vowels and consonants. Probably the most important thing about each of these sounds is that it is not any of the others. What matters about a **p** is that it is not a **b** or a **d** or a **g** or any other English sound. Because the sound **p** is different it keeps the word *pay* distinct from the words *bay*, *day*, and *gay*. The same can be said for other languages; each language has a small set of distinct sounds that contrast with one another. French has 36 contrasting sounds. Some of the click languages of Africa may have over a hundred contrasting sounds. Hawaiian has only 13, represented by the letters 'a, e, i, o, u; p, k, m, n, w, l, h' and the apostrophe ('), which is used for the glottal stop. There are no words in Hawaiian containing the sound of **s** or **t**, or many other sounds that we have in English. Hawaiian words tend to be rather long, but speakers of the language are not in any way limited in what they can say in their language.

We will underestimate the number of different sounds in a language if we count just the contrasting sounds that make different words. In English, for example, **h** and **ŋ** never contrast. One always occurs at the beginning of a syllable and the other at the end. They are clearly different sounds, but it would be perfectly possible to transcribe English unambiguously using a single symbol, ɦ (which is not an IPA symbol). We could transcribe *hiss* as ɦɪs and *sing* as sɪɦ. We would then have a rule saying that when ɦ was at the beginning of a syllable it was pronounced as **h**, and when at the end of a syllable it represented **ŋ**. This would be like one of the spelling rules that we use, telling us that 'i' is pronounced aɪ when it is in a word such as 'bite' that has a silent 'e' at the end of it, but is pronounced ɪ in 'bit', which lacks the silent 'e'.

English has other sounds that never contrast because each of them occurs only in specific places. We saw earlier that most of us have a glottal stop ʔ, in words such as *bitten*, bɪʔn. In some senses this ʔ is only a kind of **t**. It never contrasts with **t**, occurring only in special places, such as after a vowel and before **n**. It cannot be used to distinguish words. There are other varieties of **t** that never contrast in English. We saw in chapter 12 that Thai has a contrast between an aspirated and an unaspirated **t**, as in **tʰâː** 'landing place' and **taː** 'eye'. In English, **t** is usually like the Thai **tʰ** in **tʰâː** 'landing place' in words such as *tie* and *tomato*, where it could be transcribed **tʰ**. But **t** is unaspirated when it occurs after **s**, as in *sty* **staɪ**. Yet another form of **t** is found in American English when it occurs between vowels, as in *city* and *Betty*, where it is pronounced more like a **d**. In fact, most American English speakers make no difference between the words *betting* and *bedding*.

All these different **t** sounds are very similar to one another, differing from some abstract central form of **t** in only a minor way. If we are thinking in acoustic terms, even ʔ is not so far from **t**. On a spectrogram both correspond to very similar gaps in the pattern. Linguists have a term for a group of similar sounds of this kind. They call it a phoneme. In English **t**, **tʰ**, and ʔ are all members of the /t/ phoneme. The slash lines / / around the symbol are used when it is necessary to point out that one is referring specifically to a phoneme, a group of sounds.

Phonemes are often thought of as different sounds that can change the meaning of a word. We talk of the difference between *kit* and *pit* being the use of the phoneme /k/ as opposed to the phoneme /p/. There is usually no harm in expressing things this way. But it is important to remember that it is a kind of shorthand. A phoneme is not a single sound but a group of sounds. The difference between *kit* and *pit* is in the use of a member of the phoneme /k/ as opposed to a member of the phoneme /p/.

In Thai, **tʰ** and **t** belong to different phonemes because they can both occur at the beginnings of words. When the one occurs in place of the other it changes the meaning. In English **tʰ** and **t** belong to the same phoneme because they cannot occur in the same place within a word; **tʰ** typically occurs at the beginning of a word or before a stressed vowel, and **t** occurs after **s** (and in other special circumstances). These two sounds never contrast with each other so as to form English words with different meanings.

We can now get back to the problem of deciding how many sounds there are in the world's languages. It basically rests on considering whether a sound in one language is really the same as a sound in another one. We have to decide whether the two sounds could be used to distinguish words if they happened to occur in the same language. My colleague Ian Maddieson and I wrestled with this problem when we wrote a book *Sounds of the World's Languages*. We often came across sounds that seemed to have different forms in different languages. For example, we had to consider if any of the three Polish sibilants that are illustrated in table 13.8 is the same as any of the four Toda sibilants illustrated in table 13.9. If you look back at those tables, you will see that I have used **s, ş, ç** to symbolize the Polish sounds and **ş, sʸ, ʃ, ş** for the Toda sounds. That's six distinct symbols, with only **ş** appearing in both languages. The implication is that the other sounds are different in these two languages (which we believe to be true). But we do not know of any languages that contrast all of these sounds. From our observation of how these sounds were made, Ian Maddieson and I tentatively concluded that they were all distinct. Now we are busy looking for languages with contrasts that support this hypothesis. We'll probably never find them, and for that reason we will never be able to say for sure whether they are all distinct sounds, or whether they could make a difference between words in a language.

Without knowing this sort of fact we cannot say how many sounds there are in the world's languages. If I were to make a guess, based on what we know at the moment, I would say that there are probably about 600 different consonants. It is even harder to estimate the number of different vowels. If we say that vowels that differ in voice quality are to be considered as distinct (like those in Mpi and Mazatec), then there may be about 200 different vowels.

15.6   Features that Matter within a Language

When we were discussing the International Phonetic Alphabet we noted that phonetic symbols stand for the elements of a sound, but we did not explicitly say what the elements were. Linguists refer to them as the distinctive features, or phonological features, recognizing them as the elements that distinguish one sound from another within a language. Instead of saying, as we did earlier on, that the sound **p** keeps the word *pay* distinct from the word *bay*, we can say that the feature Voice (the feature distinguishing **p** from **b**) keeps these words distinct. This feature also keeps *Kay* and *gay* distinct, and *tie* and *die*, and lots of other words that differ only in the presence or absence of vocal fold vibration. Similarly, we could say that there is a feature Nasal that distinguishes *may* from *bay*, *nay* from *day*, and *bang* from *bag*. In each of these words the only difference is that one has a sound in which the vocal tract is blocked at some place in the mouth, but air can escape through the nose, and the other has a sound in which the airstream is blocked in the same place in the mouth, but it cannot escape through the nose.

Putting Vowels and Consonants Together

Table 15.1 A hierarchical arrangement of the features required for English

Feature			Value	English examples
Vocalic	Height		[high]	iː, uː
			[mid-high]	ɪ, ʊ, ɝ
			[mid-low]	e, ɔː, ʌ
			[low]	æ, ɑː
	Backness		[back]	uː, ʊ, ɔː, ɑː
			[central]	ɝ, ʌ
			[front]	iː, ɪ, e æ
Consonantal	Place	Labial	[bilabial]	p, b, m, w
			[labiodental]	f, v
		Coronal	[dental]	θ, ð
			[alveolar]	t, s, z, n, r, l
			[palatoalveolar]	ʃ, ʒ, j
		Dorsal	[velar]	k, g, ŋ
	Manner		[stop]	p, t, k, b, d, g, m, n, ŋ
			[fricative]	f, θ, s, ʃ, v, ð, z, ʒ
			[approximant]	w, r, l, j, h
	Nasal		[nasal]	m, n, ŋ
			[oral]	b, d, g, v, ð, z, ʒ, w, r, l, j, p, t, k, f, θ, s, ʃ
	Lateral		[central]	b, d, g, v, ð, z, ʒ, w, r, j, p, t, k, f, θ, s, ʃ, m, n, ŋ
			[lateral]	l
	Voicing		[voiced]	b, d, g, v, ð, z, ʒ, m, n, ŋ, w, r, l, j
			[voiceless]	p, t, k, f, θ, s, ʃ, h

The features that distinguish English sounds can be arranged in a hierarchy as shown in table 15.1. There are several possible ways of arranging this hierarchy, and table 15.1 is meant to be only illustrative of the notion of a feature hierarchy for English sounds (or phonemes as we can now say). The first division is into vowels and consonants – whether a sound is Vocalic or Consonantal. If a sound is in the Vocalic section, we have to assign values to the features Height and Backness. (Note that the name of a feature is usually given a capital letter, and the possible values for a feature are put in square brackets.) In a language such as French, we would have to add Round to the features in this section, because French vowels can differ simply in lip rounding.

If a sound is in the Consonantal section, a larger number of features have to be assigned values. The Place feature can itself be said to consist of three features, Labial specifying whether the sound involves the lips in some way, Coronal being a cover term for all the sounds made with the tip or blade of the tongue, and Dorsal implying involvement of the back of the tongue. In some ways table 15.1 can be considered as a way of combining the relevant parts of the vowel and consonant sections of the IPA chart into a single table, and showing how the features relate to one another.

The features shown in table 15.1 can be used to describe the contrasts that occur in English. Many of them can be used as they are or simply extended to describe the sounds of other languages. For example, the uvular stops that we saw in Aleut require an additional possibility for the feature Dorsal. Dorsal stops can be [velar] or [uvular]. Similarly we can extend the Manner feature. English does not distinguish between a trilled and a non-trilled form of **r**. Spanish does, having words such as *pero*, **pe***r***o** 'but' and *perro*, **pero** 'dog'. We can handle this by adding [trill] as one of the possibilities for the Manner feature, along with [stop], [fricative], and [approximant]. With this addition we can also specify the lip trills we saw in Kele and Titan, ʙ having the feature values [voiced], [bilabial], and [trill].

We might ask whether there is a universal set of features that can be used to describe all the sounds of the world's languages. First we have to decide when we need more features and when we simply want an extra possibility – an extra value – for an existing feature. Some linguists get round this problem by requiring all features to specify only two possibilities, making a so-called binary system. When describing vowels, instead of the feature Height with the possibilities [high], [mid-high], [mid-low], and [low], they use features such as High and Low, with the possible values [+high] and [–high], and [+low] and [–low]. Given this constraint, any newly discovered sound will require a new feature.

Even with this restriction we still have problems. How can we tell whether a feature that distinguishes sounds in one language is the same as a feature that characterizes sounds in another? Again we can exemplify this from material that we have already discussed. The creaky-voiced vowels of Mazatec were illustrated in table 12.7 and recording 12.7. The stiff or tense-voiced vowels of Mpi were illustrated in table 12.8 and recording 12.8. There is no doubt that the creaky vowels of Mazatec are different from the stiff vowels of Mpi, but I do not know of any language that uses this distinction to make a difference between words. Should we say that the same feature is involved? There is no precise answer to this question. It is a matter of opinion as to whether this difference is too small or too difficult to use as a means of distinguishing words. It might be that this is just an accidental gap in the set of known possibilities, and somewhere there is – or has been, or will be – a language that uses this contrast.

In trying to decide what can and what cannot occur in the languages of the world we also have to note that some sounds occur in only one or two languages, and perhaps in a handful of words. We can conclude this introduction to the sounds of the world's languages by an example from Oro Win, a language spoken by a handful of people in Brazil. This language has a sound

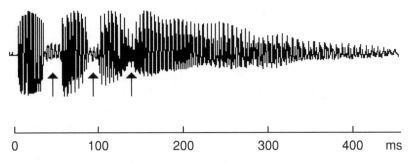

Figure 15.3 Waveform of the Oro Win word ʙum 'small boy'. The arrows indicate the moments when the lips come together or nearly together.

that occurs only in it and the closely related language Wari' (the apostrophe at the end of Wari' stands for a glottal stop, and this is how they spell it in their language). It is a combination of the gesture for a **t** and a trill in which the lips vibrate. I've heard a number of languages that have lip trills, including Kele and Titan, which have already been illustrated. But Oro Win and Wari' are the only languages in which the trill is started by the release of air from a preceding **t**. As we have seen, the IPA symbol for a voiced labial is ʙ, a small capital 'B'. To show that the parts of the Oro Win sound are combined into a single unit I have transcribed it ʙ. The Oro Win word for a small boy is ʙum. Figure 15.3 shows the waveform of this word as produced by a female speaker. You can hear this speaker and her husband saying this word in recording 15.4. As the sound goes by rather quickly, I have used a computer to produce slowed-down versions of these recordings, which you can also hear.

Do we need separate features to describe this sound? It's unlike anything that occurs elsewhere in the world, so I suppose we do. But I heard this sound in only a small number of words in Oro Win and Wari'. Moreover, there are only four known speakers of Oro Win in Brazil, so, whether we like it or not, this language is unlikely to be spoken in 50 years' time. The Wari' community is larger, around 2,000 people, but they are becoming more assimilated within Brazilian culture. They have learned to play soccer, Brazil's national pastime, and the younger ones come into town and watch TV. Some of the younger speakers no longer use the sound ʙ. I expect that in a century or so nobody in the world will use this particular sound in any language.

But who knows what the future may bring? Maybe my three-year-old grand-daughter will continue to talk about Tinkywinky and Lala using an l sound made by touching her upper lip with the blade of her tongue in a peculiar way. Maybe she will grow up to be the President of the United States and everyone will start imitating her. Maybe all English speakers will use this sound. We can never know what languages might do. This book is only an introduction to some of the sounds of languages.

15.7 Summary

Talking involves skilled rapid movements, and listening involves rapidly matching complex auditory patterns. The evidence from slips of the tongue such as spoonerisms can be interpreted in different ways, but my view (which is not that of many speech scientists) is that it indicates that we organize our speech movements in terms of units more like syllables than individual speech sounds. Listening to normal conversational speech is probably a matter of interpreting syllable- or word-size units. The alphabet, which regards syllables as consisting of separate pieces such as vowels and consonants, was only invented once, by the Greeks. It is a clever invention allowing us to write down words, rather than a natural breaking up of words into their component sounds.

The International Phonetic Alphabet is an attempt to provide a way of symbolizing all the distinctive sounds of the world's languages. Sounds within a language that change the meaning of a word can be called phonemes, although a phoneme is more precisely defined as a group of sounds. The members of the group of sounds forming a phoneme always occur in different places – before a vowel, between vowels, before **n**, or in some other phonetic context. The distinctive sounds – the phonemes – of a language can theoretically be described in terms of a universal set of features that applies to all languages. But nobody can give a full account of this set of features because languages are, and always have been, constantly changing. Who knows what the future may bring?

Glossary

Terms defined elsewhere in this glossary are shown in **bold**.

affricate   A **stop** followed by a **fricative** made at the same place in the mouth.

alveolar   Articulated in the region behind the upper front teeth.

approximant   A sound in which the vocal tract is only slightly narrowed.

articulation   A **gesture** of the vocal organs.

aspirated   Having a period of voicelessness after the release of a closure.

back (of the tongue)   The part of the tongue below the **soft palate** (velum).

bilabial   An articulation with the two lips coming together.

blade (of the tongue)   The part of the tongue below the **alveolar** region.

breathy voice   Vibrations of the **vocal folds** that are sufficiently loose to allow a greater than usual airflow.

central   A term with two distinct meanings: (1) Made with the center of the tongue, which is defined as the section below the highest part of the roof of the mouth. (2) Made with an articulation in the midline of the **vocal tract**, allowing air to escape over the sides of the tongue so that the articulation is central as opposed to **lateral**.

creaky voice   Vibrations of the **vocal folds** that are held together so that only part of their length is moving. There is a comparatively small airflow.

dental   An articulation with the tip of the tongue near the upper front teeth.

diphone synthesis   Synthesizing speech by joining together prerecorded pieces going from the middle of one speech sound to the middle of another.

diphthong   A **vowel** sound forming a single syllable, but including a change from one vowel quality to another.

ejective   A sound (usually a **stop**) produced by holding the **vocal folds** together and moving them upward so as to compress the air in the **vocal tract**.

epiglottis   The flap at the root of the tongue that can be lowered so as to help direct food into the esophagus (the food passage).

formant   One of the ways in which the air in the **vocal tract** vibrates, forming an **overtone**, or group of overtones, that characterize a sound.

frequency   The rate at which part of a sound wave is repeated. Frequency is measured in hertz (Hz), indicating the number of repetitions that occur in a second.

fricative   A sound made by air being pushed through a narrow constriction in the **vocal tract**.

fundamental frequency   The rate of repetition of the longest piece of a sound wave that is repeated.

gestural economy   The tendency of languages to use the same **gestures** in many different sounds. For example, languages that use movements of the tongue to produce **t** often use these same movements to produce **d** and **n** as well.

gesture (of the vocal organs)   A controlled movement of the vocal organs that will make a particular sound.

glottal stop   Complete closure of the **vocal folds**.

hard palate   The part of the roof of the mouth with a bony structure.

homophones   Words that sound the same (such as *mail* and *male*), but have different meanings.

implosive   A **stop** in which the **vocal folds** move downward, thus expanding the **vocal tract** and decreasing the pressure of the air within it.

International Phonetic Alphabet (IPA)   An internationally recognized set of symbols for designating the phonetic characteristics of (theoretically) all the distinct sounds in the world's languages.

labiodental   An articulation with the lower lip near the upper lip.

labiovelar   An articulation with the two lips approaching one another, and the **back** of the tongue raised towards the **soft palate**.

lateral   An articulation in which there is an obstruction in the midline but in which one or both of the sides of the tongue do not make a complete closure, as in an **l** sound.

nasal   A sound in which the air in the **vocal tract** is prevented from going out of the mouth, but allowed to escape through the nose.

nasalized   A sound in which part of the air in the **vocal tract** escapes through the nose and part through the mouth.

overtones   Regular variations of air pressure at a higher rate than the **fundamental** rate of repetition of the sound wave.

palatal   An articulation in the region near the highest part of the upper surface of the mouth, where this surface is hard, with a bony structure.

palatoalveolar   An articulation with the blade of the tongue near the forward part of the hard palate just behind the **alveolar** ridge.

parametric synthesis   Synthesizing speech by stating the values of components (parameters) such as the **formant** frequencies at each moment in time.

pharynx   The region of the mouth near the **root** of the tongue.

phoneme   Loosely speaking, a distinctive sound that can change the meaning of a word in a language. More precisely, a group of sounds that cannot, separately, distinguish words in a given language, such as **t, t^h, ?** in English.

resonance   The way in which an object (e.g. the body of air in the **vocal tract**) will vibrate when it has been set in motion.

root (of the tongue)   The lowest part of the back of the tongue, immediately above the **epiglottis**.

soft palate (velum)   The part of the upper surface of the mouth where this surface is soft and movable. Raising the soft palate blocks air from going out of the nose.

spectrogram   A picture of a sound showing how the component **frequencies** change with time.

spectrum   The component **frequencies** that make up a sound during a given (usually fairly short) interval of time.

stop   A sound in which the air in the **vocal tract** is completely blocked.

stress   The use of a greater amount of respiratory energy (and, usually, increased tension of the **vocal folds**) on a syllable.

Text-To-Speech (TTS)   Systems for turning written material (texts) into the sounds of synthesized speech.

tip (of the tongue)   The most forward part of the tongue, in front of the **blade**.

tone   A particular pitch that affects the meaning of a word.

uvula   The small appendage that hangs down from the back of the **soft palate**.

velar   An articulation in the region of the mouth corresponding to the under side of the **soft palate**.

velum   See **soft palate**.

vocal folds   Two small muscular flaps in the larynx.

vocal tract   The air passage between the **vocal folds** and the lips.

voiced   Made with the **vocal folds** vibrating.

voiceless   Made with the **vocal folds** not vibrating.

VOT (Voice Onset Time)   The interval between the release of a stop (e.g. the coming apart of the lips for **p**) and the start of vocal fold vibration.

vowel   A sound at the center of a syllable in which there is no obstruction of the **vocal tract**.

Further Reading

The sounds of languages are described in most standard textbooks in phonetics, such as:

Clark, J., and Yallop, C. (1990). *An Introduction to Phonetics and Phonology*. Oxford: Blackwell.

Borden, G.J., and Harris, K.S. (1984). *Speech Science Primer: Physiology, Acoustics and Perception of Speech* (2nd edn). Baltimore: Williams and Wilkins.

Lieberman, P., and Blumstein, S.E. (1988). *Speech Physiology, Speech Perception, and Acoustic Phonetics*. Cambridge: Cambridge University Press.

I, of course, am biased in favor of my own textbook:

Ladefoged, P. (2001). *A Course in Phonetics* (4th edn). Orlando: Harcourt Brace.

A more comprehensive, but more technical, book describing a very wide range of sounds is:

Ladefoged, P., and Maddieson, I. (1996). *Sounds of the World's Languages*. Oxford: Blackwell.

The principles of phonetic transcription are explained and demonstrated by reference to a large number of languages in:

The Handbook of the International Phonetic Association (1999). Cambridge: Cambridge University Press.

Phonetic symbols are well described and displayed in:

Pullum, G.K., and Ladusaw, W.A. (1996). *Phonetic Symbol Guide*. Chicago: University of Chicago Press.

A comprehensive account of all aspects of phonetics (including chapters on the instrumental techniques used in this book) is:

Hardcastle, W.J. and Laver, J. (eds.) (1997). *The Handbook of Phonetic Sciences*. Oxford: Blackwell.

The best introduction to acoustic phonetics is:
Johnson, K. (1997). *Auditory and Acoustic Phonetics*. Oxford: Blackwell.

Additional aspects of acoustics and computer speech processing are discussed in:
Ladefoged, P. (1996). *Elements of Acoustic Phonetics*. 2nd edn. Chicago: University of Chicago Press.

A very readable introduction to the evolution of speech is:
Lieberman, P. (1998). *Eve Spoke*. New York: W.W. Norton.

A more comprehensive account is:
Hauser, M. (1996). *The Development of Communication*. Cambridge, MA: MIT Press.

The most readable introduction to general linguistics is:
Fromkin, V.A., and Rodman, R. (1998). *An Introduction to Language* (6th edn). Orlando: Harcourt Brace.

Index